THE EARLY HISTORY
OF THE REPUBLICAN PARTY

THE EARLY HISTORY OF
THE REPUBLICAN PARTY
1854-1856

ANDREW WALLACE CRANDALL
Eugene C. Pulliam Professor
of American History
DE PAUW UNIVERSITY

THESIS

*Presented to the Faculty of the Graduate School of the
University of Pennsylvania in partial fulfillment
of the requirements for the degree of
Doctor of Philosophy*

GLOUCESTER, MASS.
PETER SMITH
1960

PREFACE

The Early History of the Republican Party was prepared
initially as a doctoral thesis at the University of Pennsylvania
under the direction of Professor St. George L. Sioussat. As a
thesis study it was strictly research based on materials from a
wide range of libraries and repositories. The volume was
printed by the Gorham Press in 1928, and only a small edition
was circulated.

Several considerations have prompted reprinting the book.
The original edition has been exhausted for a long time. Copies
were not available in used book stores and there were inquiries
for the work. The current observance of the Centennial of the
Civil War furnished a second motive. The origin and early
history of the Republican Party stands at the front of developments that led to war and also determined to a great extent its
course and outcome. The publication, though strictly research,
deserves a place in the mass of material appearing on the period.

There were motives for the re-issue more of a personal nature.
The retirement of the author set up the re-publication of the
book as a sort of memorial. Furthermore, the establishment of
the Pulliam Chair of American History at DePauw University
and extending to the author the honor of being its first occupant
made the re-publication of a work from the heart of the American
scene very much in order.

CONTENTS

PART I

THE EMERGENCE OF A NEW PARTY

PART II

THE ATTEMPT TO CONVERT THE NORTH

PART III

THE PARTIES AFIELD

PART IV

THE VERDICT OF THE PEOPLE

PART I

THE EMERGENCE OF A NEW PARTY

THE EARLY HISTORY OF THE REPUBLICAN PARTY

CHAPTER I

POLITICAL CHAOS IN THE NORTH

Finality

The controversy over slavery in the United States was the source of far-reaching political events. In the region south of Mason and Dixon's line chattel slavery had survived the period of the American Revolution, and the forming of a new national government under the constitution left it undisturbed. Servile and unskilled labor was found well adapted to cotton growing, and slavery accompanied the spread of the plantation system into the fertile lands of the Southwest. At the same time, states and territories based on a system of free labor developed in the western hinterland of the North, and the original line of demarcation was prolonged by the Ohio River. The free states of the North soon surpassed the non-free of the South in the number of representatives sent to Congress, in spite of the fact that three-fifths of the slaves were counted as part of the population. Against this superiority in numbers, the South found an acceptable safeguard in the Senate; for the number of states, free and slave, had remained equal. With the country divided geographically between the two systems, and the number of states admitted from each section kept equal, no serious crisis arose on the slavery question during the first three decades of the nation's history.

In 1818 Missouri Territory applied for admission to the Union. As part of the Louisiana Purchase, it had been open to slavery, and now petitioned to be admitted as a slave state. Missouri extended north into the latitude along which the free states were expanding, and for the first time the North mustered its numerical supremacy to check the extension of the labor system of the South. A crisis ensued which alarmed many. The Union seemed in imminent danger, but the Missouri Compromise came as a solution. This provided that Missouri enter the Union as a slave state but that Maine be also admitted and thereby the balance in the Senate retained. It provided further that no more of the territory received from France in 1803, north of the southern boundary of Missouri, be opened to slavery. Though the crisis had been passed and the old order of equally dividing the territory and the number of states maintained, from this time on the slavery question was insurgent in American politics.

The ensuing years saw a gradual widening in the scope of the sectional controversy and by 1850 another crisis was reached. Professional abolitionists in the North began to attack slavery. This, and resistance to the operation of the fugitive slave law was the source of bitter complaint in the South. On the other hand, the presence of slavery and the slave trade in the District of Columbia exercised anti-slavery enthusiasts in the North. The question of extension, however, was the one that again brought the controversy to a danger point. In 1846, in the form of the Wilmot Proviso, the North once more threatened to use its numerical strength to exclude slavery from any territory that should be acquired from Mexico by the war then in progress. With the war over, and a vast area added to the public domain, the question of the extension of slavery demanded solution. Northern spokesmen argued that since the new territory had been free under Mexican rule it retained that status on becoming part of the United States—that the principle of the Wilmot Proviso applied automatically. Their Southern antagonists argued that the extension of the jurisdiction of the United States made it accessible to slavery and that Congress could not intervene to check it. Between the two extremes were several possible adjustments. Some would leave the question to the Supreme Court; some would extend the Missouri Compromise line; others would leave the territory open to slavery and leave the final decision to its citizens. Several modifying features were also to be considered. Texas, a slave state, had claims to a considerable portion of the territory acquired from Mexico, but at the same time had a large debt which made a way of access to the claims. California, a part of the newly acquired territory, had organized a state government, disregarded the extension of the Missouri Compromise line, and applied for admission as a free state. The key to a solution lay in what the northern majority in Congress could be brought to concede and the South to accept. The North had recently succeeded in making Oregon a free territory. Radicals in the South began to assume a threatening attitude, and called a convention to meet at Nashville. A grave responsibility rested with the first Congress of the Taylor administration.

The Compromise of 1850 was the salutary response to the crisis. The leadership of Clay and Webster was a powerful force in the direction of amicable settlement. The death of President Taylor and the accession of Vice-President Fillmore made possible the support of the administration. By taking the several items involved in the settlement as separate bills, it was found possible to secure a majority for each. The South was given a new fugitive slave law; the North was compensated by the abolition of the slave trade in the District of Columbia. Texas was given ten million dollars for her claims. California was admitted with her constitution, and consequently without slavery. The remainder of the Mexican cession was organized into two territories—Utah and New Mexico. Each was to determine the status of slavery in its boundary when it adopted its constitution. In the measures of the Compromise were gains and concessions for both sides, but doubt remained as to whether the radicals in the South would accept it. In the contest that ensued the conservatives won the day and the danger of disunion subsided.

After the tense period in which the compromise was worked out, there came a momentary lull in the controversy. The settlement was pronounced final, and politicians added "finality" to their professional vocabulary. Though erroneous, the platitude was apt. It taught a doctrine of tranquillity. The recent measures were pronounced a final settlement of the question that had distracted the country for so long. Its advocates assumed with sublety that the people were tired of the strife and glad to have it concluded for all time. "Finality" had power as a popular appeal, and had a brief but important vogue in politics.

Both Whigs and Democrats endorsed it in their platforms of the campaign of 1852, though it belonged of right to the Whigs. The compromise measures were the work of the Fillmore administration, and as a matter of course should have yielded them an advantage. But the Whigs failed to secure the reward justly theirs. The South could not whole-heartedly endorse their candidate, General Scott, because he refused to endorse the platform adopted by the convention; and many of its prominent party leaders withdrew.[1] In the North "conscience Whigs" were unwilling to accept the status of slavery under the compromises as final, and would not lend complete support to the platform. General Scott's speeches as he played between the two extremes lost rather than gained support. Nor did the fact that he was a military hero strengthen his candidacy. The vote of the foreign-born population in the North was another menace to the Whigs, and Scott's puerile attempt to win it did little more than make him absurd. Confronted by many difficulties, the Whigs did not develop the self-assurance or the fighting spirit necessary to win against odds. Henry Clay, demi-god of the party, had just died; before election day, Webster too was dead, and Whig papers had been kept repeatedly in mourning. There were many forebodings of evil as the party entered the fatal campaign of 1852.

The Democrats made themselves masters of the situation. To harmonize with a platform that endorsed "finality" they secured as a candidate General Franklin Pierce of New Hampshire—"a northern man with southern principles." They also set about repairing and reoiling a machine that jealousy, faction, and defeat had nearly destroyed.[2] Their work of re-organization was well done and the result of the election was the best proof of its success. They swept the Northwest, leaving in the wake of their victory the Whigs demoralized and the Independent Democrats stranded on anti-slavery radicalism. In Pennsylvania, in the northern tier of counties, free-soilers of the Wilmot school supported General Pierce and the platform. In New York where schism had become chronic in the Democracy, the factions were re-united. The "Softs," more numerous and more inclined to be anti-slavery than their rivals, the "Hards," were accepted as regular in the new administration, and were to enjoy the patronage. This might prove a stabilizing influence in the event of any gravitation to a "dominant South." In New England as in New York, the Democracy that supported Pierce, had an anti-slavery tone. Still, he was acceptable at the South, where the conservatives had so recently triumphed, and the sweeping victory showed no surface marks of sectionalism. The Democratic party had been returned to power by a distinct majority and with it went a mandate to make "finality" a fact.

Undercurrents

But the assurance of quiet that the Democratic victory brought, merely obscured the possibilities of political upheaval that existed. The extremes that had been brought to the support of Pierce made the party itself unstable. Such anti-slavery factions as the Wilmoters of Pennsylvania were not likely to remain long in a combination that included the Democracy of the South. The slightest recurrence of the old controversy would prove a parting of the way. If the strife were renewed in earnest, other northern adherents than professional anti-slavery men would begin to leave the party. Were "finality" realized, and no measure that involved the perennial controversy over slavery taken up, there was promise of stability. In a reopened controversy, the party in power would be sure to feel the rending force of sectionalism.

There was a more promising source for a political landslide than the possible disruption of the victorious Democratic party. The Whig defeat proved fatal. Although not overwhelmed by numbers, their campaign showed a strong sectional cleavage, and their existence as a national party was menaced. The impression grew that the party was dead in spite of the fact that Whig papers, led by the *National Intelligencer* of Washington, fought hard to discredit the idea. The disintegration of a great party was in itself a political revolution. Its voting strength was thrown into the field for re-alignment. This left a large voting population in the North without a firm political mooring. The Whigs of the North were more inclined to oppose slavery than the Democrats, and the course of their new alignment could be easily predicted should the slavery issue come to the front again.

Besides these two sources from which votes might be drawn with revolutionary effect, there was also a nucleus around which they might crystallize. A small third party in the North—the Independent Democrats—stood out against "finality." The machinery of the old Liberty and Free-Soil parties had been renewed at a convention in Cleveland in 1851, and

their successor became a reality when the major parties endorsed "finality" in 1852.[3] The number of votes the ticket
polled was not significant; but the Independent Democrats
had several claims to importance. They had an organization
that could be used readily. Their immediate predecessors had
canonized non-extension of slavery in their Buffalo platform
of 1848. With an organization and a clearly enunciated platform they stood ready to give leadership to any political
combination on the anti-slavery basis. It is also significant
for Republican history that Salmon P. Chase of Ohio had
stood with the Independent Democrats. The Democratic
victory had isolated him and he was to lose his seat in the
United States Senate. It is of further importance that the
vote of the Independent Democrats indicated a change of
base for anti-slavery leadership. In the Northwest their vote
was as large as that of the Free-Soilers of 1848 but such was
not the case in New York and New England.[4] A major
party on slavery would doubtlessly take its leadership from
west of the Appalachians.

But the political revolution of 1854—1856 cannot be entirely accounted for by the instability of the party in power,
the disintegration of a major party, and the presence of a
minor one of anti-slavery principles. A great political change
requires a state of mind. This was also present. Since the
middle thirties there had been an avalanche of "isms" in the
North. A list might begin with transcendentalism, continue
with abolitionism, nativism, liquor-lawism, Fourierism, spirit-
ualism, vegetarianism, feminism, free-love, Millerism, and
conclude with various minor "isms." Some of these were bound
to exert a political influence, and abolitionism, modified to
non-extension for political purposes, was only one among
several. The presence of slavery and the issue raised by its
possible extension to territory that had been free under the
Missouri Compromise forced anti-slavery reform to the front.
Here it finally eclipsed the others; but in the formative period
of the party that it built, opposition to slavery fought side by
side with the temperance issue, and fought for its life with
nativism. In all the "isms" the seed was sown for the final
triumph of one, and the period just before the origin of the
Republican party was active with the seeding. In this work,
the greatest single factor was Horace Greeley and the *New*

York Tribune. In estimation of his influence Professor Commons says "that it was the fifteen years of revolutionary talk that made the party possible. Men's minds had been unsettled. Visions of a new world had come down upon them. Tradition had lost its hold and transition its terrors."[5] Opposition to slavery, which led to the forming of a great party, has been given a large place in history, while its co-workers in breaking the ground, have been quite forgotten. A study of the period of formation, however, demands a specific consideration of liquor-lawism and nativism.

Liquor-lawism resembled its fellows in time and place of origin. It had gone through an evolutionary process, and had attained success in a state prohibitory law in Maine in 1851.[6] This was the "Maine Law" so well known to the political history of the time. Within the next four years every free state and Minnesota Territory had taken steps towards prohibitory laws; some with success, others with failure. It did not spread to the South, if for no other reason than that the type of law was considered dangerous and classified as "legislative meddling." In the North the Democrats quite regularly opposed it, and the courts almost as regularly declared against such a law when passed. The liquor law advocates lined up with the forces opposed to the Democrats and were as a general rule a factor in the coalitions that created an opposition party. Prohibitory laws played an important role until civil strife came, when the issue was submerged and had to be taken up anew in the post-bellum period.

Nativism played a major part in the politics of the time. The American people have been addicted to sporadic outbreaks of opposition to the newer ingredients of the "melting pot," and the stage was set in the early fifties for one of these occurrences. Foreigners, chiefly Germans and Irish, had been coming to the country in large numbers. The Irish and many of the Germans were Catholics, and this led to a reaction that was anti-Romanist as well as anti-foreign. An extraordinary series of events fanned the anti-Catholic feeling in the country to a white heat, and furnished an exhaustless supply of material for preaching and writing.[7] The personal characteristics of the foreigners also supplied material for attack. The Germans with their Turnverein societies were accused of being exclusive, atheistic, and radical in politics. The aptitude

of the Irish in political affairs was resented, and the idea of a
son of the American Revolution being challenged at the polls
by a drunken Irishman became a sort of obsession with the
nativists. These critics of the new citizenry also turned to
statistics and began to compile records of insanity, criminal-
ity, and pauperism for political use.

The doctrines and methods of the Democrats had secured
for them the adherence of most of the adopted citizens. The
Pierce administration gave a large recognition to this portion
of the party. Postmaster General Campbell was a Catholic,
and Belmont and Soulé, both on foreign missions, were foreign
born. Cherishing this as a grievance, nativism was ready to
assail the Democracy as the "party of foreignism."

As an organized political force, nativism was soon to prove
itself a foe to be dreaded. Small parties based on the principle
had been in existence in the cities of the eastern seaboard since
the thirties, and as small fires they were sufficient to light a
great conflagration when the fuel was ready. The pent-up
forces behind the movement were sufficient to give it tremendous impetus when the spell of "finality" was broken in 1854.
Its form of political organization was a secret, oath-bound
society whose members prior to a certain stage of advance-
ment might reply that they knew nothing when asked concerning the organization. This won for the party, when it
definitely became a party, the name of "Know-Nothing." [8]
The name stayed by it throughout its career and was used
interchangeably with "American," the title of its own choosing,
calculated to exemplify its principles.

Many of the "isms" were irreconcilable; but they had one
point in common—the desire for reform. They leavened the
mind of the North with the idea that a renovation was needed.
The Democratic party was old, in it things had tended to find
their place, and to embrace reform in a convincing way was
beyond its power. The opportunity lay with an opposition
party. Out of the situation came an advantage of being re-
formers. Republicans and Know-Nothings were both to make
use of it. When the Republicans finally emerged as the
dominant party, they came as a party of reform.

Chaos

To the undiscerning observer there was not a cloud in the political sky when the Pierce administration began to run its course. The Whigs were dying of decrepitude, not violence, and most of the anti-slavery sentiment that had been cajoled into the Democracy was sluggish with the spell of "finality" and large helpings of the spoils. There were instances of insurgency, but they were rather targets for the finger of scorn, than indices of a potential unrest. People believed and politicians insisted that balm had been found for the wounds of agitation. On December 6 President Pierce ushered in the new era with a message on "domestic tranquillity."

January 4, less than a month after the peace message, Stephen A. Douglas introduced the Kansas-Nebraska bill in the Senate This measure created two new territories—Kansas and Nebraska—in the portion of the Louisiana Purchase that was still unorgainzed. These were to come into the Union with or without slavery as their constitutions might provide. The Missouri Compromise which had excluded slavery from this region was repealed on the ground that it was inconsistent with the principle of non-intervention by Congress as applied in the compromise legislation of 1850. The same section of the act that blotted out restriction north of the compromise line went further to declare that it was not the purpose of the act to legislate slavery into the territory nor to exclude it but to leave the citizens free "to form and regulate their domestic institutions in their own way, subject only to the constitution of the United States." Although no provision was made as to when or how, the people of the territories were to decide upon their institutions, the problem was turned over to them for solution. "Squatter sovereignty" was to be employed to settle the question of the extension of slavery.

There is disagreement as to the motive behind the Nebraska measure.[9] Certainly its authors did not realize what an apple of discord it would be. The act did not show bad reasoning, though it proved to be bad politics. The principle of squatter sovereignty that was applied to the newly created territories had already been used in organizing Utah and New Mexico. This application disregarded the idea of a compromise line like that of 1820, as did also the acceptance of California as a free state. If the idea of dividing the common territory had thus been given up, and a new principle of settling the extension of slavery reached, the applying of squatter sovereignty to Kansas and Nebraska was not an unreasonable measure. But that territory was covered by the Compromise of 1820, by it reserved for free soil, and to open it even tentatively to slavery, was to throw down the gauntlet to all anti-slavery elements. The controversy re-opened with tremendous energy, and the unstable political conditions in the North made it a promising field in which to build a new party on slavery.

There was opposition to the bill as it made its way through Congress. Those who made a record in the fight against it groomed themselves for leadership in what grew out of it. Two men from slave states distinguished themselves—Sam Houston of Texas in the Senate and Thomas H. Benton of Missouri in the House. Men from the North with anti-slavery records already established added to their laurels. Hale of New Hampshire and Sumner of Massachusetts both broke lances "for freedom." When the bill became a law Senator Seward accepted it as a challenge to "freedom" to fight for the territories opened to slavery.[10] Chase, hearing the guns that celebrated the passing of the bill, spoke prophetically of its eventual result.[11] Both men had placed themselves for leadership in what was to prove a new era.

It was a special opportunity for Chase, since his recent secession to the Independent Democrats was to cost him his seat in the Senate. Few men were ever more ambitious than he, and now on the promise of the new issue he not only saw a way of escape from his political isolation; he dreamed of the presidency. Unlike Seward who placed his reliance on the anti-slavery Whigs, Chase would have to have a new order, one more comprehensive than the Independent Democrats, to vindicate his position and to advance him politically. Ohio politicians acted at once, and before January was over the "Appeal to the Independent Democrats" appeared in the Washington and New York papers. Joshua Giddings, veteran anti-slavery agitator from the Western Reserve wrote the first draft; the final form, based on it, was the work of Chase.[12] Though developed for a time as an Ohio move, Sumner's name was added to Chase's for the Senate, and Gerrit Smith and Alexander DeWitt joined Giddings and Edward Wade for the House. This document, essentially the work of Chase, broke ground for a national Republican party.

The "Appeal to the Independent Democrats" contained several suggestive features. It furnished a point of departure for a new political movement, and called to leadership in it a party that stood on the Free Soil Platform of 1848. It utilized the strategy of attacking the repeal of the Missouri Compromise as a breach of compact. When a major party began to form on the issue that there be no further extension of slavery, they could ask no better vantage point for their radical departure than that they could not compromise, for, they could argue, true to its nature, slavery would not keep faith. In declaring that the Missouri Compromise was constitutional and that the legislation of 1850 did not affect its status, the "Appeal" laid the corner stone for a long drawn technical argument that followed. In referring the matter to the people, it was suggestive of method—"We shall go home to our constituencies, erect anew the standard of freedom and call on the people to come to the rescue of the country from the domination of slavery."

While Congress was busy with the measure a storm was arising in the North. Public meetings were called to protest, pulpit and press became clamorous, and the New England clergy sent their famous petition to Congress.[13] The *New York Tribune* which had spent so many years educating the mind of the North for reform began to preach a crusade. The passage of the bill, it said, would be tantamount to a declaration of war between freedom and slavery. Neither territory should be admitted with slaves, and to prevent it they would "necessarily be compelled to carry the war into Africa and fight against the admission of new slave states from any quarter whatsoever."[14] Before the bill was law, the pioneer of the Republican party had thus laid its gage of battle on ground marked out by the Free Soilers of 1848. The coming together of two such factors on a common issue was indicative of the extreme combinations necessary to form the Republican party. The crystallization, however, was a matter of two years' development, and was the result of the political, clerical, and press attack on the measure about to be consummated in Congress.

The reaction to the bill took on a political aspect almost immediately. State legislatures in session made the adoption of resolutions a test question. Of the free states, nine legislatures were in session at the time. Five: Maine, Massachusetts, Rhode Island, New York, and Wisconsin, adopted resolutions of protest. The remainder either wavered or were non-committal, except Illinois which endorsed the measure. There were also nine slave states whose legislatures were in session. Georgia alone gave the measure supporting resolutions. There seemed an indifference about the whole affair in the South, and conservatives who feared political strife regretted that so much capital was being made of it in the North.[15] With the new legislation enacted and made a test of orthodoxy, the Democratic structure, modelled with such care by politicians in 1852 started to disintegrate. The whole political instability of the North began to appear.

Local reactions to the Kansas-Nebraska Bill furnished the germs of a new party. Some of the meetings held in protest to the measure took the form of organizing a party on an anti-slavery basis. Any of these movements which sought to fuse, on the anti-slavery basis, any or all parties, regardless of former principles or affiliations, might be defined as Republican. The stand taken on the slavery question was characteristically that of the Free Soil Platform of 1848—no more slave states. This can be accepted as the true Republican position. The factions that made up the opposition to the Pierce administration varied greatly from the orthodox Republican, ranging from as conservative a position as the mere restoration of the Compromise to that of the Garrisonian abolitionist. Two years of organizing prior to the campaign of 1856 did not reduce them to a common denominator on the slavery question, and a great portion of the forces behind their first national campaign could not be defined as Republican.

There is neither point nor purpose here to undertake a search for the germs of the party or to enter upon the controversial subject of origin. The meeting at Ripon, Wisconsin, February 28, fathered by Alvan E. Bovay, has a very respectable support in its claim to first place,[16] although it is not universally accepted.[17] Careful study of the numerous political meetings and conventions in the North both before and after the Kansas-Nebraska Bill, still seems necessary for a satisfactory story of genesis.[18] The convention at Jackson, Michigan, on July 6 is accepted as the first to organize a state party.[19] The naming of the party like the story of its origin is still on a controversial basis, and the credit given Bovay for suggesting the name to Greeley is likewise attacked.[20] Regardless of who suggested the name, meetings and conventions that organized new parties began to use it. June 16 the *New York Tribune* in an editorial on the political situation recommended by the name.[21] By September 14 the *National Era* which had worked vigorously for a new party, but desired to retain the name Democratic for its own sake, acquiesced in the new. The press was using the term, new organizations had adopted it, and the *Era* pronounced its use necessary in order to be understood.[22]

The strength of the reaction in the North which had led to so many forms of protest was soon registered in the spring elections. New Hampshire, the President's native state, went on record in March. Although the Whigs and Free-Soilers were not united on a ticket, a lower house was returned that was anti-Nebraska. The virtual defeat of the administration in the President's own state was portentous.[23] In April two more New England states, Connecticut and Rhode Island, held elections. The Democratic hold was not so powerful in them, and the Whigs scored a thorough victory. Connecticut, which had gone Democratic by 1217 majority the year before, was lost to the administration. Two days later Rhode Island followed despite its Democratic majority of 2143 of the preceding year. That the reaction had not lost impetus during the summer was registered in September by two more of the New England group. In Vermont, a fusion party which was Republican in everything except its name elected Royce governor.[24] All three congressmen were Whig-anti-Nebraska, and the legislature which would fill both seats in the United States Senate was overwhelmingly against the administration.[25] The Maine election came September 11. A fusion of liquor-law men and free-soilers carried the governorship over Democratic, Whig, and anti-liquor-law candidates. Morrill,

their candidate, fell short of an election by the people; but
the legislature which was largely Republican assured him the
office.   Five of the six congressmen were Republicans[26]
All the New England states had gone on record save Massachusetts, and its election was not until November.

The strength of the anti-slavery sentiment in New England
was generally conceded; and the action of the Northwest was
looked to as a better test.   Early in August the election in
Iowa indicated the force of the reaction here.   James W.
Grimes, running for governor on a Whig ticket, with a Free-
Soil endorsement, after a famous campaign, defeated the
Democrats.[27]   The combination supporting Grimes was in
reality a Republican party though not so named.   It controlled
the legislature but lost one of the two seats in Congress to the
Democrats.

It was not until the October election that the West was
heard from further.   Ohio and Indiana both had held conventions on July 13, the natal day of the ordinance that made
them free states.   Their purpose was to unite all opposition to
the administration.   All the tickets placed in the field by
these conventions were overwhelmingly successful in October.
In Ohio all twenty-one of the congressmen elected belonged to
the new opposition party.   In Indiana the opposition secured
seven of the eleven seats in Congress, and controlled the
legislature by a majority of fourteen in joint ballot.   The
newly elected Ohio legislature would have the privilege of
filling one seat in the United States Senate.   In both states,
Know-Nothings were an important factor in the combination
that defeated the Democrats.

Among the October states was one of the populous common-
wealths of the Middle Atlantic seaboard.   Pennsylvania which
had wandered from the fold of Democracy but rarely since the
time of Jackson was swept out of its control.   Bigler, the
Democratic candidate, would not denounce the Nebraska Bill,
and all the anger it had generated piled up against him.   His
plea that national affairs should not influence state politics
availed nothing.   The Wilmoters in the "Northern Tier" of
counties rose in revolt.   The Know-Nothings, powerful but
still working in secret, supported the Whig candidate and
Bigler was overwhelmingly defeated. The Democrats retained
six of the twenty-five seats in Congress; the others represented

a wide variety of opposition. The legislature was equally confused. This heterogeneous opposition which had broken the grip of the Democracy in the Keystone state was destined for a large share in the political struggles of the next two years.

The November elections added to the avalanche. In New York several important developments were brought to the surface. The Democracy had, as usual, two tickets.[28] The Hard Shells endorsed the national platform of 1852 and denounced the administration for meddling in state politics. The Soft Shells endorsed the platform of 1852 and denounced the Kansas-Nebraska Bill; but decided to let it stand, for the reason that agitation for the repeal of the bill would be useless. Their platform was free-soil in tone, but so mild in its declaration of purpose that Preston King and Abijah Mann, men of "Jacksonian" traditions and anti-slavery inclination, withdrew. Philip Dorsheimer, influential German politician, and others, protested. The prospect of victory for either faction of the Democracy was not bright unless the opposition proved even more out of unison than they.

The nature of the reaction that was sweeping the North worked to the advantage of the anti-slavery faction of the N. Y. Whigs led by Seward and known as "Wooly Heads." Besides this, there were other elements of strength. A distinct anti-Nebraska party which had organized in August gave the Seward ticket its endorsement. To these anti-slavery credentials was also added the support of the temperance advocates. Furthermore, Seward's political record and his friendship for Bishop Hughes of New York, made it possible to vie with the Softs for the vote of the Catholic and foreign-born citizens. On the other hand, the anti-Seward, Silver Gray faction of the Whigs, of which ex-President Fillmore was a leader, became the dominant element in the Know-Nothing party of the state, and brought to it a tolerant attitude towards slavery. This newly formed party nominated Daniel Ullman, a friend of Fillmore, for Governor. Its opponents busied themselves during the campaign in proving that Ullman was not even a native, that he had been born in India, and Know-Nothings of the Silver Gray kind were henceforth known as "Hindoos."

But the "Hindoos" were too few, and the Democrats too schismatic to check the "Wooly Heads" and their allies.

Their candidate, Myron H. Clark, was elected, with Henry J. Raymond of the *New York Times* as his lieutenant. Of the thirty-three congressmen returned, three could be identified as Softs and one as Hard. Some of the remainder were Know-Nothings of the "Hindoo" brand, but the greater part of the representatives of the Empire state were anti-Nebraska men. Besides carrying the state, the Seward Whigs made themselves champions of anti-Nebraskaism, anti-Know-Nothingism, and reform.

On the same day that New York scored the victory for Seward, four more states held elections. New Jersey returned four Whig-anti-Nebraska congressmen, and one Democrat. There was also a Know-Nothing complication here. Illinois, the home state of Senator Douglas, had been watched with interest. Here, Whig-anti-Nebraska combinations succeeded in carrying five of the nine seats in Congress and in controlling the legislature that would dispose of the seat in the Senate occupied by James Shields. Michigan, with its new Republican machine, elected Kinsley S. Bingham to the governorship and returned three Republican congressmen out of its coterie of five. Wisconsin, which had also evolved a Republican party, went over to the new order by a narrow margin. The Republicans won two of the three seats in Congress and controlled the state legislature by a very small majority. In all, it seemed that East and West were at one in their response to the opening of Kansas to slavery.

Massachusetts was the last of the free states to hold its election. A convention in Worcester in September organized a Republican party and nominated Henry Wilson for governor. The Know-Nothings nominated Henry J. Gardner. The Whigs and Democrats also made regular nominations. The result of the campaign was a victory for Gardner and a very poor showing for the new party led by Wilson. The Know-Nothings also carried the eleven seats in Congress. The whole product of the Bay state election, though Know-Nothing, was opposed to the administration and the Nebraska legislation.

When the Massachusetts returns were in, the revolution was pronounced complete. There would be an anti-Nebraska majority in the next Congress, and Democratic losses to Whig and Know-Nothing forces in the border slave states assured an overwhelming majority against the administration. Apparently the Democratic party had been swept out of the North. Its enemies, exulting over this, pronounced it the party of slavery and now justly confined to the section where it belonged. Senator Douglas, champion of the Nebraska Bill, and sword and buckler of the Democracy of the Northwest, did not accept their verdict. In a speech at Chicago, November 9, he threw down the gauntlet. "The allied forces of abolitionism, Whigism, and Know-Nothingism, have by stratagem attained a partial victory over the Democratic party," he said. But they would soon fall to pieces over "responsibilities and spoils." They must now act affirmatively; so he bade his followers "be of good cheer. . . Though the skies are partially overcast, the clouds are passing away."[29]

The victorious opposition that would have to act affirmatively was chaotic except in the common sentiment on the slavery issue as raised by the recent legislation. This being the case, the best prospect for concerted action lay in the completion of the new party that had taken form on a free-soil basis. Party machinery existed in Michigan, Wisconsin, and for a while in Illinois.[30] Iowa was secure and was to go directly to the new order.[31] Massachusetts had a minor party calling itself Republican, and Maine and Vermont had fusion parties that were for all practical purposes Republican. Ohio and Indiana had fusion machinery that might be useful for further development. It would seem a natural thing that the Republicans unite the North at once on their positions and purpose.

But there were other considerations. Although it was generally believed that the Whig party was dead, its demise added several points to the political uncertainty. Whig disintegration would leave a residue of "Old Liners" in the field who would stay by the old organization to the last. In some states, especially in New York, it could claim to be *the* anti-slavery party. Besides this, Know-Nothings had made their appearance. In some states they were already acting as a distinct party, and in one they had been victorious. When they emerged completely, which they most certainly would do, they might assimilate the anti-Nebraska sentiment in the North which had contributed greatly to their rise in power there. On the other hand, some of them were Silver Gray,

as in New York, and could cooperate with southern brethren
without serious difficulty over the slavery question. Possibilities were many. Douglas had correctly appraised his
opposition. The North was a political chaos.

1. Cole,A.C., *Whig Party in South, pp.* 261-265.
2. For account, Nichols, R.F., *The Democratic Machine,* 1850-1854.
3. Smith,Theodore Clark, *Liberty and Free Soil Parties in the Northwest,* p. 259.
4. *Ibid.,*pp. 257-258.
5. Commons,John R., *Horace Greeley and the Working Class Origin of the Republican Party,* p. 469.
6. Fehlandt, A.F., *Century of Drink Reform in the United States,* or Krout,J.A., *Origins of Prohibition* give good accounts of the development of the temperance issue.
7. A good account of this is given in the Monographs on the subject by Haynes, Scisco, and Schmeckebier. See Bibliography.
8. Ritual in Clusky,M.W., *Political Text Book,* pp. 47-58.
9. Ray,P.O., *Repeal of the Missouri Compromise* and Hodder, F.H., "Genesis of the Kansas Nebraska Act," in *Wisconsin State Historical Society Proceedings,* 1912; also "Sidelights on the Missouri Compromise" in *American Historical Association Report,* 1909.
10. Bancroft, Frederick, *Life of Seward,* vol. 1, p. 360.
11. Schuckers,J.W., *Life and Public Services of Salmon Portland Chase,* p. 156.
12. Schuckers,J.W., *Life of Chase,*p. 140.Unsigned mss. draft in the Chase papers. P.H.S.
13. Pamphlet: *Appeal of the 3050 Clergymen of New England.* The presentation of this embarrassed Senator Everett. His resignation soon followed, and Sumner who sponsored the appeal became the mouthpiece for Massachusetts anti-slavery sentiment in the Senate.
14. *New York Tribune,* May 18, 1854, quoted in Pike,J.S., *First Blows of the Civil War,* p. 230.
15. *National Intelligencer,* March 18, 1854. The *Intelligencer* printed a series of excerpts to show that the South was not pushing the bill and to allay the fury which the Northern politicians were generating over it.
16. Viz.Curtis,Francis, *The Republican Party 1854-1904* accepts this, but at the same time reviews other claims to priority; Wilson, Henry, *Rise and Fall of the Slave Power;* Gilman,A.F., *Origin of the Republican Party.*
17. Turner,A.J. in *Genesis of the Republican Party* places the first Republican meeting at Exeter, New Hampshire, October 12, 1853.
18. Turner's article does this with considerable thoroughness, but holds a brief for a nomination at Grand Rapids, Mich., as the first on a Republican basis.
19. See Channing, Edward,*History of the United States,vol.VI,p.140* foot-note.

20. Turner thinks the credit belongs to Medill while still with the Cleveland *Daily Forest City.*
21. Editorial:*Party names and Public Duty,* quoted Curtis,vol.1, pp.214-215.
22. *National Era,* September 14. The *National Era* was the official organ of the Free-Soilers.
23. Statements on the election are based on official return in the *National Intelligencer* and *Whig Almanac. 1855.*
24. Lawrence Brainard ran independently on the Free-Soil ticket.
25. October 14 Brainard and Jacob Collamer were elected to the Senate.
26. Candidates of fusion parties were referred to as Republican whether the party had adopted the name or not.
27. Pelzer,Lewis, *Origin and Organizaton of the Republican Party in Iowa;* Slater, William, *Life of James W. Grimes,* pp. 55-61.
28. The "Hards" and "Softs", after their reconciliation in 1852, had parted company the following year.
29. Reported in *National Intelligencer,* November 20.
30. Cole,A.C.,*Centennial History of Illinois,* vol.III, p. 129.
31. Account in Pelzer, Louis, *Origin and Organization of the Republican Party in Iowa;* and Slater, William, *Life of James W. Grimes.*

CHAPTER II

ANTI-SLAVERY VERSUS NATIVISM

Organization of the Americans

National organization was the natural sequence to the activities of the Know-Nothings in the election of 1854. In some states they were already a political party, and in almost every state where the Democratic party had been overwhelmed, their influence was felt. Stimulated by this taste of power they moved rapidly in the direction of making a national political organization, and a general council to be held at Cincinnati was arranged for November 15.

It must be borne in mind that the Know-Nothing movement had not been confined to the North or to districts where Catholics and foreigners were found in any considerable numbers. It swept over the South. With a large following in the South, and with most of its northern support anti-Nebraska in sentiment, a nation-wide Know-Nothing party would have the same sectional cleavage that had disrupted the Whigs. The Cincinnati council faced this situation and attempted a remedy. A plan sponsored by Kenneth Raynor of North Carolina was adopted.[1] This added a third degree known as the "order of the American Union," which pledged its members to support no one for office whose election threatened the safety of the Federal Union.[2] The Republicans feared this because it put them in the light of Union breakers,[3] and the Democrats welcomed it as an antidote for the fusion movement. To make the Republican position more pointed, the *Cincinnati Enquirer,* coming from the scene of the Know-Nothing nationalization, began a series of editorials and exchanges entitled, "Know-Nothingism vs. Fusionism." The fact that a fusion party on slavery was sectional and that it intensified the ever present threat to the Union, gave the Know-Nothings a great opportunity. Breathing union and patriotism, standing on compromise ground on slavery, by

28

offering Americanism as a leading principle in its stead, they established themselves between the two extremes. This was the secret of the national life of the party and the source of its strength. Its chief promoters, politicians of the compromise of 1850, were enthusiastic, and were looking towards the presidency in 1856. To carry on their work they founded at Washington an official party paper and called it *The American Organ.*[4]

Its compromise position made the party a gathering place for conservatives, especially those from the disintegrating Whigs. It also brought out the free-soil sentiment that had companioned the movement in the North, and which would not compromise on slavery. Counter secret organizations were formed that made slavery the leading issue, namely: the "Know Somethings" and "Sag Nichts." The "Know-Somethings" were reputed to have had their origin in Philadelphia. The idea had been transmitted thence to Cincinnati, and by the following June there were organizations in seven different states.[5] They were used to counteract the nativist principle in favor of anti-slavery, were especially valuable to leaders like Chase and Seward, and were part of the process of Republican emergence. The "Sag Nichts" had their chief strength in the West, and to some extent in Kentucky.[6] Another way in which anti-Nebraska sentiment came to the surface was by the refusal of the northern state councils of Know-Nothings to approve the new national party. For example, that of Maine went so far as to refuse to make nominations, to leave its members unobligated, and to recommend accepting the Republican nominees.[7] All varieties of sentiment on slavery would be represented when the Know-Nothings, greatly increased in numbers, should meet in their next national council.

The next meeting was at Philadelphia June 5, 1855. The council organized, indulged in a few patriotic manifestations, and then began to fight over the slavery question. The committee on resolutions brought in both majority and minority reports. The majority report was the work of the Southern members who dominated; the minority report was signed by twelve leaders of northern delegations.[8] A split was imminent. Kenneth Raynor, always sanguine of a national party based on Union sentiment, tried a compromise resolution to no avail. The majority report was accepted and a number of northern delegates bolted.[9] The platform adopted contained the celebrated *Twelfth Article.*

"The American Party having risen upon the ruins and in spite of the opposition of the Whig and Democratic parties, cannot be held in any manner responsible for the abnoxious acts or violated pledges of either. And the systematic agitation of the slavery question by these parties having elevated sectional hostility into a positive element of political power, and brought our institutions into peril, it has, therefore, become the imperative duty of the American Party to interpose, for the purpose of giving peace to the country, and perpetuity to the Union. And as experience has shown it impossible to reconcile opinions so extreme as those which separate the disputants, and as there can be no dishonor in submitting to the laws, the national council has decreed it the best guarantee of common justice and of future peace, to abide by and maintain the existing laws upon the subject of Slavery, as a final and conclusive settlement of that subject, in spirit and in substance.

"And regarding it the highest duty to avow their opinions upon a subject so important, in distinct and unequivocal terms, it is hereby declared as the sense of this national council that Congress possesses no power under the constitution to legislate upon the subject of slavery in the states where it does or may exist, or to exclude any state from admission into the Union, because its constitution does or does not recognize the institution of slavery as a part of its social system: and especially pretermitting any expression of opinion upon the power of Congress to establish or prohibit slavery in any territory, it is the sense of the national Council that Congress ought not to legislate upon the subject of slavery within the Territory of the United States, and that any interference by Congress with slavery as it exists in the district of Columbia would be a violation of the spirit and intention of the compact by which the state of Maryland ceded the district to the United States, and a breach of national faith."

Thus the national council of the Americans in its "platform of verbiage" accepted the recent legislation on slavery, pronounced it final, and asked the country to leave the dangerous question and turn its attention to letting "Americans rule America." The bolting northern delegates would have none of it.

The bolters—the "North Americans"—met in separate session and adopted a report read by Foster of Massachusetts. They resolved:

"that the repeal of the Missouri Compromise was an infraction of the plighted faith of the nation, and that it should be restored, and if efforts to that effect should fail, Congress should refuse to admit into the Union any state tolerating slavery which shall be formed out of any portion of the territory from which that institution was excluded by the Compromise."

Pennslyvania, New Jersey, and New York were not among the seceders. New York because of the Silver Gray composition of the party had no need to secede. Pennsylvania and New Jersey protested separately and many from their delegations would not support the victorious faction. The seceders appointed a committee of correspondence headed by Orth of Indiana. Their purpose was to get in touch with all anti-slavery factions. Though their position on the slavery question was less radical than that on which the Republicans were trying to fuse all parties, they took steps towards cooperation. It might be that with their milder platform they could take the North away from the Republicans. Whatever their prospects, the seceders would not accept the Twelfth Article, and the new Union-saving party had gone to pieces on the issue it organized to avoid.

State Elections of 1855

The elections of 1855 were important as tests of strength. The Know-Nothings were now in the field as a party. In the states where they had cooperated in secret the year before, they would now be giving support to a definite party ticket. They would be distinct in the mass of anti-Nebraska votes, and unless their cooperation with the Republicans was thorough, the chances of repeating the victory of the preceding year were few. In this state of affairs the Democracy might see the clearing of the sky which Douglas had predicted.

New England elections were a disappointment to the Republicans. In Maine, Morrill received only a plurality for

governor, and thereby failed of election by the people. The
Whigs of Maine had a large following of the "Cotton" or
"Webster" variety, which gave their candidate a numerous
vote, and their strength along with the anti-liquor law sentiment, defeated the Republicans. The Whigs then combined
with the Democrats in the legislature and controlled the state.[10]
New Hampshire went anti-Nebraska; but it was Know-
Nothing rather than Republican. In Massachusetts the
Know-Nothings swept the state again, and re-elected Gardner
over Rockwell, Republican, and Beech, the Democratic Candidate. Gardner stood on the "Massachusetts Platform" of
the Know-Nothings which was anti-Nebraska, and his victory
was considered a calamity by friends of the Republican movement. In Connecticut and Rhode Island there were sweeping
Know-Nothing, anti-Nebraska victories. In Vermont alone
of all New England was there a Republican triumph. Here
the Republicans elected Royce governor over Democratic and
Know-Nothing candidates, and secured the legislature. But
considering the results in Massachusetts, and the block of anti-
Nebraska Know-Nothingism in Connecticut and Rhode Island,
where no ray of Republicanism had yet penetrated, it might
seem that the Americans had the better chance of being *the*
anti-slavery party.

The states of the Middle Atlantic seaboard brought still
more discomfort to the Republicans. The great coalition
victory of the preceding year in New York was checkmated.
The victory of 1854 had been a Seward triumph and had practically assured his return to the Senate. Early in February a
Whig caucus put his name before the legislature, anti-slavery
support rallied to him and his return was made good.[11] He
went as a Whig, intent upon using the anti-Nebraska feeling
to rebuild the party.[12] His success in this depended on the
coming election. The Know-Nothings came into the field on
a platform moderately anti-Nebraska in tone and nominated
Headly for Secretary of State which was the key office of the
election.[13] All attempts to reconcile Hard and Soft Democrats had failed, and each with a due amount of maneuvering
put up a candidate. This year also saw the creation of a
Republican party by the Whigs and free-soilers of the state.
They organized harmoniously at Syracuse in September and
nominated Preston King for the secretaryship which was to be

the test of strength. Horace Greeley, E. D. Morgan, and Henry J. Raymond were active, and behind the scenes was Thurlow Weed.[14] The "Wooly Heads" had been anti-slavery champions for a long while, and did not make the change of front with alacrity. October 12 Seward gave the new party his blessing in an address delivered at Albany.[15] His *coupe de grace* added zest to the last days of the canvass but did not bring victory. The Know-Nothings carried the state.

The New York election had results that were far-reaching. The victorious "Hindoos," in spite of the minor concessions made in their platform to the anti-slavery feeling of the state, were still essentially Silver Grays. This meant the triumph of a party that was unfriendly to anti-Nebraskaism, as such, and above all, hostile to Seward. This Silver Gray complexion had made it possible for them to stay by the supporters of the Twelfth Article in the June Council, and now, after their victory, was to make it possible for them to dictate a presidential candidate. Though defeated, the Republicans felt that they had accomplished a great deal, and had assurances of a future.[16] More significant still, Seward, whom many considered the greatest champion of political opposition to slavery, had come definitely into the Republican ranks.

The Pennsylvania election was nothing less than a disaster for the anti-Nebraska cause. The victory of the previous year had netted nothing; for the legislature came to a deadlock on the senatorship and the election had to be postponed until a new legislature should convene. The election of canal commissioner, an office to which considerable importance was attached, furnished the test. The Democrats, purged by the Know-Nothing movement, but more unified by it,[17] went into the field with good prospects of regaining the state. The Know-Nothings had come out as a party and a state council at Reading made nominations on an anti-Nebraska platform.[18] The Whigs also made regular nominations. A fusion convention responding to a call to organize a Republican party met as Pittsburgh September 5 and nominated Passmore Williamson for commissioner.[19] Williamson was a fugitive-slave-law martyr.[20] His nomination was the result of an outburst of anti-slavery feeling, and sober second thought showed him to be politically impossible. A conference was called at Harrisburg, and Nicholson substituted for him.

This was done only a short time before the election and support was not entirely withdrawn from either Williamson or the original nominees of the Whigs and Know-Nothings. The result was a Democratic victory.

The reassertion of control over the second largest commonwealth north of the Mason-Dixon Line challenged the accuracy of the assertion that the administration party was extinct in the North. The victory, won on a platform that was orthodox on Nebraska, placed Pennsylvania in a position of Democratic leadership in the North, equal to that enjoyed by Virginia in the South since the signal overthrow of the Know-Nothings in the spring elections there.[21]

Although the Democrats were victorious, the opposition was numerically stronger, and could control the state if it would unite. This caused Pennsylvania to be regarded as the "keystone" state in the presidential canvass the following year. The innate conservatism which had made it secure in normal times made it pivotal now in a time of political revolution. The fact that the Know-Nothings of the state were not coherent, that a faction of them were supporters of the "twelfth section"[22] gave the political situation further complexity. Although there was hope for Republicanism, its prospects were scarcely bright. Even the state organization set up by the Pittsburgh convention, though it called itself Republican, was in the hands of the Know-Nothings.[23]

The Northwest contributed little to the outlook for Republican success. Iowa and Michigan held steadily to the ground they had taken. In Wisconsin the Republicans elected a supreme court judge, but the returns showed a defeat for the governorship. These were contested on the ground of fraud and the supreme court decided in favor of Bashford, the Republican.[24] In Indiana the local elections which served as the only index, went in favor of the Democrats. In Illinois the only Republican gain was local organization in the northern counties.[25] Douglas was gaining ground and the Democrats were successful in some minor elections. In the block of states of the old Northwest only three had Republican organizations, and the presence of the Know-Nothings with free-soil principles cast a sinister shadow across their way. The Democrats actually claimed Indiana and Illinois, the home state of Senator Douglas.

It was left to Ohio to give the only substantial gain of the year and by it to make an essential contribution toward the dominance of the Republican party throughout the North. The loss of his seat in the Senate which had been Chase's reward for his anti-slavery partisanship, made him the rightful claimant for vindication in the governorship at stake in the October election. Several considerations, but especially the rise of the Know-Nothings, made his nomination at once doubtful. Many old Whigs who hated him on a long score of accounts were acting with the Know-Nothings and trying to block him. The nationalization of the party at Cincinnati the preceding fall had alarmed Chase; but he hoped to save the state and took his stand on the ground that anti-slavery was paramount.[26] On December 28 he gave the public the result of his resolution in form of the Paul Letter.[27] In this he declared a hearty approval of the "People's" movement which had swept the state the preceding October, but he refused to endorse the Know-Nothing movement which he feared would ruin the anti-slavery cause by subordinating the principle. Still, he was too practical to refuse to cooperate with them, and soon decided upon what terms it could be done.[28] His demands were a platform declaring for no more slave states, equal representation on the state ticket, and that the nominations be made by the "People's Convention" which was to be held after the fashion of the one the preceding year. The Know-Nothings were working to incorporate anti-Nebraska principles in their platform, and then to have the "People's Convention" endorse, not only their platform, but their nominees. This did not square with the Chase position and a battle royal for the state was in prospect.

While Chase was still at Washington, prior to the adjournment of Congress, papers throughout the state began to present his name as their choice for governor. They made trouble for him at once. About the time his political arrangers were ready to approach the Know-Nothings on the question of cooperation with the anti-Nebraska principle in the lead, his free-soil friends were lashing them furiously.[29] Chase's attitude was conciliatory. The Know-Nothings forced the issue by maturing a plan to nominate Brinkerhoff, reputed author of the Wilmot Proviso, for governor, and to offer Chase a minor position on the ticket. L. D. Campbell, influential anti-

Nebraska Know-Nothing, broached the subject by a letter to
Chase on May 28. In the heated correspondence that ensued,
Chase's ultimatum came immediately.[30] If they could have
cooperation, both sides represented on the same ticket and the
anti-Nebraska principle in the lead, he was willing to cooperate. If not, they must "fuse on the paramount issue."
Furthermore, the Independent Democrats would support no
other candidate than himself, and with the withdrawal of his
name the Germans would flock back to the administration,
and the Democrats would win the day. Giddings spoke for
the Western Reserve in terms of no cooperation save on the
basis of the "principles of liberty."[31] The Chase men also
began to consider the restoration of the machinery of the
Independent Democrats to have it ready, if the Know-Nothings should dominate the ensuing "People's Convention" at
Columbus.

The Republican ultimatum soon brought a favorable response. The split of the national Know-Nothings at Philadelphia early in June and the action taken by a Know-Some-
thing convention at Cleveland immediately afterward cleared
the way. The "People's Convention" of July 13 gave Chase
the nomination, adopted a platform with anti-Nebraska
principles the leading issue, adopted the name Republican,
and appointed a committee of correspondence to organize a
national party.[32] The rest of the ticket that went into the field
with Chase was largely Know-Nothing. The combination was
none too satisfactory, and only a tremendous effort could
bring victory. Furthermore, Chase was not popular. His old
Whig enemies could not give up their resentment. They nominated Trimble in order to draw off votes and defeat him. In
spite of it all, Chase won, though he ran a good many thousand
votes behind his ticket.[33]

The importance of the victory for the Republican cause was
almost beyond estimation. The progress of the party had
narrowed down to the single victory in Ohio. But in this it
lived and maintained the preeminence of its principles at the
same time it cooperated with the Know-Nothings. Although
many Republicans of free-soil purity did not like the close
affiliation of the Nativists, the election demonstrated the
power of the anti-slavery issue to dominate and the possibility

of an arrangement that would assure a numerous party. It also placed Chase in a position to continue the process of national organization.[34]

Outside the North the elections of 1855 had results that had a distinct bearing on the struggle for control of the nation the following year. The Know-Nothings presented a solid front in the Border Slave States, and they carried California. In Virginia they were defeated for the governorship by Henry A. Wise in the spring elections, an event of great moment for the Democrats.[35] There was much rejoicing, for in their victory the Democrats felt that they had made a significant beginning in breaking the power of the Know-Nothings in the South. In Tennessee there was a hard fight for the state which the Democrats won by a small margin.[36] The Know-Nothings did not accept either defeat as final, and in Louisiana, North Carolina, and other states of the Lower South they remained a force not to be overlooked. The Know-Nothing party in the South would be a factor in the ensuing presidential campaign.

The elections of 1855 had given less comfort to the Republicans than to any other party. In the Northwest they held Iowa, Wisconsin, Michigan, and Ohio; but Illinois and Indiana were still in the grip of Douglas. In the great states of New York and Pennsylvania they had been defeated. In New England Know-Nothingism had all but usurped the championship of the anti-Nebraska cause. In the Ohio victory alone was there prestige to sustain them in facing the ensuing presidential contest. Furthermore, they met a Democratic party that was encouraged, hopeful, even boastful. The Democrats had checked the flood of Know-Nothingism in the South and hoped to crush it soon in the Border Slave States. They had carried Pennsylvania and driven back the anti-Nebraska forces of the North. They claimed a restoration in the heart of Douglas' Northwest. They could come to the new Congress insisting that they were only temporarily in the minority. If those opposed to the Nebraska legislation were going to prevent its operation by erecting a solid North against it, they must overcome no mean antagonist in the Democratic party there. The "come back" of the Democracy taught its opponents a lesson, and the lesson was that only by a thorough cooperation of all the opposition could they hope to carry the country in the coming presidential election. That cooperation would depend largely on the success of the Nativists in submerging the slavery question in a national platform.

Second Attempt of the Americans

The Know-Nothings were assured a place of importance by their victories; but the prospect for a party of national extent was not flattering at first. The acceptance of the twelfth article by the national council at Philadelphia in June had raised a storm of protest throughout the North. Papers denounced it, local councils rejected it, and sooner or later most of the state councils disapproved it by reasserting their anti-Nebraska sentiment. The Pennsylvania state council in a meeting at Reading in early July took a very significant step. A majority led by ex-governor Johnston rejected the twelfth article and took the ground of the seceders at Philadelphia.[37] A minority composed chiefly of Philadelphia delegates led by Jacob Broom, bolted, accepted the twelfth article, created a separate state council which they declared to be orthodox, and elected Joseph W. Hunsicker as president. The majority group issued a call for an anti-"twelfth section" convention at Cincinnati in November. There were many in the North who wished a Know-Nothing party that would absorb the anti-Nebraska issue, and the Cincinnati convention seemed promising.

But the "compromise men" were again on the job and were unwilling to give up the idea of a national party. Their problem was to reduce the coming anti-"twelfth section" convention to a compromising state of mind and to induce it to make overtures to the regular council. They began to undermine the Republican victory in Ohio. Even some of the men who had been elected to state office joined the movement, and the Democrats declared that the Know-Nothings had no intention of associating with any one "presidentially" and that the "Chase bargain" was over.[38] Enthusiasm arose as the date for the convention approached. So promising was the movement for renationalization that Henry Wilson who had toured thirteen states in an endeavor to make Republic-

ans out of Know-Nothings was pronounced an ostracized man
on his return.[39]

The anti-twelfth section convention that assembled at
Cincinnati in November contained inharmonious elements in
spite of the newly generated enthusiasm for a national party.
In it were friends of the Republican cause who were unwilling to enter a further project for nationalization on a compromise basis. The committee on resolutions divided and submitted majority and minority reports.[40] Spooner of Ohio,
friend of Chase and Republican at heart, led the minority
and brought in a report that was in reality a Republican
platform. The majority report called for a restoration of
the compromise line but not for restriction of slavery in
all the territories. Most of the Ohio and Michigan delegates
with a few from Pennsylvania sustained Spooner, but the
majority stood by the major report. On this basis they were
prepared to go into "convention with the South" and attempt
to compromise on the "twelfth section." The scheme was to
hold a session of the national council at Philadelphia, Feb. 18,
a few days before the convention met,[41] and there reduce the
twelfth article to an acceptable form. So promising was the
outlook that the *American Organ* declared any attempt to
form a northern party absurd—the prospect for success in
1856 was too good for that.[42]

The regular council met at Louisville on November 27.
Although poorly attended, it did some important work. E.B.
Bartlett of Kentucky was elected national president, the
"twelfth section" was endorsed, and an apology offered for a
terrific riot that had occurred in Louisville in August.[43] The
regular organization with its new head did not withhold a
response to the compromise victory of the Cincinnati Convention. The day following adjournment Bartlett reissued the
call for the convention at Philadelphia for February 22[43a] and
with it a call for a meeting of the national council on the 18th.
With a united front the Americans were going to Philadelphia
to try conclusions again. L. D. Campbell of Ohio, despite
his recent alliance with Chase, busied himself circulating a
sample platform. Many fond hopes were cherished and the
mouthpiece of the party declared that "slavery must be put
out of the way."[44]

But there were many possibilities. It was possible that the "twelfth section" be reduced to neutrality, and a national Nativist party realized. However, there were friends of the Republican party in the delegations that would assemble at Philadelphia who would do their utmost to disrupt the council for the advantage of the anti-slavery party. Many of the northern delegates would be distinctly anti-slavery in sentiment, would concede little in compromise, and might revert to their program of making the Know-Nothing party of the North *the* anti-slavery party. There was the further possibility that the "twelfth section" men would dominate the council as they had done the preceding June. They would have sufficient strength to do this, since the Silver Gray "Hindoos" of New York and the Hunsicker organization of Pennsylvania could stand by the South. With this bloc of support in the North to give them national extent geographically, there was great likelihood of their using their strength. If they did, the party would split in two again. The council and convention soon to be held in the Quaker city were full of possibilities, and whatever happened would have an important bearing on the course of the Republican party.

1. *Cincinnati Enquirer,*Nov.28; Wilson, Henry,*Rise and Fall of the Slave Power,*vol. III,pp.420-422; Scisco,L.D., *Political Nativism in New York,* pp.137-140.
2. Degree in Cluskey,M.W., *Political Text Book* (1857), pp. 56-58.
3. Chase to E.L.Hamlin,Nov.21,1854. Chase MSS. L.C.
4. *The Daily American Organ* edited by Vespasian Ellis and R.M. Heath began publication Nov.13,1854.
5. *Philadelphia North American,*Jan.19 and June 15, 1855.
6. *Ibid.,*May 18,1855.
7. Council at Bangor May 30, reported in *Philadelphia North American,* June 9.
8. Reported in *Philadelphia North American,*June 13,14,15;also Wilson, *Rise and Fall of the Slave Power,* vol.II,pp. 425-432.
9. Henry Wilson was active in this bolt. He had gone to the Know-Nothings by the *coup d'etat* that secured him Everett's seat in the Senate. His deliberate purpose to break them up, in which he afterwards prided himself, is well substantiated by the correspondence of his contemporaries.
10. Statements relative to the facts in the election of 1855 are based on reports in the *Philadelphia North American, Tribune Almanac,* 1856, and biographical work covering the period.
11. *Albany Evening Journal,* Feb. 2 and 6. Bancroft,Frederick, *Life of Seward,* vol. I, pp. 375-377.
12. Treated in Chapter III, "Capitalizing Anti-Nebraska Sentiment".

13. Alexander, DeAlva S.,*Political History of New York*, vol.II. pp. 209-215 gives a good account of the election.
14. Alexander, DeAlva S.,*Political History of New York*, vol.II, p. 213.
15. *Albany Evening Journal*, Oct. 13. Also in pamphlet form.
16. *Albany Evening Journal*, Nov.9.
17. Simon Cameron with his following had gone into the Know-Nothing party. The Democrats considered it a good riddance and decided to keep him there.
18. There was a significant split in the Pennsylvania Council below, "Second Attempt of the Americans."
19. Call issued by a mass convention at Harrisburg Aug.8. It was instigated by the recent Ohio convention that nominated Chase for Governor. See, Going,C.B., *David Wilmot*, p. 469.
20. See Chapter V.
21. See below.
22. Term applied to adherents of the national platform of June 5.
23. Russell Errett to Chase, Nov. 16. Chase MSS. L.C.
24. The Bashford-Barstow controversy which resulted from the contesting of the returns had a large political vogue.
25. Cole,A.C., *Centennial History of Illinois*, vol. III., p.140.
26. Chase to E.L.Hamlin, Nov.21,1854. Chase MSS. L.C.
27. Chase to Dr. Paul, Dec. 28,1854, in Schuckers, *Life of Chase*, pp. 156-158.
28. Chase to J.S.Pike, March 22, in *First Blows of the Civil War*, p. 294.
29. O. Follett to Chase,May 2. Chase MSS. L.C. E.L.Hamlin of the *Columbian*, Chase's organ, was the chief offender. Chase had protested, had even denied official relation to the paper and talked of securing another editor. Chase to Hamlin, Jan.22. Chase to ——— Feb. 1. Chase MSS. L.C.
30. L.D.Campbell to Chase, May 28. Chase to Campbell, May 25, May 29. Chase MSS. L.C.
31. Ultimatum in *Astabula Sentinel* clipped by *Ohio Daily Statesman*, June 24.
32. Reported in *Philadelphia North American*, July 14, *Ohio Statesman*, July 14.
33. Chase to Kinsley S. Bingham, Oct. 19. Chase MSS. P.H.S. gives his own account of the canvass.
34. The election of Chase to the governorship is taken up again in Chapter III as a point in the organization of a national machine.
35. Hambleton, James R., *The Political Campaign in Virginia, 1855*, a contemporary account shows the importance attributed to the campaign.
36. For account, see Sioussat, St.George L., "Tennessee and National Political Parties 1850-60" in *American Historical Associations Report*, 1914, vol. I, p. 256.
37. Reported in *Philadelphia North American*, July 9.
38. *Ohio Statesman*, Nov. 17.
39. *American Organ*, Oct. 21.
40. Reported in *Ohio Statesman*, Nov. 24; *American Organ*, Nov. 23.

41. The Council of June 5 had set Feb. 22 as the time for a national convention.
42. *American Organ*, Nov. 23.
43. Reported in *Philadelphia North American*, Nov. 28.
43a. See note 41.
44. *American Organ*, Dec. 6.

CHAPTER III

MOBILIZATION

Capitalization of Anti-Nebraska Sentiment

It was obvious at once that the furor in the North over the Nebraska Act had political value for any person or party who could utilize it. Politicians and party manipulators saw this and began to act immediately. Thus it was that Chase had moved for a new party and Seward had tried to use the reaction to revive the anti-slavery Whigs. The election of 1855 had committed Seward to the new party project, but since he had held out so long and "demonstrated himself a partisan and demagogue," Chase had the advantage. Likewise the North Americans had tried to capitalize the reaction in order to become the leading anti-Nebraska party. The prospect of a new platform to be drafted by the Philadelphia council in February lessened their claims to anti-Nebraska preferment, but did not eliminate them. Besides the new party men and the North Americans there was still another group that welcomed the political upheaval as timely.

Since the renovation of the Democratic party in the Polk administration, there had existed an isolated group of politicians who regarded themselves as "Heirs of Jackson."[1] For the most part they were derelicts from the old Jackson party, and had been for a long while practically powerless. Frances P. Blair Sr., Jackson's editor, whom he had also chosen as executor of his political estate, was the leading figure. Associated with him were Thomas Hart Benton, Senate leader of Jackson's time, and Martin VanBuren, Jackson's successor to the presidency. This trio of original leaders were not all to be active in the new role the "Jacksonians" were to play. VanBuren was busy collecting data for his memoirs and took little aggressive interest in politics. Preston King and Abijah Mann who had recently withdrawn from the Softs kept the "Jacksonian" faith in the Empire state. Benton likewise proved unsusceptible to a new dispensation. Gideon Welles held an outpost in New England, and the editors of the *New York Evening Post*[2] were willing to open their columns to the "Jacksonians." Though the group was small, it was rich in tradition, and in forming a new order, traditions have power. These politicians who claimed to be the keepers of the creed of Jackson tried still another method of using anti-Nebraska capital.

The attack on the administration created a long sought opportunity. The "Jacksonians" had attributed their eclipse in the Democratic party to the ascendency of Slavery and had never wearied of denouncing the authors of their overthrow. Now, when all the North was stirred over the Kansas-Nebraska Bill, they could pronounce it a natural product of the conspiracy that had turned them out. Since the Democratic Party was to be disciplined, they could suggest as the best method its return to the true democrats—the followers of Jackson. Their free-soil belief and professed martyrdom because of it, gave them kinship to sentiment for the restriction of slavery wherever found. If the anti-Nebraska wave took political form that was radically sectional and threatening, they had the advantage of the Blair-Benton following in the Border Slave States, of being conservative, and also of being heirs to a union-saving tradition. Furthermore, if the method of redress for the recent legislation were to be an appeal to the people to rise in the name of democracy, they, as disciples of Jackson, would have much to say. There was opportunity in every aspect of the situation. Certainly a new day had dawned, and they were not slow to react. In fact they had been the first to move.

The strategy of the "Jacksonians" lay in a revolt within the Democratic Party—an uprising of "true democracy." Hence they would have no occasion for a new party, or for collaboration with the anti-slavery Whigs. Any hope of forcing a breach in the Democratic machine or of controlling the next convention was a forlorn one. Consequently they began to advocate an "anti-convention" nomination—one that took its candidate from the people, just as Jackson had been taken. Opinions varied as to exact method, but in general they wished to have some aboriginal Democrat taken up by local organizations, sweep the country, and then accept the nomination as coming spontaneously from the people. On such an arrangement it was hoped to put Benton or Houston in the field in 1856.[3] Their platform was the restoration of the Compromise with its attendant tranquillity—a position more conservative even than that of the North Americans. This would have to be fortified by a declaration asserting the power of Congress to legislate on slavery in the Territories. So conservative a position was resented by those who insisted on no more slave states. The conservative, anti-conventionists thus early began to measure swords with more radical opponents of the administration—men who wished a new party based on entire exclusion.

Benton and Houston were both available as counterparts of "Old Hickory," and the "Jacksonians" were confronted with the problem of selecting one or the other. Houston with his pioneer background and his signal speech against the Nebraska act was popular from the first. Before Congress adjourned he made a scouting trip and returned satisfied of support in the North.[4] He became the center of political interest in Washington, and his name was freely associated with an anti-convention nomination. J. S. Williams at Washington took up the task of king making. He got in touch with Gideon Welles and through him sought to approach Benton in order to get a proper letter to place with a friend in Ohio prior to the North American Convention to Cincinnati.[5] Houston added to the zest of his friends by his susceptibility, and he proved a good actor. He travelled about the country, was wined and dined, and made numerous speeches. He gave out that he did not intend to return to the Senate, to show that he had mended his ways he became a church member, and he named his newborn son Andrew Jackson.[6]

Just as the fall elections were registering the strength of anti-Nebraska feeling in the North, some of his friends attempted a *coup d' etat*. On October 11, a body styling itself the "General Democratic Committee" of the state of New Hampshire, met at Concord and issued an address recommending Houston for president.[7] Edmund Burke, editor of the *State Capitol Reporter* published at Concord had engineered the move, and at once committed his paper to the project of making Houston a popular candidate.[8] It eventually proved a premature and futile attempt of disgruntled politicians;[9] but it had a suggestive value. Coming from New Hampshire and

proposing to forego the machinery that nominated such men
as Pierce, the maneuver created a sensation. It also invited
the administration supporters to attack.

With the return of Congress, Houston came back to Washington to be "the lion of the session." Washburn of Maine,
Grow of the "Northern Tier" of Pennsylvania, and Banks of
Massachusetts were declared to be for him,[10] though Banks
insisted that he should not go to Boston and associate with
the Abolitionists. The Know-Nothing Convention at Cincinnati had considered him.[11] The Know-Nothings could not resist
his potentiality for popularity and flocked to him. August 1,
in a letter to the *Houston Telegraph* he had expressed warm
sentiments for them but he did not claim membership.[12]
Truman Smith settled down in New York to feel the pulse of
politics and declared that Houston would be the next president.[13] At the opportune moment a biography appeared which
made the most of an anti-convention program, Houston's
Jacksonian points, and his current work in the Senate.[14] A real
boom was under way, and the administration felt the necessity of a counter-stroke. Democratic Senators attacked his
conduct and motives, and accused him of angling for the
presidency by being a Know-Nothing and by super-sentimen-
tality over his Indian bills.[15] A pamphlet by Green of Texas
accused him of undue demonstrations when the body of the
great Compromiser, Clay, was being returned to Kentucky.[16]
But an attack from administration sources could not greatly
injure his popularity.

Early in the session an event took place which cleared the
track for him among "Jacksonian" friends. Benton, while
away conferring with Boston capitalists, had authorized his
colleague, Oliver, to read a speech in the House.[17] In it he took
a stand on two points that were vital to any prospective anti-
Nebraska candidate, namely: restoring the Compromise line
and resistance to the admission of Kansas with slaves. He
opposed both, the first because it would embarrass rapid
settlement so much needed to foster a Pacific railroad through
the Territory, and the second, because under the Louisiana
Treaty Kansas had a right to enter with slaves. This ruined
Benton for anti-convention purposes, and his most ardent
friends finally conceded that he was not a candidate.

Blair now came to Houston's support and was very much

in his company. He assumed a sort of political guardianship
for the "old Hero," and there was real need for a pilot.
Houston was constantly in the good graces of the Know-
Nothings. They spoke of him as their candidate. Belonging
to this nativist and patriotic organization was referred to as
"seeing Sam," and the inquiry: "Have you seen Sam?" was
a current saying. Houston's name fitted the expression, and
it was used with ever increasing insinuative value. Nor were
his friends able to keep him away from Boston.[19] The Abolitionists did not hurt him but the Know-Nothings did. He was
reported as attending their meeting during his trip.[20] "Jacksonian" friends became alarmed. Welles sent him an ultimatum on his relation to the Know-Nothings.[21] The only position
he might assume was to stand independently and let the
Know-Nothings support him, if they wished. It was questioned whether they would support one not of their own order.
They claimed Houston and the best he would do in giving
assurance that he was not a member was to say that he "knew
nothing." He also remained non-committal on Kansas, and
mindful of what Benton and VanBuren had done,[22] many
began to question his eligibility as an anti-Nebraska candidate. During the summer and with the developments of the
elections (1855) his support dropped away. The Houston
boom had spent its force and the "Jacksonians" were in search
of a *new man*. The year of the presidential election was approaching and nothing definite had been accomplished. The
anti-convention project constantly met opposition from the
men who were more radical in their views on the slavery
question and who wanted a new party. The elections of 1855
left the necessity of unity well demonstrated and any make-
shift to unite the two would be progress towards a new, great
party.

The new party idea had already passed a number of mile-
stones on its course.[23] Back of it was the ambition of Salmon
P. Chase, and his appeal to the Independent Democrats had
been a departure point. The first attempt at a new party of
national extent, according to Henry Wilson, was made in a
caucus at Washington the morning after the passing of the
Nebraska Bill.[24] Most of the members present favored the
party but some were for the Whigs. The various meetings in
caucus and otherwise that took place during the remainder of

the session and during the succeeding short session amounted
to nothing. In spite of the effort of Chase and his friends,
adjournment found a party still unorganized.[25] The Whigs
stood obstinately in the way, and Seward, encouraged by his
New York victory, vowed that he would die a Whig.[26] The
only way that was open to Chase was to make a demonstration in the West that would be "so hard, and vigorous, and
united as to compel the assent of the foolish Whigs of New
York and the East."[27] The spring elections in New England
which indicated the increased strength of Know-Nothingism
afforded Chase some consolation for they would have nothing
of Seward.[28]

At the same time that Chase was preparing for the demonstration in Ohio, he was active elsewhere. Early in the
summer he had been as far north as New York, and later in
the summer he made a visit to New England. There was talk
of him for 1856 in the East.[29] Nor were his activities confined
to this point of the compass. He had been in touch with
Grimes of Iowa since the very first of his governorship and
had his promise of support in April.[30] He had dictated the
creed of Governor Bingham of Michigan, and was assured of
his support as a political kinsman.[31] Besides laying hold of the
heads of the Republican states, he took the more important
step of starting to form a national machine. A Know-Some-
thing convention met at Cleveland June 13, just the time the
Know-Nothings were going to pieces at Philadelphia. All the
free states and Virginia and Kentucky were represented.[32] A
group of Chase's friends headed by James M. Ashley worked
the entire session of three days to get a resolution for a committee to correspond with seceding Know-Nothings everywhere and all other elements opposed to the administration
who would unite without distinction of party on an anti-
Nebraska platform.[33] The resolution finally passed and Ashley
was made chairman of the committee.[34] They, and those who
were found to sympathize with the action were empowered to
call a mass meeting about September 10 for the purpose of
consulting and making preliminary arrangements. The date
was set this early to be ahead of any other organization that
might be for Seward or Hale. Pittsburgh was chosen as the
place of meeting because it was centrally located and because
they intended to hold the nominating convention at Cincinnati.

Here was the genesis of the first Republican national convention. The project was bound up with the progress of Chase towards the nomination, and it was found impossible to do much constructive work while his fate hung in the balance in the Ohio election.

However, Chase tightened his political ties and acted as though the governorship were assured. He wrote to correspondents and friends in the East and again confided in Grimes and Bingham.[35] The convention that nominated him aided further by reporting in favor of a corresponding committee to reach other Republican organizations.[36] As soon as the nomination was secured, biographers began to appear. J. P. Jewett of Boston wished the job, and would get Sumner, who was reported favorable to Chase, to edit it.[37] D. W. Bartlett of Hartford sent for data and E. L. Pierce of Milton, Massachusetts, was doing a brief sketch.[38] Chase also began strengthening his press connections in Wisconsin.[39] J. C. Vaughn of the *Chicago Tribune*, an understudy, was enthusiastic, and was especially interested in securing the German vote.[40] Great things were in prospect for Chase, and when the election returns assured him the governorship,[41] the way seemed clear. With the New York elections two weeks later a new danger arose. Although the election took away the Whig menace, Seward's Albany speech had brought a new leader of national repute to the Republicans. It was creating a sensation.[42]

With his election Chase had passed another milestone and felt triumphant. The North Americans were quite as great a threat as the Whigs had been, and he felt that his relation to them in Ohio might have a suggestive value, though pure blood free-soilers feared that he had temporized.[43] He felt that he had united, besides anti-slavery Whigs and Democrats, also the "liberal Americans and anti-slavery adopted citizens." He expounded it thus to Governor Bingham:

> "The elements required for the presidential election have been harmonized by my election in Ohio and without that harmony I could not have been elected. They would be harmonized in a much greater degree in a presidential election. My uniform opposition in Congress to extravagant appropriations would probably rather injure than benefit my nomination, but after my

nomination would be an element not of incred-
ible value."
Still, if the friends of the cause thought another better fitted
to lead, "he would cheerfully and sincerely acquiesce."[44] As a
Republican governor he was in a position to continue to
harmonize the essential elements of his party and to put himself at the front in anti-Nebraska leadership. His play for
this and with it the coveted nomination is the story of a cause
that was destined to be lost.[45] With the victory, Ashley's correspondence committee was ready to begin work in earnest.

The full scope of the activities of this committee is hard to
ascertain, though its correspondence for the specific calling
of a convention was very definite. Its members travelled as
well as wrote and the work was open to any friendly assistance.
Chase aided personally, but as originally planned, in the
background.[46] His trip East during the summer had a direct
bearing on his plans. He was in Pittsburgh in November and
had an interview with D. N. White, editor of the *Gazette*, who
took up the matter of corresponding with the State Commit-
teemen.[47] Ashley was in Pittsburgh on November 16, inter-
viewing Errett of the *Gazette* on the subject of securing the
support of the Pennsylvania Chairman. Although the committee was in the hands of the Know-Nothings, Errett thought
that Wilmot, the chairman, would favor calling a convention,
and advised putting him in touch with the move through
A. P. Stone, the Ohio Chairman.[48] Brainard of Vermont was
also approached on the subject.[49] J. Z. Goodrich, Massachusetts chairman, seems to have entered upon the project
independently. The state committee had voted to begin
corresponding, and a few days later, on his own responsibility,
he broached the matter to Chase.[50] Iowa and Michigan had
been regularly in touch with the plans, although neither
chairman signed the call that finally resulted. White of
Wisconsin was the ony signer of whom there seems to be no
record in relation to plans made prior to the convening of
Congress. Wilmot, on whom special effort was being expended
and Goodrich, who came of his own accord, were not, as developments proved, friends of the movement as Chase wanted
it.

The meeting of Congress which brought politicians together
in large numbers soon convinced Chase that it was time to

strike. There was much interest in a candidate, and the general talk was for a convention of all the opposition to the administration in March. December 12 he wrote Stone that it was time for a call.[51] Stone wrote forthwith to Cassius M. Clay of Kentucky who was to furnish Southern support.[52] Ashley flooded the friends of the Republican cause with letters and circulars.[53] The call was to be for a convention at Pittsburgh, and February 22 was set as the time. The early date set by Chase and his friends was destined to meet opposition.

When the capital city became headquarters, politicians found the "Republican Association of Washington" organized and in shape to act as a clearing house for their transactions.[54] This club had grown up under the guidance of Louis Clephane who was an understudy of Doctor Bailey of the *Era*.[55] December 1, Blair had given it his blessing although he refused to become its president. His letter was printed and distributed "to aid the Republicans in bringing the Government back to the principle of Freedom."[56] This gave it prestige, and it needed nothing by way of impetus for work in the details of organization. Before December 25 it had already worked out a plan to perfect the organization of the new national party which was to be called into existence.[57]

The "association" was too officious and too open to the influence of the politicians who trooped about Washington to please Chase and his friends. It sent out sample calls to the state chairmen for their approval and signature and the date did not correspond with that set by Chase.[58] A fight was the result. There was abundant reason why Clephane and his associates who knew all the political currents at the capitol did not accept February 22 as the date. Seward's friends might feel that it was too closely identified with Chase, though there is no evidence to that effect. Though few, the "anti-conventionists" were a power in Washington. Blair had given up his antipathy for conventions and was now talking of three of them—Insurgent Democrats, Republicans, and anti-Slavery Know-Nothings—all to be held at Cincinnati when the Democrats met at that place.[59] North Americans were opposed to the forming of a new party on anti-slavery principles prior to their February meetings at Philadelphia. They were looking forward to forcing a postponement of the nomination or else to a bolt. In either event they would be an influence in the anti-Nebraska field and did not care to have a new party formed until they were free to play a part in it. There was also a general feeling that acting on a convention now would interfere with the election of speaker for the new congress and should be postponed.[60] Conservatives in general wished delay and deliberation rather than to answer a call for a new party, sponsored by Chase and taking as radical a ground as the non-extension of slavery.

The contest was a sharp one. Ashley wrote twenty-five letters to urge the date Chase desired.[61] Mott who was directing the Chase forces at Washington refused to yield ground, and the Michigan committee stood by the twenty-second for the convention, even if they had to attend it alone.[62] The opposition finally yielded and just as Governor Chase was being congratulated for his Kansas message—a masterly anti-Nebraska performance—the date for the call was changed to February 22.[63] The fixing of date had more significance than to commemorate the natal day of the father of the country. In gaining it, Chase saved the Pittsburgh convention to Republicanism.

The following call bearing the date, January 17, was issued by the Republican Association:

"In accordance with what appears to be the general desire of the Republican party, and at the suggestion of a large portion of the Republican press, the undersigned chairmen of the State Republican Committees of Maine, Vermont, Massachusetts, New York, Pennsylvania, Ohio, Michigan, Indiana, and Wisconsin, hereby invite the Republicans of the Union to meet in informal convention at Pittsburgh on the 22d of February, 1856, for the purpose of perfecting a national organization and providing for a national delegate convention of the Republican party at some subsequent day, to nominate candidates for the presidency and vice-presidency to be supported in the election in November, 1856."

> A P. Stone, Ohio
> J. Z. Goodrich, Massachusetts
> David Wilmot, Pennsylvania
> Lawrence Brainard, Vermont
> William A. White, Wisconsir

Before the time for the proposed Pittsburgh Convention had arrived, something of great importance happened to the growing national party. Blair and the "Jacksonians"—what was left of them—cast their lot with it. Although Blair still cherished the idea of a mass meeting at Cincinnati that would "take from the dough-faces the name they used as Imposters," he found occasion to go to Pittsburgh. An invitation reached him from a Republican club at Baltimore to represent them there. Louis Clephane had formed this club of Quakers for the specific purpose of securing Blair.[64] Blair sent his son-in-law to investigate, with the intention of accepting, should they be found as respectable as friends had represented them.[65] If in a slave city, he found men who wished him to represent them "in maintaining if adopted the temperate middle issue of the restored compromises" he felt it his duty to go. Blair's resolution brought the Jacksonians into the fold of the new party, and with them a position much more conservative than that of the followers of Chase, the free-soiler. Although it did not insure harmony, the combination would be an added assurance against North American dominance. Blair also brought with him the mantle of Jackson, and some ideas about a *new man* who should be his counterpart and successor.

Control of the House

Chase had managed to secure the call for a preliminary convention in spite of the desire of many politicians to leave it alone until the organization of the House of Representatives was completed. This significant political battle to which they wished to give precedence had begun when Congress convened December 3, and was to continue for two weeks after the call of January 17 had been given to the public. It was the first meeting of all the political forces and factors that were to contend in the ensuing election and its outcome would have a marked influence on the future of the party which would make a national debut February 22.

Though the Democrats of the new Congress were in a minority, their morale was superb. Their recent victory in Pennsylvania had put the Keystone state in the fore-front, and the position of floor leader fell to one of her representatives—J. Glancy Jones of Berks county. On the Saturday before Congress convened they met in caucus and defined their position. Though temporarily in a minority, the Democrats thanked their "fellow citizens of the whole union for the recent victories of the principles of the Kansas Nebraska Bill, and the doctrine of civil and religious liberty." It was their duty to defend every class and every section.[66] As a candidate for the speaker-ship they nominated Richardson of Illinois. He was a Douglas protégé, and thus well chosen to vindicate the Kansas-Nebraska legislation. Better still, he was on record as believing in the constitutionality of the Wilmot Proviso, and to support the Nebraska measure now, with such a background, was a tribute to the new principle and a testimony that it was not southern. Although they could give Richardson only seventy-four votes out of two hundred and twenty-five, they were confident of the inability of their opponents to give a majority to any nominee.

Joshua Giddings became the spokesman of the opposition that made the anti-Nebraska principle the supreme issue. He had been censured for anti-slavery activity in the House and to organize it now when it contained a majority opposed to the Nebraska bill, afforded him great satisfaction. Those who supported Giddings and who were customarily referred to as Republicans (Black Republicans by their ardent opponents) held an informal meeting which they refused to pronounce a caucus and came to a general agreement to support no one for speaker who would not appoint committees that would do the utmost to "restore freedom to Kansas." [67] The distinct anti-Nebraska vote was at first thrown to L. D. Campbell who had been designated as a candidate in the Ohio elections. On the first ballot he received fifty-three votes, and on the twelfth his vote was two in excess of Richardson's. But all the "anti-Nebraska-ites" had not united on Campbell. Some of the New York congressmen led by Sage and a considerable number from New England supported Nathaniel P. Banks, Jr. of Massachusetts. Since Campbell could not unite the votes an agreement was struck to throw him as large a vote as possible by way of compliment; then drift over to Banks, and failing to concentrate on him to go next to Pennington of New Jersey.[68] On the fifteenth ballot Campbell received eighty votes and then his support began to diminish.

There was some consternation at his reluctance to take a hint for he did not withdraw his name until after the twenty-third ballot and then with an explanation.[69] He could not be elected, he said, unless he gave pledges "directly or indirectly" on forming the committees which he felt would mean a sacrifice of self-respect and make him an object of public contempt.

Banks' support increased until on the thirty-fifth call of the house he had a hundred and seven votes. This was about the maximum number to be expected, and it fell five or six short of a majority. Organization might be effected if a group of "recusant" brothers could be drawn into line. This group was led by L. D. Campbell, with Dunn, Indiana's "off-ox," and Scott and Scott Harrison of Ohio as conspicuous associates. They voted for Pennington and consistently refused to go to Banks, in spite of the war made on them in the press. Banks could not be given up for their sake, for it was felt that it would be dangerous to attempt to unite on another candidate. Just before the thirty-eighth ballot, when the Banks' support was near its maximum, Thorington of Iowa moved for a plurality rule. There was a good precedent for this in the Cobb-Winthrop contest of 1849, and it became the Republican objective. Their greatest problem was to keep steadily supporting Banks. Greeley, who had over-ruled the wishes of both his subordinates and come to Washington himself, undertook to discipline any wavering member by exposure in the *Tribune*. Some of the more ardent and practical Republicans formed a club which met every other night, and which did much to prevent bolts by keeping up telegraphic communication with anti-Nebraska constituents.[70] The Banks' vote became as unwavering as that of Richardson.

The concentration of the large vote in support of the Republican candidate was due in part to the action of the Americans. A distinct majority of the House was Know-Nothing in its sentiment, but many North Americans had put the anti-Nebraska issue first. Both Campbell and Banks were Know-Nothings, and their candidacy was calculated to win all their fellow believers who were also opposed to the Nebraska bill. A few Americans from Pennsylvania led by Broom and another small group from New York headed by Whitney made a bloc of Know-Nothings from the North that would not unite in support of an anti-Nebraska candidate. This was important

and on it, and on such Know-Nothings from the South as
could not be readily driven to the Democrats, the security of
the party rested for the ensuing fight.   However precarious
their position might be, the prospect of agreeing on a new
national platform in the council to be held in February, led
the Americans to take the offensive and to clear the way for
the work they proposed to do at that time.   After a preliminary skirmish they centered their votes on Fuller of Pennsylvania.   He was a northern man, was known as an opponent
of the Kansas-Nebraska bill, and had defeated a Nebraska
Democrat for his seat in Congress.   His supporters numbered
about thirty-five and regardless of a bitter press attack on
those from the North, the group stood as securely as its opponents.   Although fewer than either antagonist, the Americans
were able to do considerable toward making a record that
would sustain their prospective compromise platform.   On
December 17 Broom offered a resolution to the effect that the
main points at issue in the slavery controversy be left to the
Supreme Court.   Before the battle was over, Eustis of Louisiana had, with some dissent, put the party on record for a more
lenient policy towards Catholics—only "foreign Catholics were
objectionable." [71] Zollicoffer of Tennessee succeeded in getting
a resolution passed whereby the candidates were "catechised"
and the middle-ground position of the Americans magnified.
Emphasize their compromise position as they would, they
could scarcely avoid being ground to pieces between the upper
and nether mill-stones of the slavery issue.

So long as each party stood by its guns, there could be no
organization, and none seemed inclined to yield.   Each accused the other of preventing organization and all assumed
that the people were distressed and the country in danger
because of their failure.   On December 15 with fifty-nine
ballots already on record, the first vital move was made—
Hickman of Pennsylvania introduced a resolution to eliminate
all candidates until only the two highest were left.[72] The
Americans met this proposition for their destruction by
thrusting forward their compromise position, but at the same
time read out of the party all those who did not stand by the
twelfth article.[73] The next tactial move was led by Percy
Walker, Know-Nothing from Alabama, who declared their
position on the slavery question to be the same as the Demo-

crats, and called for a common caucus which meant that the Democrats reciprocate by supporting Fuller.[74] This overture met a sharp rebuff at the hands of the floor leader, Jones, and Congressman Cobb of Georgia. The failure of this attempt led to a renewed effort to scatter Banks' support. All the ingenuity of skilled parliamentarians was directed against his motley following to no avail. A resolution from the Ohio Legislature, read January 9, sealed the fate of further efforts to disrupt the Banks forces. The last hope had been that someone be substituted who might secure the "recusants" led by Campbell, but now Ohio, whence came most of the recalcitrants, had denounced them. The vote for Banks and the plurality rule remained constant.

Increased assurance of Republican solidarity led to a renewal of the attempt to bring Americans and Democrats together. Although Walker had declared the oneness of the two parties on the principle of "non-intervention" the Americans refused to endorse Richardson as a proof of it.[75] Walker renewed his proposition substituting Boyce, Democrat from South Carolina, for Fuller; but was again blocked by the Democrats. However, the Americans were offering a way out, and the Democrats at last decided to make such concessions on candidates as were necessary. Clingman of North Carolina began the work of effecting a combination. Richardson withdrew his name and Fuller asked his followers to vote for another. A. K. Marshall of Kentucky, as spokesman for the Americans, declared their group ready to act with the Democrats, asking only that their candidate be not supported by caucus resolutions. Clingman, acting on the American declaration of oneness in principle, declared his intention of putting the responsibility squarely upon them, and moved for a plurality rule.[76] The Democrats and Americans were approaching each other, though Marshall insisted he had not joined the Democracy. The next day, February 1, Cobb of Georgia presented the name of William Aiken of South Carolina, and Orr, who succeeded Richardson, but who had the support of caucus resolutions, requested his name withdrawn. Whitney of New York, American bellwether from the North, sustained Aiken, and the vote showed that the Americans would support him. The crisis had come; the house adjourned, with organization assured for the next day.

With full assurance of Aiken's success, Smith, Democrat of Tennessee, moved for a plurality rule.[77] The motion was sustained. After three votes, if no candidate had a majority, one more vote was to be taken, and the candidate who had the most votes, provided it was a majority of a quorum should be speaker.[78] On the first vote about half of the Americans went to Aiken; the next two saw no change. Fuller asked his friends, who could not drop him so abruptly, to support another candidate. The roll call for the fourth vote was then begun. A. K. Marshall, spokesman for the maneuver for the Americans, when his name was called, explained the basis of the arrangement.

"We have demanded from our Democratic friends a recognition of our existence, our respectability, our patriotism, and an acknowledgement upon their part that they did us an injustice in the opinion they expressed by the resolution in the first caucus, and the declaration made in regard to us in that resolution. We have fought the good fight for our party and we have done more— we have conquered for them. The Democracy have no candidate for the office of Speaker before us now. Is there a nominee of that party here? Is there a Democratic platform now presented which bears on its face an offence and indignity to the American party? No sir, neither is before this body now. They have lost sight of both and why should we remember them longer?"

But Marshall had miscalculated the result. The concentration of the American vote on Aiken would mean the annihilation of the party in the North, and prominent Americans had spent a greater part of the preceding night making sure of a few votes to stand by Fuller.[79] There was great interest as the call proceeded. The tellers reported the results; four Republican recusants voted for Campbell, six Americans voted for Fuller, Aiken received a hundred votes; Banks received a hundred and three, and was declared Speaker of the House of Representatives of the Thirty-Fourth Congress.

The nine weeks of time and the hundred and thirty-three ballots that had been required to elect Banks had not been wasted. Significant among its results was the fact that the Americans had maintained a nucleus in the North, had not been submerged completely by the slavery issue, and the ensu-

ing council at Philadelphia might work out a national platform on the ground where Fuller had stood. The outcome,
however, had been a triumph for the Republicans. The
anti-Nebraska issue had again dominated the Nativist. It
gave them self-assurance in going to the Pittsburgh Convention, there to start their party without deference to what North
Americans might do at Philadelphia. There was almost
positive assurance now that the new "party of the North"
would be fusionist in nature and non-extensionist in principle.
The Republicans also secured the committees they wished but
failed to elect a printer. With their committees and their
anti-Nebraska majority they were ready to attack the program of the administration and thereby teach the country the
meaning and the purpose of the new party.

The Pittsburgh Convention

Less than three weeks after the election of Banks to the
speakership, the Republicans met at Pittsburgh in response to
the call for a convention to organize a national machine. The
assemblage was accounted especially large, considering the
inclement weather, and the immediate profitlessness of the
mission.[80] All the free states and five slave states were represented.[81] Blair and his followers had joined themselves to
the original movers. The prospect of complete ascendency
over the North Americans led to further accretions, and the
result was a group complex in background and lacking unity
of purpose. A preliminary meeting held at the Monongahela
Hotel showed how utterly confused the delegations were, and
alarmed those who hoped for concerted action. Out of it
grew the appointment of a committee of one from each state
to meet at eight o'clock the following morning and work out
a program before the heterogeneous convention should assemble.[82] The committee met at eight and everything was arranged
for the work of the day.

The pre-arranged organization worked smoothly. Owen
Lovejoy, brother of the Alton martyr, prayed. He asked the
Supreme Being to remove President Pierce, or else give him a
new vision. John A. King was made temporary chairman
and Francis P. Blair was given the permanent chairmanship.

He was received with enthusiasm and brought dignity, tradition, and conservatism to the meeting. His presidential address, presented as voicing the sentiment of southern constituents, was conservative and much in contrast with most of the utterances. Greeley, who brought the advice of Washington friends for caution, had a tilt with Giddings who questioned any sort of suggestion that came from Washington. The necessary committees were set to work and then the convention indulged in an outpouring of anti-slavery enthusiasm. Charles Remelin, German politician of Cincinnati, who had recently left the Administration Party, made a brilliant speech. The burden of his plea was that the new organization denounce the principles and methods of Know-Nothingism.[83] There was apparent harmony but the first day threw into relief the unfused elements: anti-slavery American, German, Republican proper, and the element introduced by Blair.

The committees were not ready to report when the convention met again the second day, and speaking continued. Burroughs of New York sounded a note that was much in contrast with the anti-slavery hurrah of the preceding day. It was part of the caution that Greeley had advised and related to the presence of Blair and of those who were North Americans at heart. It would be easy, he said, to create a small party on slavery. For that, they need only "borrow Gerrit Smith's patent right." The Americans and others he thought might be included.[84] A letter was read from Cassius M. Clay of Kentucky which had the import of representing Republican sentiment in the South. Later in the day Remelin tried again to get a resolution against Know-Nothingism in order to bring in the German vote but failed. The expression of the Convention was neutral as to these two groups. The Germans might take consolation in the claims of the archenemies of Know-Nothingism—that it was so little a part of the convention that it was unnecessary to mention it at all.[85] The tone was distinctly Republican, but the convention pointed out a great field for combination and assimilation— a problem of including elements in one place that would crowd others out elsewhere.

The national machinery which had been the objective of the convention was put in running order. The national committee, composed of one member from each state, was led by E. D.

Morgan of New York.[86] Some of the southern states present had no members on the committee, but it was empowered to add to its own numbers and to fill vacancies. The committee was also empowered to arrange for a nominating convention to be held at Philadelphia June 17. This was to be a delegate convention in which each state was entitled to twice as many delegates as it had representatives in Congress. The task of completing state organization was likewise given to the committee. Thus, the Republican machine was launched.

The platform of the convention, and its tone were essentially Republican, and practically came up to the standard of the platform of 1848. There was to be no slavery in territories once dedicated to freedom, and constitutional resistance was to be offered to its extension into any territory. In Kansas, already the seat of civil war, the Republicans were to give aid to the "freemen," and in Congress it was their duty to admit it as a free state. Their political objective was the overthrow of the administration.[87] Besides laying down their course of action and defining their objective they began another part of their program. The committee began work on a long and instructive address on the nature of slavery and the reasons for its restrictions.[88]

1. Nichols,R.F., *The Democratic Machine,1850-1854, chapter V,* gives a description of this group.
2. This paper was "Barnburner" and was edited by William Cullen Bryant and John Bigelow. Nevins,Allen,*New York Evening Post,* gives a very satisfactory history of the paper.
3. Blair to VanBuren, August 24, 1854. VanBuren MSS. L.C.
4. J.S.Williams to Welles, July 2, 1854. Welles MSS. L.C.
5 Williams to Welles, July 14. Welles MSS. L.C.
6. *Life of Sam Houston,* 1855; also Williams to Welles, Oct. 17, July 14, Dec.11. Welles MSS. L.C.
7. Text in *Life of Sam Houston,* 1855. pp. 393-95.
8. Williams to Welles, Oct. 17. Welles MSS. L.C.
9. Burke considered himself a king-maker in 1852 but he had broken with the administration and had found a kindred spirit in Daniel S. Dickinson, leader of the Hards. Dickinson was bitter against the administration. Nichols, *Democratic Machine,* pp. 121-128. Burke MSS. L. C.
10. Williams to Welles, Dec. 11. Welles MSS. L.C.
11. Chase to E.L.Hamlin, Nov. 21. Chase MSS. L. C.
12. Notice in *Philadelphia North American,* Aug. 18.
13. Smith to Welles, Dec. 19. Welles MSS. L. C.
14. *Life of Sam Houston,* J.C.Darby, N.Y. 1855, cited above.

15. Crane, William C., *Life and Select Literary Reminiscences of Sam Houston,* pp. 219-222, gives an account of this.
16. Houston's defense, Feb. 14, 1855. *Globe* vol. XXX, p. 742.
17. *Globe,* vol. XXX, p. 79. Dec. 18.
18. Preston King to Welles, April 15, 1855. Welles MSS. L.C.
19. He made the trip and spoke at Faneuil Hall, Feb. 22.
20. Welles to John Boyd, March, 1855. Welles MSS. L.C.
21. Williams to Welles, April 20. Welles to King, April 23. Welles MSS. L.C.
22. VanBuren did not bolt when the Softs took ground that led to the withdrawal of Mann and King and the protest of Dorsheimer.
23. This was mentioned in connection with the appeal to the Independent Democrats treated in Chapter I, and the New York and Ohio Elections in Chapter II.
24. *Rise and Fall of the Slave Power,* vol.II, pp. 410-411.
25. Joshua Leavitt to Chase, March 13-14, 1855. Chase MSS. P.H.S.
26. He took his stand in the *Albany Evening Journal,* May 26; Giddings to Chase, Oct. 16. Chase MSS. P.H.S.
27. Joshua Leavitt to Chase, March 13-15, cited above.
28. Besides being their political enemy in New York, Seward had attacked them openly.
29. J.S.Pike to Chase Jan. 29. Chase MSS. P.H.S. Chase to Pike, June 20. *First Blows,* pp. 295-96 Pike to Chase,Oct.18, *First Blows,* pp. 229-230.
30. Grimes to Chase, April 8; Slater, *Life of Grimes,* pp. 68-69.
31. Bingham to Chase, Jan. 8, 1855. July 7. Chase MSS. L.C.
32. Reported in *Philadelphia North American,* June 15.
33. J.M.Ashley to Chase, June 16. Chase MSS. L.C.
34. His associates were Jas.A.Briggs of Cleveland, J.S.Sayward of Maine, Schuyler Colfax of Indiana, J.W.Stibbens, of New York, O.W.Slack of Boston, and F.H.Benson of Illinois.
35. Chase to Pike, June 20, *First Blows,* pp. 295-96; Grimes to Chase, July 16, Slater, *Life of Grimes,* p. 74; Bingham to Chase, July 7, Chase MSS. L.C.
36. *Philadelphia North American,* July 14.
37. J.P.Jewett to Chase, July 19. Chase MSS. L.C.
38. D.W.Bartlett to Chase, Sept. 18; E.L.Pierce to Chase, Nov.9. Chase MSS. L.C.
39. T.F.Withrow to Chase, Oct. 12 and 13. Chase MSS. L.C.
40. J.P.Vaughn to Chase, July 17. Chase MSS. P.H.S.
41. For account of the election in Ohio, see Chapter II.
42. Ashley to Chase, Oct. 21. Chase MSS. L.C.
43. Bailey to Chase, Nov. 27. Chase MSS. P.H.S.
44. Chase to Bingham, Oct. 19. Chase MSS. P.H.S.
45. See Chapter VII.
46. Ashley to Chase, June 16, cited above.
47. Errett, Russell, in *Western Magazine of History,* vol. VII. pp. 181-182. Errett gives Chase the entire credit for the move and the work of White credit for the call. Errett's article was written many years later, and he might have had in mind Ashley's visit.

48. Russell Errett to Chase, Nov. 16. Chase MSS. L.C.
49. Kleeberg,J.S.P., *The Republican National Machine*, p. 28, based on an interview with Clephas Brainard.
50. J.Z.Goodrich to Chase, Nov. 17. Chase MSS. L.C.
51. J.P.Stone to Chase, Dec. 14. Chase MSS. L.C.
52. Stone's Letter in *Philadelphia North American*, Dec. 27. There was always a play for Southern representation to avoid the stigma of being sectional.
53. Ashley to Chase, Jan. 18. Chase MSS. L.C. At this time he had received forty-one replies, all but one favorable to the convention, three not in agreement on the time.
54. Organized June 19.
55. For account, Clephane,Louis, *Birth of theRepublican Party*.
56. Pamplet:*"Blair's Letter to the Republican Association of Washington,Dec.1."*
57. I.Washburn to J.L.Stevens,Dec.25. I.Washburn MSS. L.C.
58. I.Washburn to Stephens, Dec. 26. I.Washburn MSS. L.C.
59. Blair to VanBuren, Jan.25. Van Buren MSS. L.C.
60. Preston King to Welles, Jan. 3. Welles MSS. L.C.
61. Ashley to Chase, Jan. 18, cited above.
62. *Ibid.*
63. G.Bailey to Chase, Jan. 20. Chase MSS. L.C.
64. This is Clephane's own story told in *Birth of Republican Party*, p. 13.
65. Blair to VanBuren, Feb. 13. VanBuren MSS. L.C.
66. *Globe*, vol. XXXVIII, p. 62.
67. *Ibid.*, p.11.
68. Giddings' letter read in Congress, Jan. 9. *Globe*, vol. XXXVIII, p. 174.
69. *Globe*, vol. XXXVIII, p. 11.
70. Hollister, J.O., *Life of Schuyler Colfax*, p.86, gives a description of this based on Colfax correspondence.
71. *Globe* vol. XXXVIII, pp. 166-67.
72. *Globe*, vol. XXXVIII, p. 34.
73. Globe, vol. XXXVIII, pp.47-48. Humphrey Marshall of Kentucky defined the position of the party in a speech that was considered a sort of guidepost throughout the campaign.
74. *Globe*, vol. XXXVIII, p. 38.
75. *Globe*, vol. XXXVIII, p. 93. The test vote was taken on a resolution introduced by Seward of Georgia, December 28.
76. *House Journal*, 34th Congress, 1st Session, January 31.
77. April 4 Smith made a speech explaining this vote.
78. *House Journal*, February 2.
79. Bailey to Chase, Feb. 21. Chase MSS. L.C.
80. Republican Party Conventions, 1856-1864, p.8; *New York Tribune*, Feb. 23.
81. Accounts vary. Greeley said eight slave states, e.g., *Tribune*, Feb. 25.
82. *Republican Party Conventions*, 1856-1864, p.8;Clephane, *Birth of the Republican Party*, p.13.Clephane says that the morning committee and the arrangements were the result of a night's work by J.W.Stone of Boston and himself.

83. *Tribune,* Feb.23. Russell Errett after thirty-two years recalled the brilliance of this speech. *Western Magazine of History,*vol. VII.
84. *Republican Party Convention,* 1856-1864, pp.10-11.
85. Julian,G.W. to *New York Independent,* Feb. 29 in Clarke, *Life of Julian,* pp.170-171. Julian and radical free-soilers of his type were uncompromising enemies of nativism.
86. The members were: Fogg,N.H.; Brainard,Vt;Niles,Conn;Chase, R.I;Stone,O;Leland,Ill;Spooner,Wis;Clephane,D.C;Paulison,N.J.; Wilmot,Pa;Blair, Mo; Field, Ky; Stephens, Ia; Gross, Ind; Dickie, Mich;Blair,Md.
87. Statements based on *Republican Party Conventions,* 1856-1864, pp.10-11.
88. Text in *New York Tribune,* March 1.

PART II

THE ATTEMPT TO CONVERT THE NORTH

CHAPTER IV

ADOPTION OF ANTI-SLAVERY PROPAGANDA

Although the Republicans could use their control of the popular branch of the national legislature for political ends, and had at their disposal the machinery of a national organization, they had merely approached their problems, not solved them. In the "Address of the Committee of the Pittsburgh Convention" they made the official beginning of the work of persuading the masses of the North to support the incipient party. It was a big task for the position of the party was a radical one. In spite of the advantage afforded them by the political chaos in the North and by the "anti-everything" state of mind that existed there, large numbers of men would still hesitate to support a party, the victory of which seemed to mean certain disruption of the Union. To overcome this difficulty and to secure a following large enough to carry the populous free states, it was necessary to undertake a program that in recent years would be termed a "campaign of education."

The Republican leaders made a practical problem out of the converting of the people of the North. Ways and means of distributing "literature" were developed side by side with the political machine. Along with the call for the Pittsburgh Convention, the Washington Association had sent a circular containing a plan for organizing local clubs.[1] The Association included its own platform with the circular to serve as an example. When a new club was organized, it was to register with the parent association, send lists of persons who should receive documents, and open regular correspondence with Washington.[2] In order to supply the necessary pamphlets, the Association contracted with Buell and Blanchard of Washington to do its printing, and secured the service of a person competent to translate documents into the German language. Later an auxiliary document committee was organized to send pamphlets to places where local clubs did not flourish.[3]

Besides their improvised machinery, the Republicans had other publicity assets. Congressmen, now in a new alignment, would frank as many documents as possible in order to strengthen their constituents in the new political faith. Many of the most influential papers of the North had part in the building of the Republican party and in its first national campaign.[4] Back of nearly every such paper was the personality of an able editor, who was independent, who made no obeisance to the party in power or the great propertied institutions attacked, and who came into the movement as a free lance. Some of these papers used their press facilities to furnish pamphlets at a very cheap rate. Smaller papers, local political organizations, and even church congregations joined in the business of producing campaign material. Funds to meet the cost of printing were to be secured locally; for, like the party, said its promoters, the money to run it must come from the people. The net result of the efforts to reach the public was a campaign that, prior to the civil war, was not excelled in the amount and variety of "literature" distributed.

The sources of propaganda available for the Republicans were very extensive. The anti-Nebraska Congress might spend the whole first session in manufacturing it. The "civil war" in Kansas could be directed to that end. The controversy over slavery, especially from the time of the Missouri Compromise, had resulted in the accumulation of a large amount of argumentive material. Although the Republicans could not endorse politically the position taken by the abolitionists, their anti-slavery works and even their methods were assets as propaganda. From an extensive back-ground, facts, falsehoods, everything was revamped, elaborated, and brought to its most effective form for campaign purposes.[5] The argument over the slavery question thus furnished the Republicans was a big factor in eclipsing the Americans with their anti-Catholic, anti-foreign creed. The Republican purpose was to use the mass of argument to convince the North and persuade it to use its preponderance of numbers to control the nation and close the territories to slavery—as Greeley phrased it— "sweep the North."

Economics of Slavery

The question of the extension of slavery to the virgin soil of Kansas invited discussion of its economic merits and demerits. All the arguments on the economic short-comings of the slavery system that had been accumulating for the last quarter of a century were reviewed, expanded, and used with a more specific objective than ever before. In arguing for the desirability of extending free-labor instead of servile, comparison of the slave-holding and free states was the most direct and convincing method.

The first thing fixed upon in the attack on the economic system of the South was the thing most obvious to travellers in that section. The scattered population, the long reaches of abandoned land, gullied, weed-grown, and uninhabited, were cited as the first fruits of slavery where it had driven out free labor. Such pictures of the South were current long before 1856. An anecdote from its own section gave the most forceful putting of this *prima facie* evidence of slavery's faulty economy. Henry A. Wise had used it in his stump speeches. A certain stranger, ran the account, while travelling in the Old Dominion, met a native and fell to conversing with him. Passing a deserted house with its eloquence of delapidation, the stranger inquired as to its owner. The native companion confessed that it was his. Passing a second, the same dialogue occurred. On the third, the Virginian said: "Yes, that's mine too, stranger, but don't think I'm so d—d poor as to own all the land about here." Slavery drove out the small owner leaving the large holder who could live by operating on a smaller margin and by selling his over-plus of servile humanity where slavery in newer lands had not yet completed its desolation. This was the "skinning system," arrayed against which were the farms, towns, and free schools of the North. Frederick Law Olmstead's *The Seaboard Slave States* was opportunely published and was received as added evidence of the condition of the South.

These observations citing evidences of the evils of slave labor, were buttressed by an accumulation of argument and the whole rounded into a many-sided attack. Besides ruining the land and preventing a numerous population the system of the South was indicted as faulty in that it was not economically self-sufficient. The production of a staple rendered the South dependent, not only for manufactured goods, but also for her food products. The lack of fluid capital characteristic of the system was interpreted as a weakness. The South ran a deficit every year, it was argued, and the North was actually contributing to its upkeep—the South was a "Penuro-cracy."[6] This might be all right for their own section, if they liked it; but when it became a question of extending it to places where the "real owners" of the country were interested, it was time to stop the "pauper dictators."

The attacks on the industrial system that the South desired to spread to the virgin soil of Kansas, were characteristically bitter and scathing. The series of commercial conventions in which southern economists discussed methods of enhancing commerce, furnished a good point of assault. The northern press considered them confessions, and reiterated their language, much to the vexation of the authors. The discovery of a *Tribune* reporter in a convention was tantamount to a riot. Nor was it remarkable that it should be. One of these conventions was held at Richmond in the early spring of 1856 which called forth comment:—

"There was lately at the home of pseudo-democracy, that center of self-sufficiently, that fathomless, bungless barrel of political small beer—Richmond, Virginia—a commercial convention. What, in one view of the case, it might be asked, could a commercial convention do there, where commerce—save in human flesh, can hardly be named, if we except too, sales of that weed, which, while it has blasted the soil, turns domestic altars, hotel parlors, railroad cars, theatre boxes, legislative halls, nay even churches into huge spit boxes—concretions of beastly filth, respecting neither age nor sex—and to which the aboriginal grease and stench of savages are attractive in comparison? O Progress! O Civilization! O Chivalry! O Refinement! Niggers and tobacco squirting."[7]

A convention occasioned the airing of the alleged economic degeneracy of the South. In words of their own speakers an impending crisis was announced:—

"In vain do men go to Nashville, and to Knoxville, and to Memphis, and Charleston in their annual farce of southern commercial conventions to build up southern commerce, and to break down the abolition cities Philadelphia, Boston, and New York. The orator rises upon a northern made carpet; clothed cap-a-pie in northern fabrics, and offers his resolutions written upon northern paper with a northern pen, and returns to his home on a northern car; or being killed, is put into a northern shroud, and buried in a northern coffin, and his funeral preached from a text from a northern hymn book, set to northern music. And they resolve and resolve, and forthwith there's not another ton of shipping built, or added to the manufacture of the South, and yet these men are not fools! They never invite such men as I to their conventions, because I would tell them that slavery was the cause of their poverty, and that it is free labor which they need."[8]

Cassius M. Clay of Kentucky was the leading exponent of this type of economic doctrine, and he left little room for originality to Hinton J. Helper's celebrated work the following year.[9] Clay dethroned King Cotton and put grass in his stead. Nine staples were of larger value he declared. The argument that the staple sent abroad favored exchanges and liquidated the public debt was erroneous, because it was offset by the importation of "questionable luxuries." "If you were to blot out the whole foreign trade in cotton, the country in the eyes of true political economy would be much the gainer; in domestic industry, in home manufacture, home labor, and a home market for ourselves." General conclusions were drawn to the effect that the whole system of the South was one of waste and impoverishment. Nor was there any help for it. Slave labor could not be made progressive or scientific; it could not develop natural resources or bless the land with a healthy, prosperous citizenry. It could only spread the curse of its blight and ignorance to new fields, and that must not be allowed.

The main reason for these conditions was attributed to the influence of slavery in either driving out or degrading free labor. The "Poor White" of the South was the result where free labor remained in competition with slavery. There was much comment and speculation on this lower stratum of the southern population. Its position had come to prominent notice in the North but recently. Cassius M. Clay and John C. Vaughn of the *Chicago Tribune* were responsible for the discovery.[10] George M. Weston's pamphlet, *The Poor Whites of the South*, gave the topic the most satisfactory treatment and became one of the great documents of the campaign.[11] Although the "Poor White" comprised seven-tenths of the population, Weston contended that he was inarticulate. The plantation system had pursued him, driving the independent farmer and small planter on to new lands and leaving this derelict on the confines of civilization, in poverty, ignorance, and viciousness. Weston maintained that he was a descendent of the old planters; it was the system that had ruined him. Most of the people migrating from the South went to the free states, and although of good stock, the ignorance in the localities where they settled, e. g. southern Illinois, testified to the conditions whence they came. Even were Weston willing to grant that slavery made negroes happier, its extension and the degradation of an equal number of Anglo-Saxons should never, he said, be allowed.

Material on the "Poor White" was especially useful in the type of appeal the Republicans were making. It was exhibit *A* of the evidence used to convince the working masses:

> "Let the honest poor of the North, to whom and
> to their children a future is possible, who are fur-
> nished with means of education to fit them for an
> improved condition and with a fair field to win
> it— let them regard the state of the white work-
> ing people of the South, and see what is the fate
> the dominant power of the country would doom
> them to, if it could have its unrestricted way."[12]

Nor was this degredation of the free laborers to be considered as a mere circumstance. The mud-sill theory as maintained by the "pro-slavery argument"[13] of the South, in the last analysis, insisted that no labor should be free. Such was the climax of the great appeal that made the Republican move an issue between the democracy of the man who sold the labor of his hands and the man who owned the hands that labored for him. This was "new Democratic doctrine"—that the white laborer should be a slave as well as the black—and it was placed before the working man everywhere in bold form. If a foreigner, it reached him in his own tongue. It was illustrated by the language of the southern press. The *Richmond Enquirer* no longer apologized for slavery.

> "The line of defense, however, is now changed.
> The South maintains that slavery is right, na-
> tional, and necessary, and does not depend on the
> difference of complexion. The laws of the slave

states justify the holding of white men to bondage."

A South Carolina paper declared:—

"Slavery is the natural and normal condition of
the laboring man whether white or black. The
greatest evil of northern society is that it is
burthened with a servile class of mechanics and
laborers, unfit for self-government, and yet
clothed with the powers and attributes of citizens. Master and slave is a relation in society
as necessary as parent and child and the northern states will yet have to introduce it. The
theory of free government is a delusion."[14]

Well to the point could the orator "ask the mechanics and
laborers of the North to mark the progress of events, to lay
to their hearts these taunting declarations, and then to remember that every slave state added to this Union gives power to
those who think that labor is benefited by being *owned*."[15]

Another economic argument was that slavery reduced northern wages. Here again, Weston gave the best rendition of
the topic.[16] In their commercial schemes the southern leaders
talked of using the "Poor Whites" as mill operatives[17] but at
the same time insisted that negroes could be used, and that
with slave labor, free labor could not compete. They also
argued that the North profited by the work of the slave, but
that eventually they would put him to manufacturing to stay
the process. Weston agreed that this must come, and when it
did, free labor could not compete. The free laborer was a
citizen and maintained a family. The slave had very little
invested in his up-keep, nothing in pleasure and education,
and women and children were available for work. The boast
of the superiority of an educated laborer in production was at
fault, for once in competition, like the "poor whites" of the
South, labor could not be educated. In wheat growing and
in industries in the border states, this competition was already
being felt. He concluded that:

"Just in proportion as the two systems of labor,
slave and free, came in contact with each other
as being devoted to the same purpose, just in
that proportion must the free laborers of the
North and West be brought within the range of

> its fatal influence which now acts with direct
> and unmitigated force upon the great mass of
> the whites of the South."

The new latitude to be opened was one in which races would
multiply rapidly, and the negro there, being able to thrive
in a less healthful climate, would soon become a menace.

The Republicans laid claim to the new territory of Kansas
for the free-laborer. The South already had the lion's share of
the area of the nation, they argued, even though its population
was less numerous. Its superior acreage and the advantage
given by the three-fifths clause should be enough for it. The
new territory should go to the millions of free-men who made
up the majority of the nation. To emphasize the territorial
advantage the South had, a map accompanied many documents. The great empire of slavery was shown in black,
the free states, like a white fringe lay along its northern
border. This appeal to the laborer had a special application
to the adopted citizen. For the German and Scandinavian,
the keeping of the public domain open to free-men and closed
to slavery was a very important question. He was appealed
to to help keep slavery out that his kinsmen yet beyond the
seas might come and enjoy free land in a free country. For
laborers of every sort, the issue raised by Kansas could be
made a winning appeal.

Morals of Slavery

Conviction in regard to the morals as well as the economics
of slavery would have a direct bearing on the political action
of the North. Tracts and treatises to this end would be
forceful and there was little chance to counteract their influence. The "Pro-slavery Argument" which had been growing
in volume since Professor Dew's famous exposition and which
would naturally be enlisted in a defense of the institution, was
not a counter-force. Robert Toombs carried it, trimmed for
the occasion into the North, by a lecture at Tremont Temple,
Boston, in January.[18] A pro-slavery discourse, delivered in
Boston, gave subtle force to a current statement that Howell
Cobb[19] had threatened soon to call the roll of his slaves at
the foot of Bunker Hill. It provoked a question as to why
the South was so careful that the happy slave hear and know

nothing to induce him to make himself unhappy. To argue in behalf of slavery was a doubtful expedient in the North.

The great "educative" work of its kind had already been done—*Uncle Tom's Cabin* had been given to the world. There was evidence of much ambition to repeat it, and its author gave the public another book, *Dred,* just before the campaign closed. The performance could not be repeated. There was really no occasion for it; since Uncle Tom and Simon Legree were already fixed in political drama. Dr. Orville Dewey's *Address Delivered at the Elm Tree* was a widely noticed treatment which put current impressions in the North into argumentative sequence. Dewey was reputed to have leanings in the other direction, and now just back from the South, he spoke with authority and with disappointment for some. His performance called out replies from both North and South.[20]

The wrangle over the sinfulness of slavery had a variety of approaches. Doctor Adams, President of the Boston division of the American Tract Society, in his *South Side View of Slavery* had stated an ugly doctrine of northern responsibility for it. Nor was it until slavery became unprofitable, he argued, that the North found a conscience against it. He wondered where the conscience was when the North forced the continuation of the slave trade eight years longer than the South wanted it. His work called for a response to prove that the North, during the national period, had been consistent in its opposition, both in sentiment and in action.[21] The Bible was invoked as a court of last resort. For the pro-slavery side, Reverend Thornton Stringfellow gave the best known argument.[22] Samuel B. Howe in a pamphlet, *Slave Holding Not Sinful,* maintained the same thesis of biblical precedent. The pulpit of the North was obliged to unhorse the scriptural knights of the opposition. The biblical precedent argument was answered on the ground that that was slavery of Bible times, that "no system of modern slavery could stand before it for a minute."[23]

A controversy of so much importance as that over slavery was bound to solicit schemes for its solution. They were forthcoming. Gradual emancipation by decreeing the centennial year 1876 as marking the point after which everyone should be born to a status of freedom, along with compensation features, was suggested.[24] The greatest effort was that of

Doctor Samuel Nott who offered a solution in a work of considerable length entitled: *Slavery and the Remedy*.[25] It was a high-flown notion of solution by sweet reasonableness:

"A Christian state philanthropic, patriarchal, is bound to abolish just so much of slavery as is injurious, and no more; to retain just so much as is helpful and no less. The Christian patriarch and Christian philanthropist need not be at variance, if they will but unite in the simple attempt to promote the well-being of the slaves, in the North the well-being of the people."

The theory of slaveholding that Nott endorsed was pronounced orthodox.[26] Northern oracles like Greeley gave it credit for its good intentions but damned its effect with the dicta that the patriarchs referred to were not Christian. The work of the Colonization Society might be included in the category of salutary measures. Robert J. Walker recommended it as such in his political pamphlet,[27] and there were occasional tilts as to its real supporters and benefactors. A little extraordinary, but perhaps significant, was the argument of Doctor Elder of Philadelphia.[28] He conceded that the negro was a child-race fitted for the crude culture of new countries. Slavery must not be allowed to expand on the basis of its self-lauded excellence, but confined and forced to stand an experimental test. The present is an age when steam and iron do the work, when the crude barbarous system must pass. With density of population, the South would be forced to manufacture and to rise from the conditions that foster slavery. Protective tariffs should be used to bring this about, for "when free trade means slave men, I'll have none of it."

Political Influence of Slavery

One of the results of slavery in the country, continued the Republican argument, had been the development of a "Slavocracy." The theory of a "Slave Power" was not new when the Republicans adopted it, but it fitted their needs as well as though it were originally their own. By the use of statistics, for which the census of 1850 was fruitful, it was found that 347,000 persons owned slaves. It was a much smaller group than this that owned most of the slaves of the South. This relatively small number of men were represented in the government by three-fifths of the slaves they owned. Dominating the South, they controlled the white masses that did not own slaves; dominating the Democratic party, with that party in power, they ruled the nation. Thus, it was argued, the control of the country could be traced to several thousand slave-owners. The "sons-in-law" and "brothers-in-law" were pictured getting together in their political conclaves and dictating to the nation. Above all other things that they maintained concerning the South, the Republicans established the belief in the existence of a malignant "slave oligarchy." Every one came to have a speaking acquaintance with it, and no editor or stump orator ever forgot its presence. So real did it become that many writers of history have accepted it at par, and only recently has its nature and influence been authoritatively questioned.[29]

The "oligarchy," according to its appraisers, had several distinct characteristics. First of all, it was hostile to freedom in every form. Aristocratic itself and grounded on unfree labor, it scorned free society. Nor were Southerners careful to avoid giving evidence that could be used to make a case. Statements were gleaned from the Southern press and given wide circulation. The brightest gem, perhaps, was a clipping attributed to the Muskogee Alabama *Herald*:—

> "Free society, we sicken at its name, what is it but a conglomeration of greasy mechanics, petty operators, small-fisted farmers, and moon-struck theorists? All the Northern, and especially the New England states, are devoid of society fitted for a well-bred gentleman. The prevailing class one meets North is that of mechanics struggling to be genteel, and small farmers who do their own drudgery, and yet who are hardly fit for association with a southern gentleman's body servant." [30]

A similar confession from the *Virginia South Side Democrat* was freely used:—

> "We have got to hating everything with the prefix free, from free negroes down and up the whole catalogue—free farms, free labor, free society, free will, free thinking, free children, free schools —all belonging to the same band of damnable

isms. But worst of all these abominations is the
modern system of free schools."

In a land born to freedom and founded in its principles, this
creed must be stamped out. So the new party, as Douglas
described it, "shrieked for freedom." They wanted it in every
reasonable category. They wanted free schools, free soil, free
press, free speech, free men and finally—Frémont.

With such a contempt for free society, the "oligarchy" was
interpreted as using its own "plantation tactics," to subdue
freedom. The events in Washington and in Kansas were cited
as evidence of it.[31] After the Sumner assault the northern
press took the matter up as presenting a grave problem. There
were plainly two civilizations in the Union. The easiest solution was to "let the Union slide;" but no Republican paper
could logically admit that such a thought existed. Disunion
was taboo, and the problem, they argued, was how a society
that produced statesmen might send them to meet in the same
governing body with one that produced bullies and sent them
thither. Must prize fighters be substituted for scholars in
order to maintain free speech and the privileges of the Senate?
It was concluded that slave-owning society was vicious by
nature. There might be a veneer of the genteel on some of the
plantation masters, but it was only an upper layer. A favorite
interpretation of the Kansas struggle was that there, in an
unrestrained border region, the slave owner revealed his real
self. The slave master was a true product of the system. It
attacked freedom in Kansas, in the Senate, everywhere. It
had a background of repression and gag-rule. Where slavery
was there could be no freedom.

1. Circular dated January 17.
2. Clephane, *Birth of the Republican Party*, p.10, says that the records show an average of fifty registrations a week.
3. For description, *New York Tribune* (w), September 13.
4. For a brief survey of the Northern press, see Bibliography.
5. The arguments sketched below are based on the most effective
   presentation during the Campaign period. Most of them had a
   background extending back a number of years, and were to receive
   additional treatment before the crisis of 1861.
6. Editorial, *New York Tribune*, April 4.
7. Editorial: *Texts for Southern Commercial Conventions, New York
   Tribune*, March 25.
8. Pamphlet: *Speech of Cassius M. Clay before the Young Men's
   Republican Central Union, New York, Oct. 24.* C.M.Clay, a promi-

nent abolitionist and figure in the campaign was a southerner and ex-slave owner. He had recently taken advantage of the bankruptcy law which gave point to his attack on the economic South.

9. Helper's *The Impending Crisis* was published the following year.
10. *New York Tribune*, June 9. Vaughn was from South Carolina and had been with the *Cleveland Leader* before going to the *Chicago Tribune*.
11. This is first noticed in the *New York Tribune* of Feb. 5, and was the inspiration of a series of editorials.
12. *New York Tribune*, June 7, 1856.
13. The "Pro-slavery Argument" of the South which began with the discourse of Professor Dew in 1832, and ran with increasing volume until the Civil War insisted on the merits of servile labor. A good treatment is given by W.E.Dodd in *The Cotton Kingdom*, chapter III.
14. These and several similar clippings had a very wide circulation. Though perhaps not typical of the southern press, enough radical papers indulged in such statements as to make an effective attack on their genuineness impossible.
15. Pamphlet: *Speech of Timothy C. Day of Ohio in the House*, April 22.
16. Pamphlet: *Southern Slavery Reduces Northern Wages*, a Speech delivered at Washington, March 25, 1856.
17. Tarver's *Domestic Manufactures in the South-West*, 1847; J.H. Taylor in *Debow's Review*, 1850; and speech of Wm.Gregg at S.C.Institute, 1851.Gregg had been conducting experiments with a mill village. Weston and others use these references.
18. *Speech of the Honorable Robert Toombs at Tremont Temple*, Jan.24,1856. Henry Wise had rejected an invitation to deliver an address in Boston. *Boston Bee*, October 15.
19. The names of Cobb and Toombs are both connected with this statement.
20. Reply to Dewy's *Address at the Elm Tree, Sheffield, Massachusetts*, Charleston, S. C.,Nov. 7, 1856; *To the People of Suffolk County, Information acquired from the Best Authority With Respect to Slavery*, by William Jaeger, Oct. 1856.
21. *The Responsibility of the North in Relation to Slavery*, anon., Cambridge, March, 1856. Greeley began a disciplinary attack and in the summer the Boston division of the Tract Society selected another president.
22. *Scriptual and Statistical Views in favor of Slavery*, by Thornton Stringfellow,D.D. This went through several editions.
23. *Bible Slaveholding not sinful: A Reply to Slave-holding not sinful by Samuel B. Howe,D.D.*, by H.D.Ganse, minister of Dutch Reformed Church, Fairfield, New Jersey.
24. *The Olive Branch and the Remedy*, by Chas.Muir, Mar. 17,1856.
25. *Slavery and the Remedy or Principles and Suggestions for a Remedial Code*, by Nott, (118 pages). This went through a number of editions.
26. Tombs to Winthrop, Feb. 22, 1856. Winthrop MSS. M.H.S.
27. See Chapter XIII.
28. *Emancipation: Its Conditions and Policy.* A lecture by Doctor

William Elder of Philadelphia at Tremont Temple, Boston.

29. For treatment of the topic see Boucher, C. M., *"In Re* That Aggressive Slavocracy" in *Mississippi Valley Historical Review*, vol. VIII.

30. Radical statements of this nature made up the type of material that was printed on one-sheet circulars and broadcast among laboring men.

31. For account of these events, see Chapter VI.

CHAPTER V

CREATION OF ISSUES

Attack on the Slave Power

The most natural place for the attack on the "Slave Power" to fall was its strong-hold—the Democratic party. The major premise of Republican argument was that the South dominated the ancient party of Jefferson and made of it an impostor. Regardless of the evidence they had in proof of their thesis, the fact could not be denied that it had a powerful organization in the North where nobody held slaves. This led them to attack it as a two fold institution—a wedding of slavery and office. The "slave drivers" dominated, they said, and their northern henchmen did their bidding for the sake of office. To characterize the Democracy of the North a term was borrowed from the repertoire of John Randolph—it was "doughfaced." To belong to it was pronounced inimical to the perpendicularity of the northern spine. Southern dominance became the basis of an appeal to sectional pride to drive the Democratic party out of the North.

The first indictment brought against the party dominated by the "Slave Power" was that it was non-democratic. Its leaders, argued the Republicans, had not merely ceased to revere the doctrines found in the Declaration of Independence; they had come to believe their very antithesis. If this could be maintained; and the literature of the South furnished abundant corroboration of it, there was a great opportunity to appeal to the masses to join in the quest for true democracy. The gift of the "Fathers," the heritage of Jefferson and Jackson, should again be restored to the people. It was the South with its ideas born of slaveholding that had taken the essence of true democracy from the party. At first, under Jefferson, slavery had begged the right to exist and the principles it begat had no place, but now its advocates were in control. This rise of the slave-holding South to power in the party had been a gradual process.[1] The original principles had been revamped and invigorated under Jackson and VanBuren; but under Polk they had been obscured by a "slave holding fog," and under Pierce the "sun of democracy" had gone from sight behind the Kansas-Nebraska bill.   It was *The End of a Great Party*:—[2]

"Having passed as it has from horizon to horizon from being the special advocate of the rights of human nature, to being the special advocate of vested rights of slave-holding and nigger-whipping—from the doctrine of the equality of all men to the doctrine of "subject races" and the special right of the free white man to make slaves of everybody else—from Thomas Jefferson and the Declaration of Independence, to Franklin Pierce and the Kansas-Nebraska bill—is it not evident that the party still professing to call itself democratic must be near its final and ultimate extinguishment."

But the dominant South had done more for the party than drive out democratic principles, it had controlled it for the benefit of itself and its "peculiar" institution.   It had managed to secure the lion's share of federal offices and influence.[3]   The annexation of Texas and the annexations due to the Mexican War were interpreted as conspiracies of the "slavocracy" to add more territory to its domain.   Its latest conspiracy, that to force slavery into Kansas, had just been worked out in collusion with "doughfaces" of the North.   This latest intrigue, however, must be the last, unless it be one to destroy the Union.   To use the party deliberately to extend slavery was pronounced subversive of the principles established by the "Fathers."   They, it was argued, had made "freedom national" and left slavery exceptional and a product of local law.   Now the Democratic party was being made an instrument for the nationalization of slavery.[4]   The "party of slavery," the party of the dominant South, must be checked in its course.   The political formula for this took the shape of a declaration of purpose to "restore the government to the principles of Washington and Jefferson."[5]

Along with the Democratic party, the Federal Judiciary was pronounced a victim of the "slavocracy," and like it, a tool for the nationalization of slavery.   The goal of the ultra South, the legalization of slave property in all territory, had been in evidence for a long while and had been clearly set

forth in the arguments over the repeal of the Missouri Compromise. The Missouri Supreme Court in the Dred Scott
case had signalized a new trend in decisions relative to the
efficacy of laws of freedom in territories made by congressional
action.[6] This soon to be famous case had been argued once
before the United States Supreme Court, and Republican
leaders had few doubts as to what was coming. Slaves would
be declared property, to be protected in the territories the
same as any other, and this recognition would be tantamount
to a nationalization of that which had existed only as a product of state law. Next in order would come its status in the
free states. A number of decisions in the district courts were
interpreted as a forecast of what was coming. Judge Kane
in a Pennsylvania case had declared slaves property with
which an owner might sojourn in a free state, its laws to the
contrary notwithstanding.[7] What, it was argued, was to hinder
its being allowed to stay indefinitely, and thus by Federal
authority be forced upon the free states. Certainly this was
a preliminary to get the North used to it by degrees. The
action of Judge Lecompte of Kansas Territory against the
officers elected under the Topeka constitution, and that of
Commissioner Pendry in the Garner case,[8] were used as
further evidence in support of the contention of judicial usurpation. A characteristic tirade from the Republican press
denounced Pendry for:

> "passing upon questions involving not only the
> highest personal rights, but also the nicest points
> of Federal jurisdiction and state authority—
> points upon which these ten dollar pettifogging,
> unconstitutional judges are authorized by the in-
> famous act to set at defiance the state courts and
> state authorities, no less than the privileges of
> the Declaration of Independence and the senti-
> ment of usual humanity, and to spend any
> amount of the public money in hiring blackguard
> cutthroats to assist them and the marshals in
> doing it." [9]

With no inconsiderable list of charges, the Republicans
presented their case against the Federal Courts. Although the
final Dred Scott opinion had not been given, the first Republican campaign, like its successor of 1860, was conducted in

hostility to the Federal Judiciary. They did not mince words
in putting the case:—

"It is well known that Jefferson was jealous of the judiciary—an arm of the government that in other countries
had greatly baffled the efforts of freedom. By long fore-
sight and skilled political action the slave-holders have
brought the offices of the United States courts under their
influence. In no part of the country, slave or free, has it
been practicable to obtain the appointment of a man who
is not proven to be right in the slaveholders' view on the
slavery question. The dexterity with which courts find
law and pleas to do what they like is proverbial; courts
of law are a dangerous foe to liberty when they have an
interest to secure against it, and that interest the appoint-
ing power."[10]

The action of the Federal Judiciary drove the Republicans
to states rights as a check for "slavery's usurpation" in the
Federal government where "the dark shadow of its sceptre
falls upon the sovereignty of the several states and menaces
them with dire disaster." For instance:

"South Carolina, abandoning her once cherished doctrine
of state rights, asserts the federal supremacy over laws
made by states exclusively for the protection of their citizens. The state of Virginia is contesting in courts of law
the right of New York to forbid the extension of slavery
within her borders. A Federal court in Pennsylvania has
denied the right of that state to decree freedom to slaves
brought by their masters within her borders and has proclaimed that slavery exists by the law of nations." [11]

The action of the supreme court of Wisconsin in the case
of Booth *vs*. Rycroft was a distinct application of states rights
to nullify a federal law.[12] Still, at the same time the Republicans maintained that Congress had power to legislate on
slavery in the territories. The Democracy denied this and
maintained that as a law of Congress the Missouri Compromise had always been void, and that its repeal could not be a
violation of compact. With the Democratic party, "states
rights" was orthodox doctrine,[13] and apart from their prodigal-
ity in regard to the action of the Federal Judiciary, the Republicans opposed the doctrine.

Any advocacy of states rights could not be ranked as a

major factor in propaganda making. The slavocracy, its
nature, its control of the Democratic party, its transgressions,
its conspiracies for power and territory made the foundation
material for the attack. Speeches and documents used this
material, wholly or in part, as suited the occasion. Any of
several major statements of primary points [14] included most
of the material. Speeches were characteristically repetitions
of the same thing. Given an occasion—and there were many
—and the orator or writer would come thundering down along
the whole line. It was a long line, and the use of the arguments that comprised it was effective.

The attack upon the "Slave Power" and its many transgressions led the Republicans to interpret the campaign as a
test as to whether democracy could be restored to the administration of the country. They acted upon the assumption
that it could, and accepted as a working theory the presence
of an essential democratic quality in the free masses of the
North, and even in the South, could the throttle of oligarchy
be released. The democratic spirit that had welled up under
Jefferson and Jackson was to be called out again. It was a
living, vital force in American life, part and parcel of it, and
essential to it. In the face of such an existence there could
be but one outcome—the triumph of freedom. Its enemies
might "subdue freedom" in Kansas, they might beat it down
on the floor of the Senate, and hold black men to servitude;
but they could never yoke the democratic masses. It was
compared to hooping a boiler, which might suffice for the
moment, but which meant that they would be blown the higher
when the inevitable explosion came.

The attack the Republicans made on the "Slavocracy" was
not free from difficulties; though the method they advocated
—that of appealing to the people to close the territories to
slavery—was simple enough. They argued that such a course
was democratic and just if a majority willed it. But their
proposed majority must come from one section, and the project was immediately beset with accusations of sectionalism.
Did one section, because it had a majority of the votes have a
right to use that majority to exclude the minority section from
the possesions of the nation, held in common by all the states?
Would the South tolerate such a rule? It raised at once the
question of disunion. To raise conviction to the point of

action in the face of this threat of national disruption was the
most difficult task the Republicans had. Their enemies took
advantage of it. The South supported the Democrats as
"union savers"—a union they themselves menaced if the
Democrats did not win. The Republicans were forced to
combat the idea that they were union breakers. The position
they took was important. They were not union breakers,
and could they control the nation, they would manage those
who were. A fighting formula was engrafted on their first
adjustment to the problem of national control, and its presence
probably would aid in explaining the recourse to war in 1861.

Convincing the masses that the thing proposed was neither
sectional nor radical called forth some of the greatest *finesse*
in argumentation used during the campaign. "Slavery was
sectional, Freedom national" according to the principles of the
"Fathers." [15] The Republicans denied that the original status
of the country had been slavery, and argued that the principles of the Revolution were for freedom. The "Fathers,"
Washington and Jefferson, had incorporated these in the new
nation. The rule of a slave-holding minority had denied these
precepts, they argued, but they proposed to return to the
original principles of freedom and to use the vote of the
majority of the people to do it. Nor did they propose to
inflict any special hindrances on the Southern man who went
to the territories. The Southerner could take there anything
a Northern man could. He could not bring his slaves, neither
could a Russian his serf, nor a Mormon his plurality of wives.
They were not waging war on a section; they were meeting
aggression of a section endeavoring to carry its local institutions to all the national domain.

The threat of disunion resulted in much speculation as to
its prospect and probable outcome. Many thought there
could be no secession without war and in that event the South
would need half of its six-million whites to keep the slaves in
subjection. There was also a belief that the "poor whites" of
the South would not support the slave owners in event of a
crisis,—

"In any serious contest that might arise, labor at the
South would inevitably array itself against capital. Once
educate the white laborer so he shall know his right and
he will never rest quiet in this degraded condition. A

bold and intelligent leader could stir the country to the center." [16]

The Republicans felt that they could gain support here if only the grip of the ruling class could be relaxed. They were not sanguine that that would be immediate, but social stratification did exist, and in case of a crisis they felt that the support of the "poor whites" could be secured. There was also the idea that the South could not live economically without the North.[17] The greatest property of the South being slaves, the lack of fluid capital was said to make it impossible for them either to borrow or produce capital to carry on a conflict. Furthermore, the South would be ruined without anybody to catch runaway slaves, the border states would be denuded, the price in the interior decrease, and the value of land forced down. Though they had an important place in the education of voters, these speculations were later found to be incorrect. Especially was this true of two fundamental assumptions— that the slaves would be an active insurrectionary force and that the South was divided against itself socially.

Any prospect of a conflict between North and South brought with it the question of foreign intervention. The Crimean War was over and peace was at hand in Europe. Britain with whom relations were strained would then be free to act, and the *London Times* was indulging in war talk. On one side was the contention that England would not permit any state of affairs that would interfere with her cotton supply, and would intervene. Some argued that she would not, and would take advantage of the condition to develop sources within her own empire. On the other side was her record as the champion of emancipation which had exercised the South a great deal. In a strife growing out of the question of slavery, it was argued that Britain would not interfere in its favor. Americans had been boasting of their democracy as contrasted with foreign despotism,[18] and the British press had nailed as absurd a democracy that held slaves. Furthermore, hints at the fate of slave property in the event of war were not uncommon. The South viewed this with no little concern. The northern papers often insinuated that the South was afraid to fight on this account and that in the case of foreign war the slave-holding region might even prove a liability in the defence of the nation. The presence of this irritation in southern minds

over Britain's abolitionism was the key to the supposed check-
mate for secession.   When sectionalization of the North
began in 1854, Attorney General Cushing thought that a war
was necessary to check it.[19] In light of this, Secretary Seward's
chimerical ideas in 1861 have a background that gives them
some claim to rationality.[20]

But for purposes of education, all these things were merely
conjectural.   There would be no disunion; the South was only
bluffing.   The same threat had been heard on the election of
Speaker Banks, but nothing had happened, and Aiken, "the
greatest slave owner of them all," had conducted him to the
chair.   The South could accept the rule of a majority guaran-
teeing them their rights under the constitution, and forbidding
slavery in new territory only.   The question of southern acceptance was in mind when the "son of a southern poor white"
was nominated for president.

Resistance to the Fugitive Slave Law

The Republicans also found a political asset in cases arising
from the operation of the Fugitive Slave Law.   The enforcement of the act had stirred up public interest in a series of
noted escapes, rescues, and martyrdoms.   Such spectacles as
the rescue of a fugitive from federal officers or the use of a
regiment of militia to return one to servitude found a ready
following in a population that had just absorbed *Uncle Tom's
Cabin.*   After the excitement was over, the litigations that
arose might continue to be useful.   Although it had been
history for some time, the Anthony Burns case had some hold-
overs of political value.   At least three current cases were of
sufficient importance in the campaign to demand a brief re-
hearsal.   These were: the Garner case; the Passmore Williamson case; and the prosecution of Booth, growing out of the
Glover rescue.

The Garner case occurred in Ohio when that commonwealth
was under the administration of Salmon P. Chase.   As one of
the first Republican governors, his handling of the case had
wide significance.   The Garners had crossed the river from
Kentucky into Ohio with the evident purpose of escaping
slavery.   Scarcely had they arrived when John S. Pendry, a
commissioner under the fugitive slave law, issued a warrant

for their detention as escaped slaves.[21] A few minutes before the United States marshal arrested them, Mary, the daughter of Margaret, was murdered with a butcher knife. This was perhaps the most telling feature—slavery was such that a mother would take the life of her child rather than return it to bondage. The Garners, four adults and three children, were placed in the county jail after the sheriff had won in a contest with the marshal for their custody. On February 8, the Grand Jury of Hamilton county brought an indictment against the adult Garners for murder in the first degree. The warrants were issued for their arrest and February 23 the sheriff made return that he had the defendants in custody. On the 26th the United States commission, sitting without the presence of the defendants, decided that they were fugitives and ordered them returned to their owners. The sheriff already had them in his possession. February 27, Judge Leavitt of the Southern District of Ohio issued a writ of habeas corpus to the sheriff demanding the bodies and a showing of why he held them. The sheriff replied that they were held for murder under the laws of Ohio and appended the indictment. February 28 Judge Leavitt decided that they were in the custody of the marshal and had been unlawfully taken and detained. The marshal took the fugitives and delivered them to their owners. The following day the prosecuting attorney reported the transactions to Governor Chase.

This was a direct clash between State and Federal authority, and made a good chance for a joust. If orthodox Democracy was a champion of states rights—if a majority of the nation, even, could not tamper with the institutions of a sovereign state—here was a chance to raise an embarrassing question, by asking how the Federal authority could take persons held to justice under the laws of Ohio. It was a powerful point; timely, though not new. If a state could not enforce its own laws, what might "Ruffians" not be able to do, if their control of the Federal government were tolerated. Chase sent a request for their surrender. Governor Morehead, although of the American party, was equal to the occasion. He replied to Chase's demand for the fugitives from Ohio law as any orthodox states rights man would have done. He also stated that of course, if any of the defendants were acquitted, the Governor of Ohio would remand them to servitude, a thing

which a Republican Governor could hardly do. But there
was little danger of bringing it to a crisis. Morehead made
little effort to detain the Garners, and the Ohio officials never
quite got in touch with them. They were shipped "down
river," the vessel on which they started was rammed, and one
of the party drowned. Even then detention was not effected;
the survivors were trans-shipped, and Margaret Garner disap-
peared into the fastness of the farther South.

The case of Booth vs. Rycroft, growing out of Booth's
participation in the Glover rescue, is better known by its
constitutional significance than by the political bearing that
it had. For his part in the rescue, Booth was arrested, and his
trial was postponed until the next meeting of the United States
District Court. By writ of habeas corpus the case was brought
before the Wisconsin supreme court and Booth dismissed on
the ground that the fugitive slave law under which he had
been arrested was unconstitutional.[22] Booth was re-arrested
and refused bail by Judge Miller of the United States District
court. The state court, out of comity to Judge Miller, refused
to release Booth again, and in his trial before the district
Court, he was convicted. Then by writ of habeas corpus the
state court released him upon the ground that the law under
which he had been convicted was unconstitutional. This re-
versal of the decision of a Federal court by the state court
called into question the jurisdiction of the Federal Supreme
Court. Booth was cited at Washington to show reason why
that body should not reverse the decision of the Wisconsin
court. The State court also allowed a writ of error, that the
release of Booth was not properly before it.[23] This injected the
question of the jurisdiction of the supreme court over state
courts in a case of constitutional interpretation, and placed
the Republicans as champions of states rights. The endorsement of the stand of the state court became part of the platform of Wisconsin Republicanism.[24]

The argument in the case became campaign literature,[25] although its ultra states rights view never became more than a
local issue with Republicans. Sumner, since he had declared
that he would never enforce the fugitive slave law was looked
to for comfort in this peculiar phase of the "resistance to
slavery."[26] Chief Justice Smith feared Seward's opinion of
appellate jurisdiction, but believed that "the maintenance of

state sovereignty as *co-equal* and *co-ordinate* with the federal sovereignty, can alone save us."[27] Justice Paine stated his willingness to leave states rights defense to Smith but examined as a legal point the question of appellate jurisdiction. In this he "came to the conclusion that such jurisdiction does not exist, that it is inconsistent with the nature of the relation between the State and Federal governments, and with the preservation of the reserved rights of the states, which is one of the leading ideas of the history of the constitution." He "was led to this conclusion very greatly by the reasoning of Mr. Calhoun in his works on the constitution."[28] Radical Republicanism could draw from the same source as the Democracy of the ultra-South.

The Passmore Williamson case had borne political fruit before it was carried into the mass of educative events that focused on the presidential campaign.[29] John H. Wheeler, *en route* to his mission in Nicaragua, passed through Philadelphia, having with him Jane Johnson and her two children, held as slaves under the laws of North Carolina. Williamson, seeing them on the boat, persuaded her that she was free under the laws of Pennsylvania, and aided, some say urged, by bystanders, she escaped.[30] They were not fugitives and could not be secured under the operation of that act. Wheeler proceeded by getting United States district judge J. K. Kane, to issue a writ of habeas corpus demanding Williamson to deliver the bodies of Jane Johnson and her children. This was signed July 18, 1855. The Marshal presented the writ, and on the 20th Williamson made return that he never possessed or confined or had aught to do with the "said" persons. District Attorney VanDyke, Wheeler's counsel, objected to the return as untrue and insufficient. Williamson replied that it was not competent to go behind it, and that untruth was a separate allegation. Judge Kane admitted Van Dyke's testimony, that it might constitute a *prime facie* case of perjury, and forced Williamson to give heavy bail to appear July 27 to answer such a charge. On the 27th Kane gave up the charge of perjury and committed him for contempt. Williamson's friends declared that the Judge's actions testified his fear to put the case before a jury. This, and the Judge turning prosecutor, gave the case just prominence, and made Williamson a martyr.

The opinions of Judge Kane were almost as useful as the

martyr he had made. His first promulgation was that he
knew "of no statute of Pennsylvania which affects to divest
the right of property of a citizen of North Carolina acquired
and asserted under the laws of that state because he had found
it useful or convenient to pass through the territories of
Pennsylvania." Further progress of the case led to a second
opinion. Jane Johnson entered petition freeing Williamson
from charges relative to holding her. Kane could not allow
the petition, for she had no status; but he declared his failure
to comprehend how it could be "that a state may single out
this one kind of property from among all the rest and deny
to it the right of passing over its soil—passing with its owner
—parcel of his travelling equipment as much as the horse he
rides on, his great coat, or his carpet bag."

There was still more to the case. Williamson tried the
recourse used by Booth in Wisconsin, but the state supreme
court refused to release him, thus laying itself open to "dough-
face" classification. He might have his freedom on recanta-
tion, which left an opening to continued martyrdom. The
associates of Williamson, the negroes who had escorted Jane
away from her master, were thrown into jail. These came up
before the Philadelphia court of Quarter Sessions with Judge
William D. Kelley presiding. Jane was produced as a witness,
and then marched away in open defiance of the Federal
authorities. States rights were vindicated; Jane could not be
retaken.

Absorption of Current Issues

Although the question of extension of slavery occasioned
almost a limitless amount of abstract argument and the enforcing of the fugitive slave law furnished exhibits of great
usefulness, the "promoters of freedom" were hardly content to
go to the country on these alone. Anything that would appeal
to voters without doing serious damage to the great principle
might be added. There were several ways the Republicans
could go on record as standing for issues although they had
had no previous existence as a party. The leaders carried
their antecedents into the new party but in doing so certainly
did not bring uniformity. There was always recourse to the
process of education, but apart from opposition to slavery,

there was insufficient agreement on fundamentals. The control of the House of Representatives gave a chance to seek a sort of common denominator, and to establish a record on some things. In all, the Republicans adjusted themselves to four current issues that had an influence in the campaign, namely: the protective tariff, the homestead law, internal improvements, and the Pacific railroad.

A protective tariff was not a natural component of the group of things the Republicans stood for—free trade both fitted and sounded better. It did not become an issue. Still, the absorbing of the bulk of the Whig party and the desire to carry certain states made it a potential factor. If the failure to include protection lost Pennsylvania, it doubtless had its recompense in sections where victory did accrue. Many leading Republicans, especially those of Whig antecedents, were apostles of protection. L. D. Campbell of Ohio, chairman of the House Ways and Means Committee, ex-Whig and Know-Nothing, was a protectionist, but Chase, a free-trader, was easily dominating the movement in Ohio.[31] Greeley was a protectionist on principle—a Protectionist for the interest of labor and the mass.[32] The *Tribune*, reaching many readers, carried his editorials, and the *Letters of an Onondaga Farmer* were appearing, to present the question and hold the argument for free trade up for refutation. Thaddeus Stevens of Pennsylvania was known to have definite interests in protection, and other individuals of such proclivities could be found leading, and affiliating with, the new move. They were accepted for their leadership, not the principles for which they stood; they did not furnish antecedents sufficient to call out an attack on the party on the ground of protectionism, much less pledge it to the protective principle.

In the matter of the tariff, the Democracy held one of its two-faced positions whereby it united North and South and presented a national front. The South in general was for free trade. Still, in Pennsylvania, where it counted for much, the Democrats got "tariffwards" of the Republicans. Buchanan had a reputation for saving twenty-five dollars a ton on railroad iron in the protectionist disaster of 1846, the same measure, support of which had ruined Dallas' political career, and made it necessary even for Wilmot to give explanation.[33] J. Glancy Jones, administration leader in the House and

Buchanan's sword and buckler in Pennsylvania during the
campaign, assumed the championship and gave assurances on
iron.[34] The speaker of the House on whom the opposition
united for its first victory had a tariff record that was objectionable to protectionists.[35]

When it came to taking action on the tariff the Republicans
found it impracticable to go on record. Most of the leaders
on the pure Republican principle were political descendents of
the Old Free-Soil Democracy, and were not favorably dis-
posed. An inclusion would be regarded by them as a further
surrender of principle to the "low level of Whig expediency."
Furthermore, the South had a record for resisting a protective
tariff as exploitation, and were it coupled with non-extension
of slavery, it would be adding to a situation that already
practically assured disunion. So the House dealt summarily
with it. August 11, L. D. Campbell of the Committee of Ways
and Means brought in a bill to reduce the tariff, accompanied
by a report.[36] The report contained a protective argument,
which aired the views of Campbell and refuted the President
who had recommended reduction. The bill was read twice and
further action postponed until the third Monday of the following December. The tariff was too dangerous to the unity of
the new party, and action on it was thereby placed beyond the
period of the campaign. Resolutions were passed asking the
Secretary of the Treasury to prepare a report on the tariff and
immigration in the industrial states. Campbell also asked
that fifty thousand copies of his report be printed. Although
nothing was actually done, a committee of the Republican
House brought in a bill to lower the tariff, a move in the direction of the law of the following year that gave us the lowest
of all our tariffs. So far as a record on the issue was concerned,
the Republicans made none—they side-stepped it.

Internal improvement by the Federal government, unlike
the tariff, became an issue. It harmonized with the Republican doctrine of the powers of Congress, and they could argue
that it would aid in extending commerce and building cities.
in opening new territory, and in bringing prosperity to the
masses generally. The Democrats were divided on it. It
was a point where Douglas might be undermined in the Northwest, yoked as he was with the ultra-South and its proverbial
opposition. However, initiative came from the Democratic

stronghold, the Senate. Early in the session a series of bills were launched. Senate bills one and two were for the deepening of the St. Clair Flats, and to balance this Michigan project, senate bill fourteen called for a deepening of one of the mouths of the Mississippi. Senator Judah P. Benjamin of Louisiana gave them an active southern support. The bills passed both houses and reached the President on May 13. He vetoed them, and in so doing made another bid for support at the South before the convention at Cincinnati should convene. On July 7 the Senate passed the bills with the necessary majorities and with only the ultra-South in opposition.[37] July 8 the bills were carried over the veto in the House.[38] The Republicans certainly did not gain complete title to being the party of internal improvements.

Only the ultra southern vote and the party tradition made it impossible for the Democracy to lay claim to the title. At that, it left a working margin for the Republicans. They could cite their record.

A Pacific railroad was the acme of all improvement questions. It, more than anything else, had carried the Democracy all but out of the time-worn scruples as to the constitutional power of the Federal government to carry on such enterprises. Several bills in Congress and a series of conventions at St. Louis, Memphis, and Philadelphia already indicated the importance of the measure. Secretary Davis' report on surveys was at hand, and sectional rivalry as to location was running high. The opinion predominated that the road should be built, and of necessity by federal aid. Several were ready to bring in bills when the House got under way. February 21, Denver of California introduced a bill for a railroad and telegraph line.[39] This bill was referred to a special committee of thirteen, created for the purpose.[40] Ohio, playing a leading role under its new Republican régime, sent joint resolutions to Congress including a Pacific railroad with other distinctly party measures.[41] July 24, with a view to bringing it in at the proper time, Denver presented a report of the special committee, and four days later a supply was printed for use by members. It was some time before the report could be brought in. August 16 it came along with a bill.[42] By this time both national conventions had gone on record, with the Republicans giving it an unequivocal endorsement. The majority report followed the national platform; the minority report was in two parts. Wood of Maine insisted that the location should be made with due reference to serving the greatest population which he argued would be north. Kidwell of Virginia questioned the feasibility of a Pacific railroad and doubted *"the constitutional power to aid."* When the report was made and the bill introduced, the session was within two days of its close. In the crowded business of these last days of the session the Pacific railroad was passed over and left for future reference.

As a Pacific railroad party the Republicans secured the advantage. They endorsed it in their platform and through their candidate. The position of Kidwell and the necessity of acknowledging the states-rights conservatives, did the Democrats injury. Though they endorsed it generally in their platform, they could not make a clear breast of the matter, and at once their Cincinnati declaration was attacked,—the Democracy was not in earnest, only shamming to secure votes. The Republican was the Pacific railroad party.

In all its attributes, a homestead law, free land for free men, was a Republican measure. Though he doubtlessly overstates the case, Professor Commons insists that in this the working class origin of the party is shown, that "only because slavery could not live on 160-acre farms did the Republican party come into conflict with slavery."[43] Above all others it contained elements to appeal to the masses, and had a background to give it weight if used in such an appeal. The *Tribune* had long been an advocate, and Greeley in his short period in Congress had championed such legislation.[44] The tendency of land legislation since the beginning of the public domain had been in the direction of free land. Politicians of Jackson's time had utilized the popularity that such a disposition of the public lands had in the West and with the masses generally. There had been no abatement of interest since their day and the Thirty-Third Congress, the same that passed the Kansas-Nebraska Bill, gave prominent place to a homestead measure. The presence of nativist sentiment led some members to hesitate to open lands to the immigrants. A bill for the care of the "Indigent Insane" which appropriated over twelve million acres and which passed both houses only to go down before the presidential veto, had a modifying influence on the homestead bill. It was its arch enemies, the South and East, however, that finally defeated the measure in the Senate.[45] The Southern opposition to a free land policy enhanced it for Republican consumption. Conspicuous among its exponents had been Galusha A. Grow, free-soil Democrat, from Wilmot's district of Pennsylvania. Grow conceived himself to be the heir of Benton's land policy[46] which he now brought to the new party. In the Thirty-Fourth Congress he was a conspicuous figure, was given the chairmanship of both the Committee on Territories and the Committee on Agriculture, and was in a position to use his antecedents for party purposes.

Before the Committees were appointed and the House in running order, Grow gave notice of a proposed homestead bill.[47] February 18 he introduced the promised bill, which was referred to the Committee on Agriculture.[48] Two days later, a homestead law as a counter proposition to the extension of slavery was thrust forward. Mace of Indiana introduced a bill to grant a hundred and sixty acres free to actual settlers, at the same time he introduced a bill to prevent the extension of slavery north of 36-30.[49] This Homestead Bill was likewise referred to the Committee on Agriculture. One week later, February 27, Grow reported his own bill, without amendment, from the committee. The action taken by the House showed that the party line was clearly drawn. The Republican press took up the advocacy of Grow's measure, the *Tribune* leading.[50] So committed, the Republican party became the party of homestead legislation although the passing of a bill was impossible. It went hand in hand with the extension of freedom; it appealed to the landless man, and it pleased the free-state man with a large family. It appealed to the immigrant, and was an antidote for the poison of incorporated Know-Nothingism.

Thus, the few issues that fell in line with the movement to generate a new party from the people, were assimilated. But even so, to pile up issues as a *raison d'etre* was foreign to its spirit. That would be Whiggery. In spite of the fact that most of the votes necessary for victory must come from the Whig ranks, the free soil element which gave the new party its basic principle dominated in the first campaign. For them, the Whig party was one of jobbing and trading off interests to formulate a policy and create a majority—it had no basic principles. There was some show of cleavage between party promoters of Free-Soil and Whig antecedents,[51] but the latter as a rule gave way to the aborigines of political opposition to slavery. The Free-Soilers carried the new party before the people as one founded on the essential principles of liberty and democracy. The Whig party with its American System was not the spiritual father of Republicanism.

Formation of a Foreign Policy

The Republicans endeavored to add to the strength of their position by their adjustment to the current problems of foreign relations. Any adjustment they made would be magnified because of the wide public interest in foreign affairs. It was a period of broad interest in the Orient and of diplomatic activity there. Expansion, Isthmian transportation, and filibustering enterprises made Central American and Caribbean relations live issues. In these, and at other points European relations were involved. Permeating it all was a spirit verging on the chauvinistic. On several occasions American statesmen had made "the Eagle" scream—it was a period of "vigorous self-assertion."[52] The Democrats were applying this strenuous policy, and all that was necessary for the Republicans to do in making their adjustment to the problems was to come out in opposition. The campaign was in a sense a struggle between foreign and domestic problems for first place. The Republicans pointed to home affairs as our first concern; the Democrats tried to divert the public mind to interests beyond our own borders.

The Ostend Manifesto of 1854, although two years old, was still important. Its proposed annexation of Cuba, and the question of slavery extension that it raised, made it fall into the torrent of sectionalism. The disrepute, in some quarters, that it brought upon Soulé, the criticism of it at the North and abroad as a specimen of diplomatic "brigandage," made it widely known and available for political use. The Republicans could use it as a specimen of slavery's "ruffianism" in diplomacy, and declare it comparable in spirit to events in Kansas and Washington. It could be used to attack those connected with it, as indeed it was when one of its authors became the Democratic candidate. On the other hand, since it was ultra southern, supporting it was a means of enhancing a following in the South. The fact is often overlooked that the Pierce administration did not accept it. Secretary Marcy shrewdly construed it as not having the meaning so definitely implied.[53] The failure of the administration to take the extreme stand was a point against the availability of Pierce for re-nomination in the Lower South.[54] Even so, the rejection applied to the method and not the objective of the Manifesto. Soulé's successor was instructed to endeavor to secure the Island,[55] and this policy of the Democratic party to add territory that would augment the region of slavery made an outstanding point of attack for the Republicans.

There was kinship between the designs on Cuba as expressed in the Ostend declaration, and Central American affairs in general. Both places were objects of our financial and fili-buster enterprises. In Central America, the relation with Great Britain was also involved. Our wrangles with that power over the interpretation of the Clayton-Bulwer Treaty, had already aroused a great deal of spleen and given any strenuous anti-British program a political fervor.[56] With the controversy over the treaty at dead-lock, Britain had entered the struggle with Russia in the Crimea, which, although it rendered a breach of peace with the United States, inadmissable on the part of Britain, led to an additional controversy with her over enlistments.

The Pierce administration began its Central America policy with vigor. British expansion along the Mosquito coast, under their interpretation of the Clayton-Bulwer Treaty, had estranged Nicaragua to us since she expected protection under the Monroe Doctrine. Solon Borland was sent to woo her back by using the Senate's interpretation of the treaty and guarantees against American expansion. At Greytown, Borland was caught up in a fight and driven from the American consulate, whence he fled, under fire, protected by the crew of the American steamer, *Northern Light*. In reparation, July 9, 1854, Captain Hollins bombarded and destroyed the city. With England confining her attention to the East, there was a lull in Central American interest until the following year. In June, 1855, William Walker, "the gray-eyed man of destiny," taking advantage of a raging conflict between the two political parties, and acting on invitation of the Liberals, came with some fellow adventurers, and soon made himself master. Patricio Rivas was elected president, and the United States agent at Greytown, recognized this government. The new government sent Parker H. French as its minister to the United States.

Here the progress of the filibuster government towards recognition ran into the storm and stress of politics. Marcoleta, representative of the Legitimist, Estrada government still held to the position as Nicaragua representative. His protracted tenure was based on the insistence of his chief that the treaty on which Walker's government was founded was null, and that the real government was the one he had set up at Segovia. It was impossible to recognize Estrada's phantom government, and yet, to refuse continued recognition to Marcoleta was to give tacit approval to the Walker establishment. This would antagonize England, which might not prove a bad move for the administration. It would also wave the red flag before the young Republican bull which was already finding too many pretexts for a change. Since the annexation of Texas there had been growing a conception of a South ever reaching to extend its empire of slavery. Walker's position, as a southern man and promoter of slavery, along with the recent Ostend declaration, fitted his enterprise into the frame-work, although he had no purpose ever to attach his projected empire to the United States.[57]

French arrived and introduced himself at the department of State about the middle of December, 1855. Marcy refused recognition in unmistakable terms.[58] The rival claimant still persevered and was the recipient of attention that gave him and the situation publicity, while French, after the rebuff, went to New York where he became involved in an embroglio over filibuster enlistment.[59] The treatment of the would-be minister laid the administration open to criticism by many who favored Walker's project.[60] Whatever embarrassment it may have had was promptly relieved when friends proved the man a scamp. After a second refusal early in February, French went his way, and Walker, seeing the way the wind was blowing, disclaimed his connection with the Nicaragua government.[61]

The administration had rejected the minister of the filibuster nation, just as it had turned aside the product of the

Ostend conference. Affairs, however, were shaping to make the recognition question acute. While French was at the gates of the State department, Pierce was "getting south" on his successive positions on Kansas.[62] The nearer approach of the June convention pointed to the availability of a northern man with a southern record. The Walker situation was receiving much attention in many strongholds of Democracy,[63] and it soon became obvious that its endorsement would be one of the Democratic issues. The growing prominence of the question, and Pierce's desire to secure a southern backing for renomination, forced him to the exigency of acting on the Nicaragua question. Walker was conscious of the advantage, and early in May the unique figure of Padre Augustine Vijil appeared as his minister.[64]

Vijil's coming was given due, perhaps undue, attention. Eight trunks of state papers made his mission impressive, but the uncertainty of Walker's position, it was announced, caused the administration to hesitate for several days.[65] May 14 the reception came, and the following day Marcoleta was told that he no longer represented a government. This made a new point on which to attack Pierce. It was proclaimed a change of policy, and a breach of consistency. It had been our policy to recognize *de facto* governments. This, it was argued, the President had refused to do when French came, and the Walker Government was secure; but now that it was on precarious footing, he recognized it—which action was "too late for Cincinnati and too early for History."[66] In light of the Ostend declaration recognition was announced a trouble maker with Spain, but as such a valuable smoke screen for Kansas.[67] The reception of Vijil was identified as part and parcel of the scheme to grab Cuba, *a la* Ostend Manifesto. The personality of the Padre was set upon, and his actions made objects of comment. A "filibuster" meeting in New York on May 23 to celebrate recognition,[68] was synchronous with the "Sack of Lawrence" and the Sumner assault.[69] The recognition of the Walker Government accompanied by many other exciting issues now demanded rejection or acceptance at the Democratic National Convention at Cincinnati. This body gave it a distinct approbation.[70]

With the sanction of the Democracy, Nicaragua became a campaign issue. It was pronounced part of a slavery expan-

sion scheme. Padre Vijil was hounded about the country,
and early in June he declared his intention to leave.[71] His had
been only a "back-door" reception after all. Bishop Hughes
had not received him graciously; he disliked the food and the
wearing of pantaloons, and the danger of carriages in the
streets by day and gas in the houses by night worried him.
John P. Heiss became *charge* until a new minister should
arrive. Walker's own activities, his election as president, opening the slave-trade, and acting confidently with prominent,
pro-slavery Americans, whether he purposed annexation or no,
gave Nicaragua a place of interest in the campaign.

The Nicaraguan recognition complicated British relations
in Central America, which Buchanan and Clarendon had already reduced to an *impasse*. Before this occurred, the
"enlistment question" which finally resulted in the dismissal
of the English minister Crampton, made a more direct cause
of quarrel with John Bull. Crampton and the consuls at New
York, Philadelphia, and Cincinnati were the chief offenders.
Marcy had protested at first, but enlistment had continued,
and now it was pending for drastic action under the influence
of heated politics. January 27 Marcy pronounced it still
second to the recognition question, on which there was a
strong unity of opinion; but that Crampton's recall had been
requested and his government would be likely not to grant
it.[72] The Peace Conference was approaching, Britain would
soon be disengaged in the Crimea, and it was intimated that
she wanted to make a bold move to retrieve the bad showing
she had made as compared with the French. With John Bull
thus circumstanced, there was a good background for a war
scare. At the same time assurances came that in the event
of war, France could be relied upon not to join against us.[73]
That the British people would not permit war on the issue
was heard from many quarters.[74] Britain must have cotton.
Forcing a settlement was pronounced a possible triumph for
the Administration, and Buchanan, feeling his way to nomination and just leaving the court of St. James at his own behest,
was considered the loser of a great opportunity.[75]

On the last day of February, Marcy had received Clarendon's statement of position. He offered to leave Central
America to a third power to arbitrate; he gave no satisfaction
on Crampton. Marcy thought that the President would re-

fuse arbitration, but declined any further action on Central
America until his note requesting Crampton's recall should
be answered.[76] Marcy was giving his correspondence a wide
circulation, with several possible motives.[77] Clarendon had
apologized for enlistment, if such a violation of our laws had
occurred, but he did not admit that it had occurred. This
was going half way, but if Marcy insisted on the recall it
meant a clash, and Marcy insisted on an answer. Conservative men showed some alarm; Judge McLean cautioned Marcy
that Clarendon had no way out under the circumstances, but
to fight,[78] and VanBuren hinted that arbitration might be
necessary for two cabinets, each with an "eye out for
buncomb."[79] No answer came. A month went by and Marcy
expressed surprise that he had had no answer.[80] A week later
he instructed Dallas to ask for an answer.

The crisis was fast approaching. April 30 Clarendon replied. He made way for Marcy to give proof of the guilt of
the four men, and some thought he extended an invitation to
be let off on the ground that his agents were over zealous,
and not prone to legal exactness.[82] Before this could reach the
department at Washington, Pierce, contrary to Marcy's advice, decided to recognize the Walker government, and penned
a message to that effect.[83] The same day, May 12, Marcy
decided that there was no other course than to give Crampton
his passport, for the recognition of Walker might complicate
matters.[84] On May 19 Clarendon's note came, but it did not
alter the purpose of the Secretary of State. He decided to
delay action ten or twelve days in which time he would write
his reply.[85] Marcy based his answer on the ground that
Clarendon had misrepresented what he had said.[86] Late in
May Crampton received his passport. This action was a
contemporary of the "Sack of Lawrence" and the "Sumner
assault." [87]

Diplomatic relations with Great Britain, merged in the
general excitement, came before the Cincinnati Convention for
pronouncement. It emerged with strong ground taken.[88] The
Democrats would thereby place foreign affairs "second to
nothing," while the Republicans insisted that the real issues
were domestic. Crampton's place was left vacant, and British
relations left in condition to supply political capital.

1. The "Address of the Committee of the Pittsburgh Convention, February 22", is one of the best reviews of the argument for the growth of slave-holding dominance in the Democratic party.
2. Editorial, *New York Tribune*, Jan.9,1856. Good sketches of the idea are found in the pamphlets: *The Democratic Party As It Was And As It Is*, and *The Humbug and the Reality, by Timothy C. Day*. See Bibliography.
3. Pamphlet: *The Record of Sectionalism*, by Dr. G. Bailey, is the best statement of the influence of the South in federal office.
4. Pamphlet: *Modern "Democracy", The Ally of Slavery*, a speech of M.W.Tappan of New Hampshire in the House, July 29, is one of the best statements of this point.
5. This statement is found uniformly in platforms, addresses, and appeals.
6. Catterall, Mrs.C.T., "Antecedents of the Dred Scott Case" in *American Historical Review*, vol. XXX.
7. For Judge Kane's opinion, see below.
8. For an account of the action of Judge Lecompte, see Chapter VI; for the Garner case, see below. Commissioner Pendry was an official with jurisdiction in fugitive cases. The fugitive slave law provided for the appointment of such officers.
9. Editorial: "Atrocious Judges", *New York Tribune*, March 9.
10. Pamphlet: *Letters addressed to Friends of Freedom and Union* by Hampden, from *New York Evening Post*, Sept. 9.
11. "Address of the Committee of the Pittsburg Convention, Feb. 22". The New York case referred to was the Lemmon case.
12. For a sketch of the case, see below.
13. Pierce's annual message, Dec. 28, 1855.
14. Good general statements of the argument are: "Address of the Committee of the Pittsburgh Convention, February 22" "Address of the Democratic Republican State Committee at Syracuse, New York, July 24, 1856".
15. *Who Are Sectional*, pamphlet by George Weston is the best treatment of the subject. It was done to meet the direct attack made in the canvass. See Chapter XI. Other Weston pamphlets on this subject were: *Will the South Dissolve the Union?; The Federal Union—It Must Be Preserved. Freedom National—Slavery Sectional*, Speech of J.W.Perry of Maine in the House May 1 was another widely used treatment.
16. *New York Tribune*, March 10.
17. See Chapter IV—*Economics of Slavery*.
18. Marcy had recently carried this so far as to order American ministers to wear only the dress of a citizen, which caused some ridiculous situations.
19. Hamilton Fish to Robert Winthrop, June 10, 1854. Winthrop MSS. M.H.S.
20. In the early days of Lincoln's administration Seward recommended war with England as a means of re-uniting the sections
21. The statements of fact are taken from the report of James Cox Prosecuting Att. of Hamilton Co. to Governor Chase, Feb. 29 1856, in Chase MSS. L.C. Chase wrote an account of the case in a letter to Trowbridge in 1864. See Schuckers, *Life of Chase*

pp. 171-176.
22. The statements of fact are based on the printed report of S.M. Booth to Sumner, Feb.25,'56, in Sumner MSS. Sumner had sent a note of inquiry. Booth included an expense account with his statement. He desired to put his paper on a firm basis for the coming campaign. A similar statement to Chase had brought no results.
23. B.Paine to Sumner, June 12. Sumner MSS. H.L.
24. Madison *Argus and Democrat,* June 5.
25. Pamphlet, report, 216 pp.
26. Letters of S.M.Booth;Justices A.S.Smith and B.Paine to Sumner, Sumner MSS. H.L.
27. Justice Smith to Sumner, Jan. 1, 1856. Sumner MSS. H.L.
28. B.Paine to Sumner, Jan. 12, 1856. Sumner MSS. H.L.
29. See above, Chapter II.
30. The statements of fact are based on "Narrative of the Facts in the case of Passmore Williamson" published by the Pennsylvania Anti-Slavery Society. One has to watch the anti-slavery bias in their presentation.
31. The relation of Chase and Campbell as revealed in their correspondence throws as interesting light on their difference as to the protective principle.
32. Commons,John R., "Horace Greeley, and the Working Class Origin of the Republican Party", *Pol.Sci.Qr.,* vol. XXIV, p. 487.
33. Wilmot's letter to B.Laporte, Jan.22,1855, in Going,C.B., *David Wilmot Free-Soiler,* pp.90-93.
34. Letters of J. Glancy Jones to Buchanan. Buchanan, MSS. P.H.S.
35. The Pennsylvania representatives had an argument over Banks' free-trade record during the speakership fight.
36. H.R. 566. House Report, No. 342.
37. *Senate Jl.* July 7.
38. *House Jl.* July 8.
39. H.R. 53, *House Jl.* Feb. 21.
40. *House Jl.* Feb. 21. The committee was headed by Denver, in cluded men from states that were prospective termini, and Wood of Me. and Kidwell of Va. represented respectively radical northern and southern positions.
41. This Resolution. *House Jl.* May 21.
42. H.R. 584. Report No. 358. *House Comm. Reports,* vol. III.
43. Commons,J.R., "Horace Greeley and the Working Class Origin of the Republican Party". *Pol.Sci.Qr.,*vol.XXIV, p.488.
44. *Ibid,*p.484. *Recollections of a Busy Life,* p.217.
45. Stephenson,George M.,*Political History of the Public Lands,* 1840-62, Chapter XII. Tiffany,Francis,*Life of Dorothea Lynde Dix,* Chapters XVII,XVIII.
46. Dubois,James T. and Matthews, Gertrude S.,*Galusha A. Grow,* Chapter V.
47. *House Jl.* Feb. 7.
48. *House Jl.* Feb. 18.
49. H.R. 43 and H.R. 44, *House Jl.* Feb. 20.
50. *New York Tribune,* May 16 and May 27.
51. Hall, B. F., *The Republican Party,* a campaign history, which

traced the descent of the party from the national Republicans,
through the Whigs, to a re-emergence in 1856, presented the
Whig claim to preëminence in the Republican movement. Doctor Bailey, champion of the Free-Soilers, reviewed the book in
the *National Era* of Nov. 13, and pronounced it untrue and un-
fair.

52. See Johnson,W.F.,*American Foreign Relations,* vol.I, Chapter
    XX, for interpretation.
53. Marcy's Reply, no.23, Nov.13,1854. Text in *Phil.North Amer-
    ican,*Mar.7,1855.
54. Letters ofCol. Seibels to Buchanan, in Buch.MSS. See Chapter
    VIII.
55. Pelzer,Lewis, *Life of Augustus Caesar Dodge,* pp. 220-221.
56. The Democrats incorporated this and the attitude of Sec.Cass
    does not rest entirely on the fact that Britain was his *bête noir.*
57. Scroggs,Wm.O.,*Filibusters and Financiers* makes this special
    point as to Walker's purpose.
58. House Ex.Doc.103, 34th Cong.57.75, cited Scroggs, p. 169.
59. *Ibid.,* p. 167.
60. *Ibid.,* p. 168-169.
61. *Ibid.,*p.172.
62. Kansas Messages, see below, Chapter VI.
63. Scroggs, *Filibusters and Financiers,* p. 171.
64. *Ibid.,*p. 172-173, for account of Vijil.
65. *New York Tribune,* May 12.
66. *New York Tribune,* May 15.
67. *New York Tribune,* May 17.
68. See Scroggs *Filibuster and Financiers,* p. 173.
69. For account, see Chapter VI.
70. See Democratic Platform, Chapter VIII.
71. *New York Tribune,* June
72. Marcy to Buchanan, Jan. 27,1856. Marcy MSS. L.C.
73. Mason to Marcy,Feb.7. Marcy MSS. L.C.
74. Mason to Marcy, Feb. 18; C.A.Dana to Marcy, March 3; L.D.
    Bradford to Marcy, Mar. 6. Marcy MSS. L.C.
75. Mason to Marcy, Feb. 18. Marcy MSS. L.C.
76. Marcy to Dallas, Feb. 29, Marcy MSS. L.C.
77. Marcy's actions at times indicated that he might like to be a
    presidential candidate.
78 McLean to Marcy, March 19. Marcy MSS. L.C.
79. VanBuren to Marcy, March 21. Marcy MSS. L.C.
80. Marcy to Dallas (Private), April 20. Marcy MSS. L.C.
81. Marcy to Dallas, April 28. Marcy MSS. L.C.
82. Dallas to Marcy, May 6. Marcy MSS. L.C.
83. Pierce to Marcy, May 12. Marcy MSS. L.C.
84. Marcy to Dallas, May 12. Marcy MSS. L.C.
85. Marcy to Dallas, May 17. Marcy MSS. L.C.
86. Marcy to Dallas, May 23. Marcy MSS. L.C.
87. See Chapter VI.
88. See Chapter VII. Democratic Platform.

CHAPTER VI

UTILIZATION OF EVENTS

The Republicans had a broader foundation on which to base their efforts to convince the North than the abstract arguments contained in the "literature" they circulated. At any time there are various problems in which the public is interested and which are bound to assert themselves in a political contest. The campaign year of 1856 held a large list of these, many of which were extremely useful for political ends. Besides those that had been in the public eye for some time there was a series of current events of absorbing interest. These kept the North in an excited state of mind and made it receptive to the propaganda the Republicans were distributing. The first campaign of the party cannot be understood apart from the influence of contemporary happenings, nor could a master dramatist have ordered and arranged them with greater effectiveness. Boutwell probably spoke more to the point than he realized when he declared that "the Republican party was a child of events."[1]

Kansas Background

Of all the current events that the Republicans found useful, there was nothing quite so valuable as what happened in Kansas. The working out of the act that had opened the territory and precipitated the conflict would as a matter of course be the core of the struggle that it projected into politics. Apart from what happened in Kansas in the process of applying the new principle fathered by the administration, the Republican genesis cannot be explained. It is scarcely making the case too strong to say that without the constant stimulus afforded by events in Kansas, the party would never have crystallized. The argument over the repeal of the compromise and the accusation that a compact had been violated by the South had power in themselves; but the application of squatter sovereignty, which was for all practical purposes, an invitation to fight for the territory, and which produced

"Bleeding Kansas," was the greatest of all propaganda factors.

Long before the time the campaign had become definite with candidates and platforms, the Republicans were in a position to make the most of Kansas. The piled-up events since the opening of the territory made a store-house of detail for editors and speakers to draw upon. Congress was in a position to accept the "salvation" of the new territory as a special obligation and to magnify its importance. There was also machinery to supply men and money to maintain the fight for the territory. For giving publicity to the "Kansas war" they were fortunate in having the services of two very able reporters, William Phillips and James Redpath. These men were radicals of the John Brown school, both produced major documents in the controversy,[2] and the pen of each contributed to the dramatic events in Kansas. Their principle press outlets were the *St. Louis Democrat*, the *Chicago Tribune*, and the *New York Tribune*. These three formed an unfailing source of information on the subject, and friends of the administration alleged with a large element of truthfulness that most of the terrible happenings in Kansas had their origin in St. Louis and Chicago.

The factors in the Kansas background were more complex than the mere problem of organizing the territory under the provisions of the new organic act. While the Kansas-Nebraska bill was making its way through Congress, Eli Thayer was pursuading wealthy New Englanders to pour their treasure into an enterprise to secure Kansas as a free state. Before the bill became a law, the New England Emigrant Aid Society was incorporated.[3] On the other hand, David R. Atchison and his associates were formulating a counter-program to secure Kansas for slavery.[4] These opposing purposes led to the fight that ensued and to the counter-accusation that each conspired to secure the territory. The priority of the alleged "conspiracies" became an important point—who started the trouble in Kansas? The presence of these extraordinary influences in the forming of the territory gave the administration a chance to maintain that the new principle, squatter sovereignty, had not been given a fair trial, and also a chance to point out the party guilty of thwarting the true purpose of its program. The indictment fell upon the Aid Society which defended its position on the ground of the strict legality of all its functions.

Administration, Aid Society, and "Ruffians" in embryo, were sure to create a situation of great public concern.

Andrew H. Reeder was appointed Governor of Kansas. The importance attached to Pennsylvania politics made a son of that state a logical selection, and John W. Forney gives himself and Asa Packer credit for recommending Reeder, a member of the "Tenth Legion Democracy" of the Keystone state, for the position.[5] It was not until October 7 that the new governor reached his post. This delay had its significance; for, said the Republicans, it was done deliberately to allow the Missourians time to take possession. When Pierce later attacked Reeder, he named the delay as the undoing of his plans, since it allowed the abolitionizing process to start.[6] Along with Reeder came the other officials of the infant territory, and the creative process began.[7] Late in November an election was held for delegate to Congress, and in this the Missourians participated. It had nothing to do with the question of passing on local institutions, and gave the Republicans an advantage in argument to the effect that it was a declaration on the part of the Missourians of their purpose to take Kansas. March 30 the election of the territorial legislature was held, and in spite of Reeder's precautions the Missourians were there again. Here was more material— the Missourians were outsiders interfering to carry slavery into the territory regardless of the wishes of the inhabitants. Soon afterwards Reeder returned to Pennsylvania. In an address at Easton he declared the elections fraudulent and began his role in the campaign of 1856.

Reeder returned to Kansas in May and began a fight with the legislature in which a majority returned by the March election dominated.[8] Shortly he reached the position of refusing to recognize it as a legal body. The technicalities involved in his position made good points for argument. On July 28 the administration dismissed him. A staunch Democrat thereby became an enemy, and Pierce was put in the position of accepting the legislature which his opponents now denounced as "bogus." Daniel Woodson, the secretary, became governor pending another appointment. During this interval a number of laws, including a "slave code" were enacted. This code enabled the Republicans to round out a case. They maintained that the laws were passed by a "bogus" legislature, elected by interference from a slave state, that slavery was recognized as existing, that the freedom of speech and of the press necessary for the people "freely to determine their institutions" were denied, and that residents of anti-slavery opinions were disfranchised by the required oath, while Missourians could come over and vote, if they paid a dollar. This was the applied squatter sovereignty that Pierce endorsed.

At this juncture another element was introduced. The free state men began a movement which led to the formation of the Topeka constitution. Although there has been disagreement as to the influence of this movement in making a free state of Kansas,[9] there can be no question of the facilities it afforded for making propaganda out of Kansas. They based their project on the right they claimed under the Federal constitution to form a government where none existed. This proceeded on the thesis that a majority of the citizens were free-state men, and that the existing government was illegal and therefore void. In the process of creating this spontaneous government Reeder had been elected to go to Congress to represent "a majority of the people" and to contest the seat held by Whitfield. Their constiututation was ratified December 15 and the Topeka government was ready to take its place in the Kansas drama. The presence of this party laid the foundation for executive interference "with freedom" and for civil war.

Wilson Shannon, who succeeded Reeder, reached the seat of government of the territory early in September. Whatever he did would reflect the administration's policy in Kansas, and pressure was at once put upon him to elicit a declaration. He soon went on record as accepting things as they were, but promised security of elections for the further application of squatter sovereignty.[10] The free state men joined issue on the ground that slavery was already established, that they were disfranchised by the law the governor recognized, and that they doubted his ability to give security. The press throughout the North kept the issue hot.

There proved to be more fascinating things immediately in store than the policy of the new governor. November 21 Charles Dow, a free state man, was killed, and shortly after it came the Branson rescue which gave Sheriff Jones of

Douglas County some processes to serve and also assurance that there was armed resistance to his exercise of authority. In response Shannon called out the militia and called on all citizens to rally in defense of the law.[11] Law-loving citizens were plentiful. They gathered along the Wakarusa, menacing Lawrence, the rendevouz of the free state men. This town was well garrisoned by men armed with Sharp's rifles,[12] and Shannon found a pitched battle imminent. He sent a dispatch to Colonel Sumner to come at once with United States soldiers.[13] Although Sumner never came, Shannon succeeded in getting a treaty between the two parties and in disbanding his militia. This "militia invasion" furnished another source of useful material. The Border Ruffians were as ready to serve at invasions as they had been at elections. The fact that Sumner never came was valuable as evidence that the administration wanted Lawrence destroyed and the Topeka movement stopped. The pro-slavery men had organized a "law and order party" to meet the Topeka movement,[14] which name the Republicans accepted for the ironic value this "invasion" episode had given it.

This first venture of Shannon's administration in governing Kansas furnished still another point. While the militia was in the field, a free state man named Barber was killed.[15] No effective action was taken against the murderer, and another martyr was added. Coleman who had killed Dow was still at large. The northern press had another point now— the "Laws of Kansas" had no cognizance of murder when committed on a free state man by a promoter of slavery.

The militia melted away leaving Lawrence untouched and its citizens still unharmed. Then came a lull while the blizzards of the winter of 1855-1856 held the territory in their grip. In January, state officers under the Topeka constitution were elected, and Charles Robinson, the New England Aid Society agent, was named for governor. Along with Reeder's challenge of Whitfield's seat in Congress, the question of the admission of Kansas with a free constitution was put before that body.

Kansas and Congress

The Thirty-fourth Congress assembled December 3. Washington became as much a center of the Kansas trouble as the

distressed territory itself. Greeley said—everybody said—
that it was up to Congress to do something for Kansas. It
was a question primarily for the House, since it contained a
majority opposed to the new régime in the territories. As an
opposition its clear duty was to demonstrate that squatter
sovereignty was a failure, and to enact measures to correct
it. The Senate with a strong administration majority would
exert its efforts to vindicate the measure and promote its
further working out along lines already introduced by
Shannon's policy. At best it could be only a deadlock, with
a slight advantage for the lower house in the fact that it had
come last from the people and could claim to represent their
wishes best. This balance, although it rendered any legislation on Kansas impossible, created an ideal situation in which
both sides could maneuver, with the securing of public
approval in the presidential campaign as an object. With the
happenings in Kansas as a background already at their
disposal, they set to work to argue out a solution.

Congress could not break in at once on the subject. The
House had to be organized in order to use its anti-Nebraska
majority, which, in itself proved to be a Herculean task.[16]
Everybody was anxious while the House wrangled away the
nine weeks required to organize, even though it was not
entirely dumb on Kansas during the process. The Senate,
though it did not intend to start work until the other house
should be ready, broke ground on the question. President
Pierce sounded the first bugle in his annual message. He was
anxious to take position on the great topic with such advantage as immediacy would give; and there was much to be
gained towards a re-nomination, especially since several southern states would hold conventions on or about January 8.
Although the House was not organized and Congress not ready
for business, the annual message was delivered. While the
House turned back with scorn "the package" the President's
secretary brought to the door, the Senate received it, referred
it to a committee, and printed it.[17]

The message was, in most of its features, a political document.[18] Foreign relations were given first place, and states
rights received a hearty endorsement. As for Kansas, the
President admitted "acts prejudicial to good order;" but
declared that none had "occurred under circumstances to

justify the interposition of the Federal executive." This would
be justified only in case of obstruction to Federal law or "to
organized resistance to territorial law assuming the character of insurrection." He hoped the good sense of the people
"free to determine their own institutions" would prevent its
necessity. It was "organized meddling" that had led to the
difficulty in Kansas; for "while the people of the southern
states confined their attention to their own affairs, not pre-
suming officially to intermeddle with the institutions of the
northern states, too many of the inhabitants of the latter are
permanently organized in associations to inflict injury on the
former by unlawful acts, which would be cause of war as
between foreign powers, and only fail to be such in our
system because perpetrated under cover of the union." The
new principle gave justice to all sections and should be accepted. The President also raised the disunion bogie—"a
sectional victory preventing the admission of Kansas with
slavery would mean disunion."

The Republicans opened on the message with unction. The
press saw more in the Kansas happening than "events prejudicial to good order." On January 3 Senator John P. Hale
moved to reconsider the vote to commit the message in order
to speak. Hale was a veteran Free-Soiler, and was now
Senator from New Hampshire, the home state of the President.
In this speech, significant because it came from the President's
own state, Hale launched the attack on the administration in
Congress, and introduced the program of destroying the
Democracy in the free states by this first stride towards taking Pierce's own state away from him. It was a direct
assault, and thereafter, affable gentleman though the President
was, he turned his back upon the anti-slavery senator. Hale
attacked the message as irregular and not worthy of recognition. It was timed, he said, for the President's political
advantage at the South; but in this his efforts were useless
because slavery, having used him, had already cast him aside.
The war talk was a blind. Kansas was the issue, and the
President did not wish to stress the subject.[19]

The Topeka movement was rapidly coming to fruition, and
on January 24 the President delivered a special message on
Kansas, even though the House had not yet organized.[20] Like
its predecessor, the Senate received it while the House demur-

red, ordered it read that it might facilitate organization, and then tabled it for future reference. The President admitted irregularity, but explained it as the result of an organized scheme to abolitionize the territory which Reeder's delay had made possible. He accepted the Kansas legislature just as Reeder had done, and declared it too late now to go behind what had already been done. A solution was to be found in further constructive acts under the organic law. He promised protection from invasion and also enforced obedience to the territorial legislature but not intervention in local affairs. Although peace had been restored he feared developments and recommended steps towards organizing and admitting Kansas. Thus, the strategy was to accept the existing machinery and to use the will of the people of the territory, unhampered from without or within, to direct further progress towards statehood. This would vindicate squatter sovereignty and reduce the territory to order—it was the official Democratic position on Kansas. It embarrassed the opposition in that they claimed to have a majority in the territory and consequently should not fear the outcome of the President's program. They met the issue directly on the ground that an unbiassed settlement under existing machinery was impossible, that the laws Pierce accepted in Kansas disfranchised free state men and made criminals out of those who sought a free constitution even though they were a majority.

Congress was not ready to take up the question, but there were other means of making much of it. The following day Reeder made a reply to the attack made on him in the message and promised to "bide his time" to expose the whole affair.[21] Greeley declared that "so base a document had never till now emanated from the White House."[22] A passing event added a further touch of excitement. The *Tribune* of January 20 commented on the motion made by Congressman Rust of Arkansas to the effect that all candidates for speaker withdraw. Greeley's statement was, that he was well acquainted with human degradation, but Rust's resolution was the "most discreditable proposition he ever heard put before a legislative body."[23] Rust met Greeley in the capital grounds, and after an exchange of remarks, beat him over the head with a cane. After this event, until Pike took his place at the capital, the editor was seen about town in the company of husky admirers.

Here was a direct way of striking at the freedom of the press. Its political value was chiefly in its place at the head of a series of similar events, all to be used as testimony that slavery ruled by violence.

Finally, on February 9, the House was organized and ready to take charge of its new ward—Kansas. With Congress ready for action and the first session of the legislature under the Topeka constitution scheduled for March 4, the President took the occasion to proclaim it an outlaw.[24] The administration was entirely on record now, and its succesive positions were summed as declaring: first, there was no cause to intervene; second, there was no right to intervene for purity of election; and third and last, the outrages were proper and the free state men outlaws.[25] The recent killing of R. P. Brown by a pro-slavery mob made another martyr and lent unction to the task of doing something for Kansas. The House called the President's message of January 24 off the table and began a wrangle as to the proper committee to which to refer it. Finally, on the 14th it was turned over to the Committee of the Whole House and not the Committee on Territories which had been organized for this work. It was a strange reference and the Republicans deprecated it as a show of weakness and a party defeat.[26] Balked in its attempt to get directly at Kansas from the President's recommendation the House had to seek other means.

Several ways were open. As proffered relief measures the House could attempt to repeal the Kansas legislation—either the organic act itself or the work done in the territory under it. It could block any constructive measure of the administration there, and above all, it could refuse to admit Kansas with slavery. Further, it could withhold any appropriations that applied to governing or protecting Kansas. As a more constructive measure, it could unseat Whitfield and thereby render the decision of the representatives of the people that the régime in Kansas was illegal. As a suggested solution, they could pass a bill admitting Kansas with the Topeka constitution. With the Senate strongly Democratic, the House could not legislate, but it could educate.

The first trend of the House was towards repeal measures. On February 14 Grow of the Committee on Territories called for the laws and executive proceedings of Kansas. On February 18 Dunn of Indiana introduced a bill "to re-establish the boundaries and reorganize the territories,"[27] which went to the Committee on Territories. This with various resolutions and memorials, found lodgment in Grow's committee. On February 25 he gave notice of a bill to be introduced to "amend certain acts of the Kansas legislature." He introduced two bills[28] on February 27: one "to amend and supplementary to" the organic act, and one "repealing some of the acts of the legislature of Kansas." These went to the Committee of the Whole on the State of the Union for debate. It was a chance to give Kansas an airing, but a great disadvantage was at once apparent. A bill to repeal the laws of the Kansas legislature recognized the legality of the body and could not be squared with the concurrent move to seat Reeder and thereby demonstrate its illegality. The shrewd parliamentarians and politicians of the Democracy would allow no such loose play, and distinctly repeal measures played little part thereafter, in spite of the fact that the Kansas laws were so open to attack that the Democrats found advantage in talking of their repeal. The second of Grow's measures finally passed the House completely changed, as the Dunn Bill, July 20. Before that time, the Kansas question had been fully thrashed out—fought in a circle and repeal returned to as a last resort.

The blocking of constructive legislation for Kansas internally, like the repeal measures, did not occupy a large place. The anti-Nebraska House would countenance nothing projected from the existing enactments; and since any such proposed legislation would add fuel to the flames already too hot for comfort, the Democrats were not persistent. On February 28, Whitfield introduced three bills of this nature.[29] These came to naught, for to the country they would make it seem as if progress were being made under squatter sovereignty. On March 10, Phelps of Missouri gave notice of a bill to mark the southern boundary, and on March 25 he introduced it. The President had recommended this in his annual message as an act for the facilitation of commerce to Santa Fé. This bill became a law July 9. It was the only constructive measure passed for Kansas and had nothing to do with internal affairs. The Republicans were quite willing to be for it as a measure fostering trade.

The real forensic possibilities of Kansas were not brought

out in these minor measures and wrangles. The first telling round was that over the contested seat of territorial delegate. Claiming to represent a majority of the settlers,[30] in which position the basic principle of squatter sovereignty fortified him, Reeder appeared at Washington to contest with Whitfield the seat in which the latter had been seated. It was a two-edged proposition. It would cast a dark shadow upon the sincerity of the administration party in letting a majority rule in the territory, and if Whitfield were ousted, it would commit the House, the popular body, to the opinion that the Kansas legislature was illegal.

On February 14 Florence of Pennsylvania presented Reeder's memorial protesting the seat. This was referred to the Committee on Elections which was headed by Hickman of Pennsylvania, a personal friend of Reeder's. On February 19 Hickman reported from committee a resolution that the committee be empowered to send for persons and papers. With this the battle started. Stephens of Georgia moved a re-committal with instructions to state "reasons and grounds" for sending, which motion failed by the casting vote of the speaker. On February 20 Hickman's resolution was carried, and then reconsidered. At this juncture Orr of South Carolina made a parry to thwart the anti-Nebraska purpose by moving an amendment to give the power to collect evidence to two Washington attorneys. The resolution and the amendment, with instructions to report reasons, were recommitted.

The first point at issue involved all the technicalities of Reeder's position on Kansas affairs, and they in turn involved all that had happened in Kansas. The administration champions argued that he could not contest the seat; that he was stopped by his own action in acknowledging the Kansas legislature as legal. Another fine point was the power of the House to go behind the laws passed by a territorial legislature. Orr's move to send attorneys and avoid the expense of sending so great a distance for persons and papers had a splendid political advantage in its appeal to economy. In this, and in the technical legality of the Kansas legislature, the seasoned parliamentarians of the administration had distinct advantage. But the Republicans also had their vantage ground. They could, and did, show vividly how the legislature came to be in Kansas. They argued that Congress could investigate

fraud in a territory, and an attempt to block an investigation
under the circumstances was certainly a confession that fraud
existed. It was a hot debate, and many cmpaign documents
were made.[31]

On March 5 Hickman reported giving reasons and submitting resolutions for power to send for persons and papers and
subpoena witnesses. Stephens submitted a minority report.
The battle started all over again. The next day Boyce of
South Carolina moved to recommit with instructions making
any cognizance of Reeder's case impossible. This was debated
until withdrawn on March 17. The same day, Dunn, taking
advantage of the popularity of Orr's suggestion of economy,
moved an amendment which was, in brief, the provision for
an investigation committee. This was debated, and on March
19, passed. The anti-Nebraska forces had won a victory. A
committee of their own making would be sent to spy out the
land. Their opponents complained of irregularity; the senders
congratulated themselves on what they would find.

Within a few days the committee was appointed. L. D.
Campbell of Ohio declined to serve and John Sherman of the
same state was appointed in his stead. Howard of Michigan
was the other Republican memb̃er. In the appearance of fairness, Mordecai Oliver, representative of a Missouri border
constituency, was made the third member. Fogg, an influential
editor of Pierce's own state, was made secretary. The committee was ready, spring was opening the frost-locked rivers
and fields, and it could soon be at its task. With the contested
seat placed in abeyance by the pending investigation, the
House well might rest from its Kansas travail; but the subject
was too valuable and its approaches too versatile to admit of
pause. The Pittsburgh Convention of February 22 had put
the Republicans on record for the immediate admission of
Kansas under the Topeka constitution,[32] and memorials from
its promoters were at hand.

The Senate, following the President's recommendation, had
moved directly towards an enabling act. As early as February
4 there was a call for papers; February 29 the President complied. Senator Douglas, chairman of the Committee on
Territories, had been delayed in his work by illness during the
opening weeks of Congress. It was not until March 12 that
his committee reported, and a bill was not yet ready. Collamer

of Vermont made the minority report. These were important
political documents and 31,000 copies were eventually printed.[33]
Douglas' argument was a review of the administration position on Kansas to date. Like the President's message it placed
the onus of outside interference on the New England Emigrant
Aid Society. In the same voice he cited peaceful Nebraska as
an example of the working of squatter sovereignty where
there were no societies to interfere. The populace had been
anxious to hear from the "Little Giant" and his performance
gave a new burst of splendor to the publicity of Kansas in
Congress. In the discussion on the report Douglas made a
remark to the effect that they intended to subdue the opposition. On it a new hue and cry arose: *subduing freedom*.
Henceforth the Democratic policy had a name, and "we will
subdue you" became a current phrase. The *Tribune* the following day announced that the free states did not intend to
be subdued.[34] But one good turn deserves another, and Douglas
pronounced *shrieking for freedom* a new political method in
use by his opponents. In platitude and sophistry he could not
be beaten; not even by the Sage of the *Tribune*. Lyman
Trumbull, Douglas' colleague, took occasion to register disapproval of squatter sovereignty from the home state of its
champion.[35] The approach of the Democratic National Convention laid the work of the Little Giant open to sinister
interpretation. Greeley announced that Pierce had thrown
the free state men of Kansas into prison, that he had this
information from good authority, but it was now necessary in
order to outbid Douglas.[36]

On March 17 Douglas brought in his bill—an enabling act
for Kansas.[37] On March 20 Seward moved a substitution to
admit Kansas as a free state. The Topeka Constitution had
not yet been presented, and was not specifically mentioned in
Seward's motion. This counter proposition opened the flood
gates in the Senate. The Topeka memorial when finally injected added little—it was already a known quantity. On
April 7 Cass presented it, not as a protagonist, but merely to
accommodate. However, its friends thought there would be
an advantage in securing the services of the father of squatter
sovereignty. It was referred to the Committee on Territories
and ordered printed, hardly noticed in the noise of the conflict
over the enabling bill and the substitute. On April 9 Seward,

as champion of the Topeka movement in the Senate, delivered his great speech on the "Immediate Admission of Kansas." It was an exampler for a series of efforts to which Sumner made a fitting climax late in May.

It would have been strange work to pass over the Topeka memorial without some excitement. On April 10 it was taken up, discussed, withdrawn from the committee and the printer released. Only three votes were cast against this—Harlan, Seward, and Sumner. The document, a copy of the original, contained technical flaws which led to the summary disposal. On the 14th, Harlan introduced a memorial of J. H. Lane claiming a senatorship when an act should be passed admitting Kansas; also the rejected memorial along with the original copy. Douglas objected to receiving it, and a debate ensued. It finally resulted in an arousal of bad blood between Lane and Douglas, whereat there was exciting talk of a duel for some time. The memorial was laid on the table and there the Topeka constitution slept its long sleep in the Senate.

Although the contested seat had been placed in abeyance until the Investigation Committee could report, the House turned to the Topeka constitution for material to continue the controversy. On April 7 Mace of Indiana presented "certain papers purporting to be the 'constitution of the State of Kansas' and a memorial of the Senators and representatives of said State" which were referred to the Committee on Territories and ordered printed. On April 10 Wakeman gave notice of his intention to introduce a bill for the admission of Kansas. The acceptance of Kansas with a free constitution brought on a debate of greater volume, and if possible, of greater violence than had been witnessed heretofore. The right of the people to meet and to inaugurate a government, even as they had the Federal constitution, was an added point. This also called up the use of every precedent in state-making —Tennessee, Michigan, Arkansas, Florida, and California. Waldron of Michigan sprang to fame with a "powerful" speech on the precedent of his state.[38] The opinion of President Jackson's attorney-general in the Michigan and Arkansas cases was wielded with political *éclat*. The debate included likewise all points involved in former debates; for the making of a new government denied the existing one and presumed a majority of the people in support. It raised the old question of legality and election fraud, for which a committee was now collecting data.

As an enabling act for Kansas made way with assurity in the Senate under the leadership of Douglas, the necessity for the House to make good a counter proposition became more obvious. Advanced thought on Republican matters declared that Kansas must be admitted under the Topeka constitution or else the administration party be defeated in the coming election. Failing in these, the territory was doomed to slavery.[39] But developments came slowly—appropriations, questions of privilege,[40] and the pending report of the investigation retarded action. Not until May 29 did Grow bring in an admission bill.[41] A majority and minority report of the committee accompanied it. The minority report endorsed Douglas' enabling project. The majority report was the Republican counter maneuver and their declaration of position to date. Discussion was postponed until June 25,[42] which placed it beyond the time of the Convention.

But before the Republicans of the House had taken this position many things had happened. Along with the varied arguments over Kansas, had gone one on appropriations. The President's war scare had occasioned his asking additional supplies. Instead of granting them, the House fell upon a deficiency bill to eliminate any portion that might have a bearing on governing Kansas. Since the administration said it was urgent, the House dallied a while before presenting a deficiency bill.[43] When it came, it was too stinted a measure for the Senate which amended it to include all things necessary for full administration of the territories. The usual debate ensued. On April 3 the House turned down flatly amendment 30 for pay for the first and second dragoons, and 31 for appropriation for temporary encampments, along with many others. The Senate grew desperate and insistent. Recourse to three successive conference committees reduced the measure to agreement. At the time it was nearing a head, the debate was hot over the question of admission, the "Marshals Invasion" was brewing in Kansas, and the House constantly showed its teeth. May 12, just before the final conference committee met, Barbour of Ohio introduced a resolution which was carried. It was an embarrassing request of the President for information as to whether troops had been used to enforce the laws of the Shawnee Mission legislature.[44] May 13 an agreement was reached, the Senate receded from fourteen amendments, the House concurred in seven, and no. 31 was left out. The bill became a law May 16, but it was only for a deficiency. Appropriation for military purposes kept its political usefulness to the last, and became the occasion of an extra session.

The *impasse* created by the solutions proposed by the majorities of either house made it possible for debate to continue indefinitely, to political end, not legislative. Outside events made a minor climax early in May before the situation in Congress had borne its best fruits. May 8 was called "the day of disasters." On that day Major Heiss assaulted Mr. Wallack of the *Washington Star* because of his derogatory articles on the Walker Government in Nicaragua.[45] The same day Padre Vijil, representative of that government, waited the hand of a friend to conduct him to the State Department, and the question of his recognition into current American politics. The same day, Herbert, Democratic Congressman from California, shot and killed Thomas Keating, Irish head-waiter at Willards' Hotel. This was an event of political importance. Herbert came to the dining room after hours for breakfast, Keating refused to serve him, words were exchanged, then dishes, then came the fatal firing. The fact that Herbert was an administration Democrat and that Keating was an Irish menial lent a splendid illustration to the argument that such was the "slave-drivers'" attitude toward all workers.[46] It was immediately acted upon as political capital.[47] The expulsion of such a member gave the House a further topic for debate. The same day as the killing, Giddings, while discussing the deficiency bill was reviewing the Cincinnati slave case,[48] with too much vehemence for a man of his years, and fell in a fit. All of this, added to the influence of the long protracted debates, placed excitement at a higher pitch. Not many days previous, in far-away Kansas, Sheriff Jones had been shot in the back by an unknown marksman.

With the coming of Spring, events in Kansas were again in the public eye. Shannon's "Ruffian" militia had faded away and left Lawrence intact and the promoters of the Topeka constitution unmolested. That movement had come to fruition, and the repudiation of the existing government had a stronger backing than ever. Along the border there had been some violence, considerable tension, and events waited only the passing of winter. The President had taken a stand against the Topeka movement, and the supporters of the territorial government, backed by the President's declaration would likely make the most of the first opportunity to strike the repudiators. The Topeka party was now facing the opportunity of being persecuted by the administration.[49] With the opening of the rivers came the inrush of armed men from both sections. It was evident that Congress was dead-locked and that only the ensuing presidential election could make a decision. To hold the territory until that time, Greeley preached an emigration crusade with a true martyr spirit in it. Free state men were to go and to take a "sharp friend."[50]

In April, Sheriff Jones found trouble awaiting him. S. N. Wood, a Branson rescue fugitive, had returned from a lecture tour and Jones attempted to arrest him. Citizens refused to function as a *posse* and made the arrest impossible. Tappan, another fugitive, put in his appearance and Jones was knocked down in an attempt to arrest him. Soldiers were necessary, and Jones telegraphed his needs to Colonel Sumner. Colonels Cooke and Sumner had been instructed by Secretary of War, Davis, to furnish troops,[51] which authorization had been pronounced a move to "dragoon" the free state men into submission. Soldiers added nothing to Jones' success; for the object of his quest had fled across the prairie. It was during his stay on this mission that he was shot in the back one night while sitting in his tent.

This was an important event, politically. Although it put Jones out of active service for a few weeks, it also came nearly compromising the position of the repudiators. They denounced the act, and offered five hundred dollars reward for the guilty party. The Missouri Border was furious and anxious for revenge. In the North it was accepted in a variety of ways. There was a tendency to regard it as just retaliation. A rumor arose that he had been shot by a woman. There would seem poetic justice in this; for a conception of Kansas had been built up in which widows were wandering insane over the plains in search of their murdered husbands.[52] The most effective reaction was that it had been done by pro-slavery men to make capital, since they were capable of any violence, or else Jones was shamming. When he turned up three weeks later as a leader of a raid on Lawrence, the thesis that slavery ruled by violence and fraud, had gained strength by the episode.

However, there were larger stakes than those placed on the serving of ordinary legal processes. The President's proclamation of February 11 had made a clear foundation whence to proceed against the free state move. Plans to determine the "future institutions of Kansas," if attempted from without were "invasion aggression," if from within, "insurrection," and in either case the general government would by "forcible intervention" maintain "the laws of the Territory as of the Union."[53] This, with the instructions to supply soldiers, put the administration in a very definite position. With this for backing, the District Court under Judge Lecompte met the second week of May. The Judge instructed the Grand Jury that refusal to recognize the laws was "construc ve treason." This was aimed at the promoters of, and officials under, the Topeka constitution. In a few days processes appeared for a number of these *quasi* officers.

The attempted arrest of Reeder upon one of these processes started a new epoch of violence in Kansas. He refused arrest in threatening terms, and claimed immunity on the ground of being a member of Congress, and actively engaged in securing evidence for a committee of Congress. In the interval afforded by his frightening off the process servers, he was advised by his friends to escape. This he succeeded in doing.[54] His flight while employed before the committee was received as a proof that pro-slavery men intended to stop the investigation and destroy its results.[55] Robinson had left the territory before processes were issued, but was stopped at Lexington, Missouri, and sent back. The "Border Ruffians" were pronounced so zealous in the enforcement of law as to be prescient of its working out. Deitzler, George Brown, G. W. Smith, and Gaius Jenkins, were later arrested and taken into custody. These *treason prisoners* proved a political asset to the Republicans. Held in custody by Federal troops, their lives supposedly in jeopardy, traitors because they had deigned to stand for freedom in Kansas; they became a vexing problem for Pierce, being politically dangerous either to hold or to loose. From their guarded rendezvous, they wrote to friends, and letters from *Camp Treason* made a new style of propaganda.

The resistance offered by Reeder and the recent discomfiture of Jones were sufficient to bring out a show of force. United States Marshal Donelson, under whose authority the duty of serving the treason warrants came, on May 11, issued a proclamation calling on the "law-abiding citizens of the Territory" to assemble at Lecompton as soon as possible in numbers "sufficient for the proper execution of the law."[56] Lawrence was the natural objective; for the men to be arrested lived there. Like Shannon's "militia invasion" it was almost certain to degenerate into a raid on the hated city. "Law abiding citizens" would likely prove inclusive enough to enlist Missouri borderers. Besides this, a South Carolina unit and "Buford's cavalry" put in their appearance. The latter gained wide renown. Though it came unarmed as a regular pro-slavery migration,[57] it took part in the struggle in progress, and the fact that it acted as an organized unit from a southern state made about the best political capital to date, and greatly stimulated the process of pouring armed free state men into the territory. In the marshal's posse of law-abiding citizens were many not averse to blood-letting and among the men from the free state were those of like mind.

There was another contingent to this so-called "Marshal's Invasion." Sheriff Jones rallied quickly when there was a chance for action against Lawrence. He had processes for several men there, and he also got an indictment from the Douglas County Grand Jury against the *Herald of Freedom* and the Free-State Hotel, the latter the property of the New England Aid Society, as nuisances. Armed with these, and relying on the marshal's strong arm of the law, he too went down to Lawrence.

The morning of May 21, the deputy marshal entered town and made the arrests desired without resistance or violence. He then turned the command over to Jones upon whose shoulders rests the responsibility for what followed.[58] The arms of the town, not the personal weapons, were turned over to him. The Free-State Hotel was ordered cleared, was bombarded, and then fired. The press of the *Herald of Freedom* was smashed and thrown into the river. Governor Robinson's house was destroyed and some pillaging done, though it is hard to estimate the amount from the glaring accounts of the "sack of Lawrence." The citizens put their case in document-ary form by a memorial to the President.[59]

This was a climax. The day that the ultra-offensive portion of Lawrence lay in ruin, Sumner in the Senate delivered the third and last installment of his "Crime of Kansas" speech. It was a masterly tirade, and still speaks for itself. That afternoon, while seated at his desk after an early adjournment, he was assaulted by Congressmen Brooks from South Carolina, and beaten into insensibility with a heavy gutta percha cane. The northern press was literally black with rage. This assault on Sumner was one of the great incidents of our political history. Along with the "sack of Lawrence" it was a sort of final incentive necessary for action. As the new party took on national dimensions, Sumner had desired to be a moving force in it, and had suggested that it be called the "back-bone" party and have some of the attributes of its name. His friends, remembering "The True Grandeur of Nations," had been urging him to use his talents to do something effective for Kansas.[60] He complied with the request, and succeeded better than anyone had dreamed.

As for Congress, each house could complete the program started by its majority, and could continue to maneuver for advantage, but there was nothing to add in excitement. Almost immediately, while the response was at its height, the parties went before the country in their national conventions. It was late in June before the making of political capital was renewed in earnest at Washington. Kansas territory settled down to a state of civil war—it was "bleeding Kansas."

Early Results

An opportunity to test the results of the program of educat-ing the voters of the North was soon at hand. In March, Pierce's home state would hold an election. In this, it would endorse either the President or Senator Hale. Early in April Rhode Island and Connecticut would hold their election. Both of these states were in the grip of the Know-Nothings, and had been practically strangers to the Republican movement. In Connecticut, the seat of Senator Isaac Toucey, a prominent administration Democrat, was the chief political stake. These elections would make up the first installment of the 1856 campaign, and their outcome was considered very important.

The Democrats made a great effort to carry New Hampshire.[61] They nominated Wells to lead the ticket again, kept as silent as possible on Kansas, and launched a very active campaign at Concord. A Peoples' convention met on the same day in the same city and was addressed by Senator Hale, Amos Tuck, and others. This cooperated with the Americans and their collaboration was the basis of the organization of a Republican party after the election. Though nominally American the opposition was potentially Republican. February 13 the Whigs held a convention and nominated Ichabod Gardner and took steps towards a general resuscitation of the party. They were not "silver gray" and were not unfriendly to the American-Republicans.

The Democrats exerted every effort. February 7 a great rally was held at Concord. Senator Weller of California, Congressmen Cobb of Georgia and Orr of South Carolina, spoke.[62] A clash with the Temperance men injured the prospects of the Democrats. During the whole canvass the administration forces were accused of using money and whiskey as well as oratory. Election day, March 11, settled the contest, in favor of the anti-Nebraska combination. Metcalfe had a plurality of eighty-eight votes over Wells. There was consequently no election by the people and the offices were left in the hands of the legislature. The Americans and Whigs controlled this by a majority of twenty-six on the joint ballot.[63]

In Rhode Island, the Democrats "opened the ball" by a nominating convention February 21. March 11 the Americans followed by one in Providence which chose Governor Hoppin for re-election. A Republican movement had been started and a Republican convention assembled in Providence the following day. After submitting a list of questions to the Americans, they recommended the same ticket except the lieutenant-governor and treasurer. The following day, a Kansas meeting gave a touch of brotherhood to the Providence conventions and success seemed assured. The Old Line Whigs held a meeting, also at Providence, but did not nominate. April 3 Hoppin was re-elected. There was no election by the people in the offices the Republicans had refused to endorse.

These went to the Legislature where the anti-Nebraska forces had elected a large majority. A senatorship was also at their disposal, but action on this was postponed until the following January.

The Americans of the "nutmeg" state met in council at New Haven January 10. They endorsed the bolt at Philadelphia in June, took ground to make themselves the leading anti-slavery party, and made nominations. February 27 the Democrats held their convention at Middletown, made nominations, and endorsed the administration. The Whigs also put a ticket into the field. They were considered anti-Nebraska, but independent. Between the Americans and the Democrats was a large block of votes that was unwilling to act with either party. This was led by Joseph Dixon and was a *de facto* Republican party.[64]

Out of this intervening group a Republican party was founded. Men like Dixon, Gideon Welles, C. F. Cleveland, and Senator Niles led the way. Welles and Niles started a paper to "knock out Toucy, Pratt, and Co."[65] A call was circulated by a group of Hartford citizens for a convention on March 12.[66] The leading elements in the combination were Whigs and Free-Soil Democrats. A great many at the convention wanted to endorse the American nominees but this was blocked by C. F. Cleveland,[67] and Gideon Welles was put at the head of a Republican ticket. In the election, which occurred April 7, there was no choice by the people but the Americans and Republicans carried the Legislature by a majority of thirty-one votes.[68] It was an anti-Nebraska victory. The new Legislature organized May 7. The Republicans held the balance and claimed a senator. All the offices were filled by anti-Nebraska men and on June 4 Dixon was elected to the seat held by Isaac Toucey in the Senate.

The first reckoning had shown the strength of the new issue, and that Greeley might be right in thinking that it could be used to "sweep the North." Three states, one the home of the President, had gone anti-Nebraska. The Republican party had been definitely established in all three. It cooperated only, but it bided its time. The anti-Nebraska members of Congress hailed it as a triumph. In a caucus April 14, they resolved:—

"That the anti-Nebraska members of Congress

tender to their fellow-citizens of the United
States their sincere and hearty congratulations
on the recent success of the friends of order,
justice, and freedom in the elections which have
been held in the states of New Hampshire,
Rhode Island, and Connecticut, and take pleasure in acknowledging these triumphs, not less on
the ground of the encouragement they offer to
our determined effort to secure the immediate
admission of Kansas into the Union than as being auspices of the speedy restoration of the true
principles of the United States." [69]

1. Boutwell,George S., *Why I Am A Republican*, p. 22.
2. *The Conquest of Kansas* by Phillips came out in 1856 near the
   close of the Campaign. Redpath's *Captain John Brown* was published in 1860.
3. Thayer,Eli, *The Kansas Crusade*, p. 27.
4. Malin,J.C., "Pro-Slavery Background of the Kansas Struggle" in
   "*Mississippi Valley Historical Review*, vol. X, pp. 285-305 consid-
   ers assertions in regard to Atchison's policy on dangerous ground
   until more research has been done on the subject. However, he
   ventures to assign him a program which involved gaining political
   control of Kansas in order to give assurance to Southern settlers.
   Slave owners would hesitate to come to a territory where the
   government would be hostile, and the comprehensive and widely
   advertised program of the New England Emigrant Aid Society,
   Malin thinks, was taken at face value, thus making political control necessary to assure southern settlers.
5. Forney,J.W., *Anecdotes of Public Men*, p. 193. Senator Broadhead of Pa. was an enemy of Reeder, and his influence had to be
   overcome in the appointment.
6. President's Message, Jan.24, Richardson's *Messages and Papers*,
   vol. V, pp. 352-360.
7. Connelly, William E. in *Kansas Historical Society Publications*
   has published documents covering the complete story of early
   Kansas. Ensuing statements of facts are largely based on these.
8. Reeder had disallowed some of the returns and ordered a new
   election. The members returned by this second election were
   turned out by the majority which was a product of the March
   election.
9. In 1899 W.E.Connelly published *James Henry Lane, The Grim
   Chieftain of Kansas*, and the following year the *Life of Captain
   John Brown, Last of the Puritans.* Giving credit to the work of
   these men called out in 1902 *False Claims of Kansas Truthfully
   Corrected* by G.W.Brown. His, *The Reminiscence of Old John
   Brown* also stated contrary views. To these Connelly replied by
   publishing in 1903 *An Appeal to the Record*, etc.Connelly as-

serts the value of the work of Brown and Lane who were not at one with the Topeka movement, maintains that the securing of Kansas was due to the inflow of citizens chiefly from the Northwest and not to the Emigrant Aid Society. He claims the writing of Brown to be directed to the purpose of appropriating credit to Robinson, the aid society agent, and his associates, and indicts Robinson's *Kansas Conflict,* and Thayer's *Kansas Crusade* as directed to the same purpose.

10. This policy was to be consistently held by the Democrats and was finally formulated into the Toombs Bill.
11. Executive minutes, *Kansas Historical Soc. Pub.,* vol.I, pp. 99-102.
12. A new model rifle given to northern emigrants. The work of Henry Ward Beecher in securing these weapons won for them the well-known name of "Beecher's Bibles".
13. Executive minutes, pp. 104-105.
14. Malin,J.C., *Pro-Slavery Background of the Kansas Struggle,* p. 299.
15. Whittier reflects the sentiment aroused in his poem *The Burial of Barber.*
16. See Chapter III.
17. *Senate Journal,* December 31, 1st Session, 34th Congress.
18. President's Message, December 31; *Messages and Papers,* vol. V, pp. 327-350.
19. Hale's Speech, Jan. 3, is a good example of an opening tirade on the Administration, *Congressional Globe.*
20. President's Message, Jan. 24. *Messages and Papers,* vol. V, pp. 352-360.
21. Reeder's Reply, *Kas. Hist. Soc. Pub.* vol. 5, pp. 257-258.
22 *New York Tribune,* January 25.
23. *Ibid.,*January 29.
24. President's Proclamation, Feb. 11. *Messages and Papers,* vol.V, pp.390-391.
25. *New York Tribune,* Feb. 15.
26. *Ibid.,*Feb. 15-16.
27. H.R. 9. *House Journal,* Feb. 18.
28. H.R. 74. and H.R. 75. *House Journal,* Feb. 27.
29. H.R. 114 relating to town sites; H.R. 115 creating two new land districts; and H.R. 116 on roads, bridges and geological survey.
30. In the election of Reeder which occurred October 9 the free state men claimed he received the vote of a majority of the settlers.
31. Republican speeches in this debate widely used for documents were: Grow (Pa.), March 5; Trofton (Mass.), March 12; I.Washburn (Me.), March 14; Damerell(Mass.), March 18; Hickman (Pa.), March 19.
32. Platform, article 8. See Chapter III.
33. Collamer's minority report summarized the Republican position.
34. *New York Tribune,* March 14.
35. Trumbull's speech, March 14. Pamphlet.
36. *New York Tribune,* March 22.
37. S. 172. *Senate Journal,* March 17.
38. Speech of Henry Waldron in House, April 8.
39. *New York Tribune,* April 25 and April 29.

40. The action of the Senate in regard to appropriations raised this question.
41. H.R. 411.
42. *House Com. Report,* 181.
43. H.R. 68.
44. *House Journal,* May 12.
45. See above, Chapter V.
46. See Chapter V.
47. *Viz.:* "The Slaughter at Willards", *New York Tribune,* May 14.; "A Democrat may kill an Irishman", *New York Tribune,* May 17.
48. The Garner case. See Chapter V.
49. Robinson maintains the motive of the Topeka constitutionalists was to prove that the territorial government did not function, and that no real government existed. They would have to do this and avoid defying federal authority. At the same time he maintained the "Ruffians" wished to bring them to blows with the Federal forces. He makes a case against Lane and Brown whose methods interfered with their program and brought on Civil War.
50. *New York Tribune,* March 13.
51. Order, *Kansas Historical Society Publications,* vol.V, p.260.
52. Brown's widow was pronounced insane of grief;widows Dow and Barber were connected with similar stories which ran in the press and were depicted in caricature.
53. Presidents Proc. in *Kas.Hist.Soc.Pub.,* vol.V, p. 259.
54. Diary of Reeder's Escape in *Kas.Hist.Soc.Pub.,* vol. III.
55. *New York Tribune,* May 13.
56. Marshal's Proclamation in Robinson's *Kansas Conflict,* p. 243.
57. Fleming,W.L.,"Buford's Expedition to Kansas", *Ala.Hist.Soc.Pub.,* no.7.
58. Malin,J.C., *Pro-Slavery Background* etc., p. 303.
59. Peoples' Memorial, text, Robinson, *Kansas Conflict,* pp. 243-256.
60. Letters in Sumner MSS. H.L.
61. The details of these elections are based on *Springfield Republican, National Intelligencer, New York Tribune,* and *Tribune Almanac* for 1857.
62. *New York Tribune,* February 11, admits that it was large and enthusiastic even in a snow storm.
63. *Tribune Almanac,* 1857.
64. *Springfield Republican,* Jan. 26.
65. C.G.Berg to Welles, Feb. 20. Welles MSS. L.C. The paper started was the *Hartford Evening Press.*
66. James Dixon to Welles, Feb. 9, William Field to Welles, Feb. 25, H.J.Raymond to Welles, March 15, Welles MSS. L.C., give an idea of the source of the movement.
67. *Springfield Republican,* March 12.
68. *Tribune Almanac,* 1857.
69. *National Intelligencer,* April 16,

PART III

THE PARTIES AFIELD

CHAPTER VII

THE OPPONENTS OF THE REPUBLICANS

Before the Republicans had made their nomination both of their major antagonists, the Democrats and the Americans, had taken the field, and some minor political movements of importance had occurred. This made the problem of defining their position easier for the Republicans; but in the unique campaign that followed, the ground taken by the opponents had more importance than simply facilitating a definition of issues. Each opposing party strove to reach as much of the loose material as possible without doing serious damage to the array that regularly belonged to it. Every party fragment or residue they could secure was that much that the Republicans lost in their endeavor to reach a maximum assimilation. Consequently, the opposition must be given a large place in an account of the Campaign of 1856.

The Americans

First in point of time and in some respects first in importance came the Americans. Although they were doomed to disappointment in their plans to form a large party, they did manage to retain a support in the North. Their position as union-savers led them to attack the Republicans as sectional and dis-unionist—their most vulnerable point. The Republicans resented their persistence on a nativist platform, since they considered it only a temporary issue and felt that it kept the real issue on slavery from triumphing in the North. They were not far from correct in their contention that the American party alone stood between them and victory.

The Americans hoped for much in their Philadelphia meetings, the first of which, the National Council, would convene February 19. Although they had narrowly escaped being ground to pieces between the upper and nether mill-stones of the slavery question in the recent fight for the speakership, they had nevertheless come through it with considerable publicity for the ground they intended to take. By the Broom

Resolution they had made it clear that they intended to substitute for the twelfth section in their Philadelphia platform[1] a declaration of the power of the Supreme Court to settle the question of the status of slavery in the territories. The statements of their leaders during the heated debates over organization indicated a more lenient interpretation of their anti-Catholic creed. They had also shown their purpose to give up their secrecy and thereby remove a source of criticism that many felt was hurting them as a political party. The election of speaker and the now certain organization of the Republicans made more room than ever for a compromise platform and candidate. But the slavery question still threatened to divide their own number. The twelfth section men had recently voted with the Democrats for Aiken save the small group from the North who had clung to Fuller. Could these be brought to unison again and any of the Americans of the ilk that supported Banks be returned to the "national" party?

The lack of unison in the American party had made the hunt for a presidential candidate exciting and full of interesting possibilities. The first National Council in the autumn of 1854 surveyed the field for presidential material and the problem of a national leader had been omnipresent thereafter. The Know-Nothings had been quick to respond to the popularity of Houston whom the "Jacksonians" had found. Their support had killed him for the faction that had introduced him, and that death killed him for all. Quite as unique a figure was Commodore Robert Stockton of New Jersey. He had a spectacular career as a background, one to endear him to any nativist, and part of the romance of the conquest of California belonged to him. There was a sustained effort to boom him for president and an attractive biography appeared.[2] Stockton was as good an actor as Houston. At a crucial moment he over-shot the mark and made statements that were too strong for the kind of candidate needed when the nomination was made.[3] Neither the small personal following which stayed loyally by him nor his record and personality as presented by his biographer made a consideration of him necessary in the choice of a presidential candidate. As the leader of a small faction chiefly confined to his own state Stockton was to play a minor role in the campaign.

The field was not limited to such personalities as Houston and Stockton. McLean of Ohio was a possibility from the first, and out of the maze of political development that marked the career of the Know-Nothing party, he finally emerged as a competitor for the Republican nomination.[4] Kenneth Raynor of North Carolina, father of the "union degree," was another possibility. Senator Clayton of Delaware possessed the proper qualifications for a candidate, and the Broom Resolutions which were for all practical purposes a reiteration of the old "Clayton Compromise," made his candidacy logical. A public letter declining to accept a nomination, if tendered, prevented further consideration of Clayton.[5] Though Clayton was unavailable and McLean too northern, there was no dearth of candidates for the "National" American nomination. Kentucky had several, and in light of her position in the party she had a right to demand consideration. In the fatal Philadelphia Council of June, 1855, the Kentucky delegation had stood firm on a compromise platform.[6] Garret Davis had worked hard to make himself a candidate and to secure the endorsement of the State council.[7] Friends of Crittenden were endeavoring to bring him out.[8] They encountered Humphrey Marshall who was trying to carry the state for Fillmore.

It was left to New York to name the candidate. The unique nature of the party there which had rendered it immune to disintegration over the slavery issue, and made it the bulwark of Americanism in the North, explained this prerogative of the Empire state. She had two presidential prospects each backed by a distinct faction of the party.[9] Ex-president Fillmore was the more promising, though his supporters were not so numerous as those of George Law, the other aspirant. Fillmore was backed by the portion whose origin was "silver gray," while the pure-blood Know-Nothings, led by Barker, national ex-president, supported Law. The Barker faction was traditionally friendly to the South, while the candidate of the other faction was also a favorite there.

The movement for Fillmore was as old as that to organize the party. When the opportunity for a compromise party was seized upon and the "Union" degree adopted to give it the breath of life, Fillmore became the logical candidate. Daniel Ullman, his friend, had been his spokesman at the first national council. From that time on his own activity as well as that of his friends shaped his course towards the nomination.[10] With his house in order and after a thorough solicitation of advice from friends, he decided to go to Europe to be out of the way and inaccessible for any further committal that might injure him.[11] He sailed in May. His record was left to plead his case, and it was well calculated to do so. He had signed the Compromises of 1850; he was a Northern man and yet was popular at the South; he could classify as a tried statesman to which the outcry against Pierce gave significance, and he would add dignity to the new party. His relation to a secret organization led to a controversy and some embarrassment, since Fillmore, like so many of the Whigs of New York, had come to political estate as an anti-Mason. His relation to the Americans was properly vouched for and his friendship for Ullman stressed as a guarantee.[12] His anti-Masonic record was accounted for on the basis that the incident which brought the response was sufficient to arouse any young man of spirit.[13] His Clay principles were useful argument for his candidacy and for his election as well.[14] Besides being a compromise man, he was for internal improvements and for protective tariff. His position on the tariff had its place in explaining why the Republicans failed to break up the Nativist party in 1856.

Though New York could name the candidate, the supporters of George Law made it doubtful whether Fillmore would be the man regardless of his qualifications. "Live oak" George, for such was the name used by his friends, had wealth, ambition, was backed by the more numerous faction of the party, and had contrived to bring the powerful *New York Herald* to his support.[15] The South would decide as between him and Fillmore at the convention soon to meet in Philadelphia.

The Know-Nothing delegations that assembled in council at Philadelphia February 19 were far from being harmonious or of a single purpose. The objective of the meeting had called out a wide variety of delegates. From the North came some who were in truth Republicans and wished to bring to naught any efforts to unify and expand the Americans. A large group, especially those from the New England states, still hoped to accomplish something towards making the party the anti-Nebraska champion. The southern delegates were in the main ready to compromise on the platform, though some were not. Such extremes as the ultra-southern and bona fide Republicans were in the motley group called to order by C. D. Freeman, in place of the president who had not yet arrived.[16] Maine, Vermont, and Michigan from the North were not present. Of the South, Georgia, Alabama, Texas, Mississippi, and South Carolina had no delegates. This poor representation from the South gave the North control of the council; but it was reported that the South did not hope to accomplish anything save in the nomination. Freeman sounded the temperament of the council and felt the influence of the poor showing of the South when he attempted a ruling for the acceptance of the work of the June council. Safely past this first jar over the righteousness of article twelve, they proceeded to the acceptance of credentials. Two Pennsylvania delegations were present of which the "Edie-anti-Twelfth-Section" group was seated. The Louisiana delegation present the first day was Catholic. One objective of the Council was to introduce leniency in their anti-Catholic creed, and the northern delegations now in control thought to secure an advantage when they seated this delegation. Delegates from Wisconsin were reported as favoring Protestant foreigners. Well might it be asked, "What has become of the platform?"

The second day brought the president, a Protestant delegation from Louisiana, and trouble. The Southern delegates had been much concerned over the entry of the Pennsylvania delegation and held a caucus with a view to bolting. However, they fell in with the Law men of New York and the Ely-Brewster resolution was carried which based voting on the number of delegates to which a state was entitled and not the number present. This threw the control to the South and led to more trouble. The next day a motion was made to reconsider this action and with it the fight started in earnest. Bennett of New York attacked Lieutenant-Governor Ford of Ohio on a charge of Republicanism. Then a heated discussion on retaining the twelfth article ensued, until it was blocked by tabling the motion and putting before the council the new Evans compromise platform. This carried by a good majority, the "North" alone fighting it.

Their new platform was a document of sixteen articles. As a party they thanked Providence for its gifts—the "Federal Union and the Constitution." As a party they accepted a special mission to protect these gifts. Entrenched as Union-savers they proceeded to relax as Nativists. Americans should still rule America to the extent that only native-born be put in office. States and territories should not admit others than citizens to office or to suffrage. Twenty-one years should be the period of naturalization, and no paupers should be admitted to the country. A great deal of liberality had already been shown the Catholics by admitting their delegation from Louisiana. In the place of article six of the old platform, was put a declaration that no one should be raised to office who recognized allegiance to any "foreign prince, potentate, or power." To free themselves of the stigma of secrecy they empowered the state councils to abolish degrees and substitute a pledge of honor, and called for an open discussion of the principles of their platform. All the objectives necessary for placing the party on a more liberal basis and broadening its support by compromising on article twelve had been accomplished save one—the "North" would not compromise on slavery.

The substitute for article twelve practically endorsed squatter sovereignty and passed the responsibility of settling the issue to the Supreme Court. They stood for:

"The maintenance and enforcement of all laws constitutionally enacted, until said laws should be repealed or should be declared null and void by competent judicial authority."

This solution, now embodied in their platform, left slavery where it was in the territories. The "North" would never accept it. Connecticut stood as a solid block, and Perkins their spokesman, objected to the new platform on the ground that it endorsed squatter sovereignty, that the new twelfth article meant nothing, and that the council had no right to declare a platform for the coming covention. This was ominous. The night after the council adjourned, the "North" went into caucus, and a bolt was assured, should the ensuing convention proceed to nominate. According to report, the Middle "Centrals" and "Nationals," pleased with the new platform talked candidates, and the "South" got drunk.[17]

The following day, February 22, the nominating convention assembled. It was called to order by Parson Brownlow of Tennessee, and Ephraim Marsh of New Jersey was made president. The move to proceed to ballot for candidates was resisted by the "North." Killinger of Pennsylvania offered a resolution:

> "That the National Council has no authority to prescribe a platform of principles for this Convention, and that we will nominate for President and Vice-President no man who is not in favor of interdicting the introduction of slavery in the territory north of 36-30 by congressional action."

This resolution was the ultimatum. It was defeated and a motion to proceed to the nomination put. Perkins unburdened his mind:

> "You can't carry the South," he said, "Not a single state in any event. We could sweep the whole North on our platform, and you do your best to defeat us. You commit a suicide. You pretend that we are to be sold out to the Black Republicans; I know no such. But we will, those of us who are driven away from you—go for our principles—our Americanism, our freedom, and the Republicans of the country will join with us."

The balloting proceeded and the "North" walked out amid shouts of "Black Republican."[18]

New York combined with the South to force the nomination, and on the first formal ballot the Southern delegates designated the choice as between her two proffered candidates. Although the New York votes stood twenty for Law to ten for Fillmore, Fillmore was nominated. Law was second, and a few scattering votes expressed pleasant memories of Raynor, McLean, Davis, and Houston. When Fillmore was nominated, ex-Governor Johnston led out a part of the Pennsylvania delegation, and others followed. The breach was complete. In securing a candidate for the vice-presidency, the Americans turned to the South, and on the first ballot nominated Andrew Jackson Donelson of Tennessee. Donelson was a southerner and the boasted owner of a hundred slaves. He was the heir of President Jackson, the great patriot and union saver, and was well chosen to fit the political niche where his party placed him. Gardner of Massachusetts who had been playing politics for the nomination was given twelve votes, and

Raynor of North Carolina and Percy Walker of Alabama were remembered with a few.

The "North" Americans who had bolted met in caucus and organized. They decided to call a convention on June 12 in New York. This was near the time the Republicans would hold theirs, and the bolters empowered their committee to change the date, if desirable. The Know-Nothings who were anti-Nebraska in principle, who nearly a year before had attached the restoration of the comprises to their creed of Nativism and tried to dominate the North with it, were now driven to the last ditch. The Republicans had organized at Pittsburg, heedless of the outcome at Philadelphia. The party based on the principle of non-extension was now sure to dominate the North. The "North" Americans would be absorbed. The only uncertainty that remained was one as to the thoroughness of the assimilation, and as to the influence on the assimilator.

There were stormy waters ahead for the "National" Americans with their new platform and candidates. All was not well in Fillmore's own state. The supporters of Law were not satisfied, and their conduct boded ill. They made a formal protest against the nomination and some of them associated with the bolters' caucus. There was promise of trouble in New York, and outside that state the schismatic twelfth section council in Pennslyvania was the only other reliance in the North. Many of the state councils there would refuse to accept the nomination and would be forthwith read into the Republican party by the national president. The Americans faced a problem of organization in the form of securing orthodox councils in such states.[19] In some states where the candidates were endorsed, the party could and would cooperate with the Republicans in state politics, if not in national. A number of things would have to be accomplished to make the new venture give any promise of success. The endorsement of its candidate by the National Council and a hearty one from that of his own state must be secured. Fillmore was not in the country, and unless a good showing were made, he might not accept the nomination. Plans were soon under way to get the proper response and to assure the union saver on his return.

The Democrats

The overthrow of the Democratic party which under the leaderhip of Pierce had passed the ill-fated Kansas-Nebraska bill, was the objective of both Americans and Republicans. The ground the Democrats took in facing their opponents and the candidates they ran would determine to a great extent the number of votes that could be taken away from them in the North. The personality of Buchanan, their candidate, and the position he was able to maintain on the slavery issue as presented concurrently in the Kansas "War" was perhaps the most important single factor in determining the final outcome. The shrewd mastery of politics that gave Buchanan the nomination, and the front that he presented to the Republicans, are essential to an understanding of his victory over the anti-slavery candidate.

A number of things made the time opportune for James Buchanan. He had been away at the Court of Saint James and had received none of the stigma of the Kansas embroglio. He was old in service and since the Nebraska upheaval under Pierce, an "untried man," had nearly wrecked the party, it was good tactics to talk of putting statesmen in the presidential chair. This began to be heard in many places. Buchanan's work at the Ostend Conference made him strong at the South.[20] It was evident, too, that a Southern man could scarcely hope to be candidate. Henry A. Wise of Virginia arrived at this conclusion, decided that Buchanan was the man and wrote to him to return and aid in uniting Pennsylvania and Virginia to save the Union.[21] Then came the victory and the restoration of the Democratic party in October, 1855, which placed Pennsylvania in a prominence equal to that held by Virginia. It was also the "keystone" state politically— the one to be held from the opposition that promised to sweep the North. That it was Pennsylvania's "day" was generally admitted. She need only to name a "favorite son."

The first step would have to be an unanimous Pennsylvania, and that was not easily obtained. A lack of unity in the Keystone delegation at Baltimore in 1852 was credited with losing the nomination for Buchanan there. A recurrence had to be prevented and a great deal of animosity that still lived would have to be overcome. Since the failure to get the

nomination Buchanan had posed as an aspirant no longer.
He had given out further that he was surrendering his diplomatic post at London to return home to spend the remainder
of his life resting at "Wheatland." To all who approached
him he was not a candidate. It was good tactics save in instances where his apparent unwillingness was used against
him—the nomination must seek the man. His friends did not
comply with his wishes. How they secured a solid delegation
from his home state is a story of Pennsylvania politics. The
Democratic convention at Harrisburg, March 4, gave him
Pennsylvania and a great deal more.

While friends were securing Pennsylvania, others were making use of the advantageous position he held, both for the
nomination and for the ensuing election. Seibels was the
chief of those who laid the foundation for his assurances of
support in the South. In touch with influential press connections in Georgia he informed Buchanan that the demands of
the South were not large. They merely demanded "that the
convention deny to Congress all constitutional power to
legislate upon the subject of slavery in the States, Territories,
etc." If Buchanan gave that, the South would go for him.
As for Pierce, *"his abandonment of the Ostend Conference
killed him at the South."*[22] Buchanan had stood for an extension of the Compromise line in 1850 and feared he should be
forced to "eat his own words," if he stated now that Congress
did not have power to create such a line.[23] Finally, Buchanan
authorized him to state that without knowing whether
Buchanan would run or not "We do not speak unadvisedly in
declaring that he will give every aid in his power in whatever
position he may be placed to the maintenance and carrying
out of the present existing laws relative to slavery, the Kansas
and Nebraska Acts included."[24] Wise and Hunter buried the
hatchet in Virginia and practically assured it for Buchanan.[25]
Daniel E. Sickles, his dashing secretary of legation, had returned somewhat earlier and was doing work for his ex-chief
among the Hards in New York. J. Glancy Jones, administration leader of the House, was his manager in Pennsylvania.
The movement in his favor was wide-spread when the Keystone state took the first required step and presented her
"favorite son" to the country.

There was great unanimity among the delegates that as-

sembled at Harrisburg March 4.[26] They gave enthusiastic
consent to an important set of resolutions.[27] Declaration of
orthodoxy and denunciation of Know-Nothingism were easy,
but the Nebraska question had to be approached with care.
Buchanan had once advocated the extension of the Missouri
Compromise line to the Pacific. The Pennsylvania Democracy
approved the Nebraska bill as a timely solution, and so
worded their statement as to fit into the position Glancy
Jones had been holding in Congress. Such a line, he had
maintained, was beyond the pale of the constitution and could
be drawn only by common consent to avoid a crisis. This
position was now to be orthodox.[28] The resolutions called for
a settling of everything by ballot. This was sound squatter
sovereignty; but the troublesome question as to when the settlers were to vote was not stated. Jones' position placed the vote
at the time of adopting a constitution as orthodox. It was to
stay there and Buchanan was to answer no questions on the
subject.[29] With a way thus made for his record, they recommended James Buchanan, a tried statesman, to the people for
president during the period of foreign and domestic stress.

There were chances for developments in the three months
that intervened between the Harrisburg Convention and the
National nominating convention. Pierce was in the field and
active. He was making use of the office-holders in the North
to secure delegates, and his conduct in Kansas affairs was
securing him a hold in the lower South despite his record on
the Ostend Conference and failure to recognize Nicaragua.
Buchanan's friends had to guard their own ranks carefully to
keep some of their members from attacking Pierce and creating such a chasm as to make it impossible for the administration ever to support Buchanan and thus make his nomination
impossible.[30] In Pennsylvania a *modus vivendi* was reached in
which Pennsylvania was to be for Buchanan first. The difficulty was avoided and by the time the national convention
was at hand Pierce had practically ceased to be a contestant.
He would get some votes at first as a recognition and then be
dropped.[31] Douglas came to the front as the only real contestant. He had worked in the Senate as champion of the
Nebraska Bill, and developed considerable rivalry with Pierce
whose program had been to "go south" on Kansas. He was
not in the ring at first; but when it became possible that

Pierce and Buchanan might "kill each other off" he began to wedge in between the two and to work for delegates as only Douglas knew how. The author of the Nebraska Bill could not expect much from the North just now and Buchanan still held the supremacy. The field was his. The only danger feared was that bitterness might be stirred up on which one-third of the delegates could be combined to defeat him.[32]

On Monday, June 2, the convention assembled at Cincinnati.[33] Thousands of citizens gathered, and Congress failed to have a quorum. The Pennsylvania delegation was both seen and heard. Along with it went the Keystone Club of Philadelphia, Beck's Band, and many citizens. To add interest, two delegations appeared from Missouri and likewise two from New York. The committee on arrangements blocked the Benton, Missouri, delegation by refusing to grant them tickets of admission, and ordered the New Yorkers to reduce their numbers. The matter was not so easily settled. The Missouri delegates, after a pitched fight at the door, rushed in, shouting, "Make way for the Border Ruffians." They later retired at the request of the convention.[34] The proper committees were put to work, and the work of the first day was finished. The next day General J. E. Ward of Georgia was made president. The committee on credentials remained in session, wrangling on the New York case, while the convention proper discussed the feasibility of clearing the galleries.

The committee on resolutions reported on the morning of the third day. There were three distinct parts to the platform. The first endorsed the traditional and orthodox. The second denounced the Republicans and Know-Nothings. And the third pronounced a foreign policy. Virginia delegates blocked a unanimous acceptance. They were not ready to act on the strong foreign policy outlined.[35] The two parts were adopted, Virginia was given time for a conference after which the resolutions on foreign policy were taken up singly and passed. A resolution in favor of a Pacific railroad was tabled. The day closed with Virginia trying to modify the foreign policy, and New York still outside.

The following morning the committee on credentials reported. The majority report was for a proportionate division on the basis of the number of votes cast in previous elections, which gave preponderence to the Softs. The minority was for an equal division between the two factions. The minority report was adopted. It was a Buchanan victory. With New York present, the convention was ready to ballot. Inge of California moved for a suspension of the rules for another test on the Pacific railroad resolution. His motion failed, and the convention proceeded to ballot. As was expected, Pierce received strong support at first. It weakened, and on the sixteenth ballot, Hibbard of New Hampshire withdrew his name. After a few more ballots a letter from Douglas was read withdrawing his name, and Buchanan was nominated with unanimity. In swinging his delegation for him, Inge of California said that the Pennsylvania delegation had repeatedly blocked his Pacific railroad resolution, but he joined with them for victory because he was satisfied that Mr. Buchanan did not approve its position. In the afternoon a resolution was carried in the convention recognizing the importance of a railroad and declaring that the federal government should do all in its power constitutionally to build one. The last day also brought the nomination of Breckinridge of Kentucky for vice-president. He was regarded a strong man and would aid in carrying the Know-Nothing stronghold whence he came.

The Democratic platform was as well chosen as its candidate. The fundamentals of the Democratic creed were re-endorsed. As for the Americans, "No party can justly be deemed national, constitutional, or in accordance with American principles, which bases its exclusive organization upon religious principles and accidental place of birth." Then they stated their position on "Domestic Slavery," and declared against agitation. "To meet distinctly a sectional party, subsisting on slavery agitation," they called for "the fellowship and cooperation" of those who wished to save the Union. This could be done by accepting the principles of the Kansas-Nebraska Bill as a solution, and insisting on *"Non-interference by Congress with slavery in States and Territory and in the District of Columbia."* They endorsed the right of Kansas and Nebraska to form a constitution when their population justified it and a majority of their lawful residents wished it. This was a good endorsement of the position taken in the Toombs Bill in the Senate.

From domestic affairs they turned to foreign. There were "questions of foreign policy inferior to no domestic questions whatever." The United States should set a telling example for "free seas and progressive free trade throughout the world." The Monroe Doctrine must be rigidly applied. In the great highway nature has put between the Atlantic and Pacific oceans "we can under no circumstances surrender our preponderance in the adjustment of all questions arising out of it." The people of the United States sympathize "with the efforts being made by the people of Central America to regenerate that portion of the continent which owns the passage across the Inter-oceanic Isthmus." The next administration would be expected to use efforts to gain "ascendancy in the Gulf of Mexico" and thereby maintain protection for the products of the American rivers that empty therein. Here was the endorsement of resisting the British and recognizing Walker in Central America; here was also an endorsement of the Ostend Conference in regard to Cuba. It was an aggressive policy in matters that were of great interest and part of the program to divert the attention of the American people from domestic affairs.

There was strength in both candidate and platform. Buchanan was a "statesman"—a "tried man"—the man the country needed for such a time. The nomination had sought him. It was the voice of the people. He could carry Pennsylvania and save the Union. With the nomination went the understanding that it was made on a single term basis. Douglas who had nailed his political reputation to squatter sovereignty would be enabled by the flat endorsement in the Cincinnati platform to support Buchanan with all his splendid energy. Though there were many adjustments to be made, the outlook was good. Throughout the North where the Democracy faced a real danger, the idea that squatter sovereignty as applied by the Toombs Bill and endorsed by the platform meant a free Kansas, began to grow up. That the South would accept the principle was assumed, and with the steady hand of a tried statesman at the helm for four years, the crisis would be passed, a solution effected, and the country given peace for half a century.

Minor Parties

Americans, Democrats, and Republicans did not absorb all the political loose ends in the country. A residue of Whiggery

—"Old Line Whigs" and the "Radical Political Abolitionists" took an active part in the campaign. The number of votes they controlled was not significant; but their relation to the major parties made them important.

Republicanism fell far short of abolitionism, even when it held fully to its own doctrine of non-extension. Abolitionism proper held its breath until the new anti-slavery party should be defined. When Blair came to the party and made his presidential address to the Pittsburgh Convention, Garrison attacked his action as an "abolition killer." Under the influence of Blair, the new party was "sliding down to a Southern level."[36] Early in April a call appeared which pronounced the dissatisfaction of the abolitionists with the Republican movement. They asked for a convention at Syracuse in May to unite on the principle of abolishing slavery in states by the action of general and local governments. The list of signers was headed by Gerrit Smith and Lewis Tappan. Thirty-three of the signers were from Massachusetts.[37]

The result of their convention was the nomination of Gerrit Smith for president, Samuel McFarland for vice-president, and the promulgation of a platform on true abolitionist grounds.[38] This maintained for them a distinct place and cleared the Republicans of the stigma of actually being abolitionists. It would have been wisdom on the part of the Republicans had they instigated this movement; but the Abolitionists needed no such incentive. They also served the Republicans indirectly in other ways. Garrison was a professed Union breaker, and he avowed the Republicans the only party that did not threaten to break the Union, if they failed to win.[39] Furthermore, the abolitionists refused to be identified with the Republicans.[40] As a final confirmation Greeley sent Garrison a collection of press statements about his supporting Frémont, and inquired as to their truth. Garrison pronounced them every one a lie—products of such lying journals as the *Pennsylvanian* and the *Boston Post*.[41]

The aligning of parties found the Whigs practically in dissolution. Those with whom the slavery question was primary had already gone to the Republicans in the North and the Democrats in the South. The middle position held by the Americans appealed to a large number of them. The few that clung to the old tradition remained so under constant pressure.

When the political strength of the country began to fall in at the extremes on a sectional issue, they were galvanized into life by their own conservatism. Though few, it was felt that organized expression on the point of the safety of the Union might be a determining influence.

The "Old Line Whigs" began to come to life. There was a small element throughout the entire country but only in places did they rise to the dignity of being worthy of notice. In the border slave states, where the Whig traditions were strong, and where reluctance to align on the slavery issue had given Americanism a peculiar hold, there was material for a resurrection. There were pockets of active "Old Liners" in some of the Northern states. Their significant group, so far as Republican precedent-making was concerned, was that centered in Massachusetts. Here a brilliant residue of "Webster Whigs" still remained. Choate, author of the statement that he belonged to no party that did not "carry the flag and keep step to the music of the Union," was a conspicuous member. Edward Everett and Robert C. Winthrop had large renown.

Late in January a correspondent of the *Baltimore American* signing himself "Old Line Whig," asked the Maryland Whigs to hold a convention in order to deliberate on how best to repudiate sectionalism, and to preserve the Union.[42] Members of the legislature took up the idea and called a convention for March 31; but soon postponed it until April 29.[43] About the same time this move was made in Maryland the *Louisville Courier* proposed an "Old Line" convention at Louisville to celebrate Clay's birthday.[44] Other local movements sanctioned the general purpose and the Louisville convention gave it utterance:—

"*To the Whigs of Kentucky and the Union.* The Old Line Whigs, as such, cannot conscientiously unite with any other existing party. They cannot join the Democratic party because they do not approve its administrative policy. They cannot join the American party because they believe its principles and spirit involve a menace against the security of civil and religious liberty, and because furthermore, that party has systematically introduced the alarming practices of subverting the judiciary to party and political influence and control. They cannot

join the Republican party of the North because it is a
fanatical and sectional party whose policy, if carried out,
will shatter the Union in fragments, and drench the land
in fraternal blood."[45]

To act on this they adopted a platform of principles and
called a national convention at Louisville for July 4.

The Maryland convention endorsed the address of the
Louisville convention, but made no response to the idea of a
national meeting.[46] On May 1, the Whigs of the Massachusetts
legislature met with others and decided that the party should
not disband.[47] Some Congressmen and Whigs of the District
of Columbia held a meeting in Washington in June, and asked
friends to attend the proposed Kentucky convention.[48] There
was a general consensus that a renewal of the party was
desirable.[49]

Other activities had accompanied the proposed renaissance
of the Whigs. The Sumner assault was used to club the
Massachusetts group into submission to sectionalism. Everett
who had been thrilling the country with his address on the
"Life and Character of Washington" refused to attend indignation meetings and suffered the cancellation of speaking
engagements as a rebuke.[50] Winthrop also refused to appear
at indignation meetings and made public his reason.[51] The
Republican press in general and Greeley in particular made
war on the "magi." Winthrop, who was alarmed at the
state of affairs, wrote to Crittenden asking him to say something in the Senate to allay the furor over the Sumner assault, and also suggested sending General Scott to settle the
Kansas "war."[52] Crittenden had already thought of sending
him, and his motion to that effect took well for a while; then
died.[53] At the same time W. C. Rives who was conducting a
Whig revival in Albamarle county, Virginia, began to exchange views with the idea of seeking the basis for a solution
of the Kansas situation.[54] Clayton of Delaware joined in this
attempt of "Old Line Whigs" to pacify the country.

With pacifist activities in progress and a convention pending, the Old Liners were met by the storm that applauded
Fillmore's return to America and his acceptance of the nomination. Many of them had leanings in his direction, and the
National Intelligencer approved him.[55] What can Fillmore
do?" was the question, and that remained to be seen.

1. Broom resolution, December 17. See Chapter III.
2. *A Sketch of the Life of Commodore Robert F. Stockton with an Appendix*, etc., New York, Derby and Jackson, 1856.
3. Letter to the Americans of Trenton, Nov. 14, 1855, *Life of Stockton*, pp. 207-210.
4. See Chapter VIII for the McLean candidacy.
5. Clayton's letter, Dec. 27; *Philadelphia North American*, Dec. 28.
6. A.T.Brunley to Crittenden, June 12, 1855. Crittenden MSS. L.C
7. Garrett Davis to Brunley, Jan. 27, Brunley to Crittenden, Jan. 28. Crittenden MSS. L.C. *National Intelligencer*, Feb. 5.
8. Letters of Robertson and Brunley, Crittenden MSS.
9. Scisco, *Political Nativism in New York*, p. 169.
10. Some of the documents relative to this are found in the Fillmore papers edited by Frank Severance in *Buffalo Hist.Soc. Pub.* vol.XI, viz: Fillmore to Isaac Newton, pp. 347-349; Fillmore to Erastus Brooks, Feb. 10, 1855, pp. 330-352; Fillmore to Hugh Maxwell, Nov. 10, 1855, pp. 351-354.
11. Fillmore to Corcoran, March 10, 1855, March 17, April 8, April 17 and 23, May 3. Corcoran MSS. L.C. F. to H. Maxwell, March 10, Severance, pp. 351-354. Cited above.
12. Chamberlin, Ivory, *Life of Fillmore*, Buffalo, 1856.
13. *Ibid.*, pp. 198-199.
14. Barre, W.L., *Life of Fillmore*.
15. The *Herald* refused to endorse Buchanan. June 5,6,7, and June 17, it endorsed Frémont. See Chapter XII for its relation to the Democrats.
16. Statements of fact are based on reports in the *New York Tribune, National Intelligencer*, Scisco, *Political Nativism in New York*, pp. 173-175.
17. *New York Tribune*, February 22.
18. Only the Connecticut delegation left in mass at this juncture.
19. *The Springfield Republican* gave special attention to securing anti-Fillmore declarations from northern councils.
20. I.I.Seibels to Buchanan, July 2, 1855. Seibels of Alabama was consul at Brussels. He took up the task of putting Buchanan right in the South.
21. Wise to Buchanan, August 10. Buchanan MSS. P.H.S.
22. Seibels,I.I. to Buchanan, October 11. Buchanan MSS. P.H.S. Italics belong to Seibels.
23. Buchanan to Seibels, Oct. 18. Buchanan MSS. P.H.S.
24. Buchanan to Seibels, Dec. 29, reply to Seibels, Dec. 23. Buchanan MSS. P.H.S.
25. J.Randall to Buchanan, Feb. 25, on authority of a letter from Wise to Robert Tyler, Buchanan MSS. P.H.S.
26. Reported in the *Pennsylvanian*, March 5. This was a leading paper in conducting the move for Buchanan, and was accounted his official organ.
27. Reported in *Pennsylvanian*, March 6.
28. Jones to Buchanan, March 22. Buchanan MSS. P.H.S.
29. Jones to Buchanan, cited above.
30. Jones to Buchanan, April 28. *The Washington Sentinal* was the chief offender against the administration.

31. George Sanders to Buchanan, May 4; H.Carrier to Buchanan, May 27; N.Clifford to Buchanan, May 27;J.C.VanDyke to Buchanan,May 30. Buch.MSS.P.H.S.
32. J.C.VanDyke to Buchanan,May 30. Buchanan MSS. P.H.S.
33. Statements of fact based on the *Official Report* and reports in *New York Tribune* and in the *Pennsylvanian.*
34. Benton was at Cincinnati en route to Missouri. On his return to St. Louis he delivered a speech that was a tirade on the convention. The nomination of Buchanan was regarded a victory for Benton.
35. One Resolution on Central America which was thought to antagonize Great Britain caused this hesitation.
36. *Liberator,* March 28, April 4.
37. *Springfield Republican,* April 12.
38. *National Intelligencer,* May 29, 30.
39. *Liberator,* August 1.
40. *Liberator,* August 29.
41. *Liberator,* October 31.
42. *National Intelligencer,* Jan. 28.
43. *Ibid.,*March 8 and March 22. As an old Whig paper, the *National Intelligencer* fostered these Whig movements.
44. *Ibid.,*Jan. 29
45. *Ibid.,*April 21.
46. *Ibid.* May 1. Kentucky politics in the proposed Louisville Convention prevented a Maryland endorsement.
47. Reported, *Springfield Republican,* May 3; *National Intelligencer,* May 5.
48. *National Intelligencer,* June 13.
49. The issue of the *National Intelligencer* for June 24 had statement from seven Whig papers and a letter of Edward Bates of Missouri favoring re-organization.
50. The Connecticut Legislature withdrew an invitation it had extended him to speak at New Haven.
51. Letter to Samuel Gridley Howe, June 2. Pamphlet, also *National Intelligencer,* June 13.
52. Winthrop to Crittenden, June 3. Crittenden MSS. L.C.
53. Crittenden to Winthrop, July 6. Winthrop MSS. M.H.S. *Senate Journal,* 1st Session, 34th Congress, June 10.
54. Rives to Winthrop, June 16. Winthrop MSS. M.H.S. Rives to Winthrop, June 10. Public Letter, *National Intelligencer,* June 19.
55. *National Intelligencer,* June 26.

CHAPTER VIII

REPUBLICAN PRESIDENTIAL MATERIAL

The Pittsburgh convention had been dominated by anti-slavery sentiment, and a Republican platform had been the result. It had adopted slavery opposition as a leading issue, but it gave evidence of influences that made the selection of a leader uncertain. It would seem only logical that some anti-slavery champion be now put at the head, but the presence of Blair and the advice of Greeley that they be cautious indicated other possibilities. The Blair influence which had just come to the Republicans was more conservative, and would add to their prestige and scope. Before the convention adjourned, the Americans in a contemporary assemblage had gone to pieces again, and the North Americans had been placed in a position to be included. The selecting of a candidate would have to be done with all these factors in view. The personality of the candidate might determine how nearly all of them could be included.

Elimination of Leaders

Salmon P. Chase merited first consideration in the search for a leader. He had a well established anti-slavery record, and with it, the proper background to lead a new party on slavery. He was the frst leader of national calibre to come out for a new organization, and he had fathered the building of the national machine. At critical periods in the contest with Know-Nothings he had tipped the balance in favor of the Republicans. In the Ohio elections of 1855 he gave them their only substantial victory, and he had intervened to save the Pittsburgh convention to Republicanism. His services merited the nomination, but his political personality made him impossible when power to secure votes became the great objective. Chase was never popular in spite of his victory in Ohio. He had many political enemies, but paradoxical as it may seem, his record as a free-soiler, and not the enemies he

154

had made, stood between him and the coveted nomination.

At the same time that Chase was working for a national party he was busy putting himself in position to become its leader. Carrying Ohio in the election of October, 1855, was his greatest bid for leadership, and it gave him a place wherein to continue to make himself felt. His inaugural address and his special Kansas message were both designed to this end. The Garner case gave him a chance for further distinction though it added little, if any to his reputation as an anti-Nebraska champion. Along with these constructive measures in the direction of the presidency he was forced to do some retrenching. His hold on the German vote, which he felt to be one of his strong points, had been alienated to a considerable extent by his close association with the Americans in the Ohio elections, in spite of the fact that he had kept the slavery issue first. Much depended on it, too, for the Germans of the West followed those of Cincinnati and New York.[1] His greatest rivals for national leadership stood much higher in their favor than he, for they were clear of any taint of Know-Nothingism. Seward was its enemy, and Sumner had denounced it in his Faneuil Hall speech in December. The German press took notice of this, and some of their leaders threatened to take the field against Chase were he nominated.[2] It was urgent that he reinstate himself. Latta, whom he chose for an appointment, turned it down,[3] and Remelin was undecided. Others were not so averse, and his friend, Stephan Moliter, continued to work among his countrymen, and to recommend appointments. Opportunities to denounce Americanism were open in both his inaugural and his message to the legislature, but he let them pass. He still chose to stand on the ground that he had taken in the Ohio campaign—that the Liberal Americans were clever fellows and did not mean to prescribe anybody. He did not wish to alienate either German or Nativist from his support, for the ability to combine them was germane to the national candidacy.

The conventions of February 22 brought developments for Chase. Spooner had gone to the Know-Nothing meeting at Philadelphia convinced that the South would dominate. He was also opposed to an independent nomination, and resolved to smash the convention.[4] It was also planned to have an editorial ready for a prominent Republican paper when

Spooner made the breach.[5] However, any open movement in Chase's favor, coming from an American convention, would be dangerous, and nothing definite was done. The nature of the work carried out by the Republican convention at Pittsburgh concerned his future more directly. His scouts reported that there was very little electioneering done there, but that things looked favorable.[6] The West seemed a unit and New England had a majority for him. Dorsheimer of Buffalo was for him, and Vaughn of the *Chicago Tribune* was still loyal. The Germans in Illinois were for him. Greeley, however, was fearful and recommended Preston King. Some thought that were it a nominating convention, Chase might have been named by acclamation.[7] The tone of the convention was anti-slavery and its platform was Republican. Chase could easily stand on the ground taken by it and at the same time retain a liberal attitude towards the Americans. June 17 had been named as the date for a nominating convention and Kimball outlined a plan of procedure for Chase.[8] In about a month a movement for his nomination was to be put under way. One or two New England papers were to lead off, then the *Cleveland Leader*, the *Chicago Tribune*, the *Milwaukee True Democrat*, and if possible, the *New York Evening Post*. In the meantime Chase would continue the work of impressing his own leadership on the country.

Progress towards the nomination was beset by difficulties even in Ohio. The problem of reassuring the Germans had still to be solved, for the convention had not aided in that. Remelin had failed to get a resolution against the Know-Nothings and had come home in a huff. His failure at Pittsburgh, the failure of a similar resolution in the Iowa Republican convention, the discussion of suffrage in Congress and a liquor law bill in the Ohio senate with which the Republicans were identified, held out enough German votes to assure the municipal elections in Cincinnati to the Democrats.[9] Chase had made this a test of his power to combine votes and it had failed. But Moliter remained active in his cause, and in April Remelin yielded and accepted a commission.[10] The Cincinnati election was not the only reverse in store. When Chase endeavored to secure the first requisite for a nomination,—an Ohio delegation wholly for himself —he also met difficulty. The "Old Whigs" did not forget their dislike for him. Soon after Congress assembled Galloway started a damaging report to the effect that Chase had agreed not to be a presidential candidate. He said that this concession had been made to the "Old Time Whigs" to secure their support for him as governor.[12] The same group of Whigs were conducting a move for Judge McLean, and Chase scouts had found Judge Spaulding at Pittsburgh working for him. Chase also encountered a Frémont boom. Early in April the *Cleveland Herald,* an old Whig paper, came out for Frémont, and the *New York Tribune,* in reporting it, pronounced him popular in Ohio and sure of carrying it if nominated.[13] These movements, both being generated from Washington, were making a solid delegation from Ohio uncertain. Chase had the cold comfort of hearing that the state was considered safe in November and that some preferred him for president.[14]

The plan to start the movement throughout the country was beset by the same difficulty as that to secure a solid Ohio delegation. At Washington politicians were trying for a candidate who could include a larger range of the available material than could a man of Chase's more radical free-soil antecedents. The platform would stand as a bulwark for the free-soil principle, consequently they planned to pass by the real leaders, Chase and Seward, with tremendous praise for their service, and move on to a man whose antecedents would include the conservatives.[15] Dr. Bailey committed the *Era* against the effort that was being made to pass by the true free-soilers, in an article which he said would show that he was apprehensive that "the Republican movement will slip from the control of men of principle into the hands of place hunters and politicians. Such men as Henry Wilson, Horace Greeley, Banks, Colfax, etc. I consider really demoralized by a passion for immediate success. Conceding and conceding, diluting and diluting, they are seeking to trim and weaken our movement so as to include conservatism. I have worked and talked and remonstrated, but our friends are infatuated."[16] Such news from Washington was alarming. Furthermore, the attempts to take the initiative produced few results. Only the Pittsburgh *Gazette* seems to have responded favorably.[17] This article Chase proposed to send to Hamlin, asked that he get other papers to print it, and that

he write an article on sentiment in Ohio.[18] He got in touch
with all possible points where it was planned to generate a
move in his favor, he wrote to every person whose support
he might invoke, and to some whose support, if given, could
be of but little value. Grimes he already knew would support Seward, a former Whig associate.[19] The tardy replies
to his letters soon gave evidence that his cause was lost. Before these responses were in, friends scoured the country in
his favor. F.D.Kimball and J.D.Baker covered the East.
Kimball found that Seward was not a candidate, and inci-
dentally that he favored Chase. The Frémont movement
he thought would die. Dorsheimer was still favorable.
Baker opened communications with Hammond at Albany
and interviewed others at New York, and he and Kimball
projected their trip to Philadelphia.[20] A.P.Stone went to
Chicago and the Northwest to see what he could do.[21]

At the same time supporters of Chase had been bombard-
ing the *New York Tribune* with letters in his favor, but the
Tribune had already put itself in line with the availability
hunt at Washington.[22] In response to the letters it moved a
little more definitely into its position of remaining uncommitted while looking for the best man to carry the doubtful
states.[23] The candidate must be safe on the question of freedom for Kansas. With assurances on this point, the probable
number of votes he could poll became the vital consideration,
for "to talk of nominating a man only because we should
prefer him for president without considering what vote he
could probably obtain or how he is to be elected is sheer
lunacy." For the sake of the cause they could not disregard
availability and the *Tribune* made itself a leader in the
search for it. To this end it promised to publish letters for
all possible candidates in order that the strongest might be
ascertained. Accordingly, it included one for Chase, elim-
inating such passages as reflected on other men.[24] The import of the letter was to counteract the impression being
given currency that he could not carry Ohio, and to stress
him as the most capable and acceptable candidate. It was
evident, however, that "availability" did not mean Chase.
The Presidential situation in New England was reviewed
without mentioning his name.[25] The current was sweeping
past the great free-soil champion.

But Chase did not die easily. He sought delegations and awaited developments. He met the McLean forces with argument. It was better tactics, he contended, to hold the center than risk it for the doubtful ends. Ohio was the center. He could make sure of it, while Pennsylvania where Judge McLean was supposed to be strong, would be uncertain with anyone.[26] The Ohio resolutions in favor of a Pacific railroad were opportunely presented.[27] They would emphasize the record in support of this enterprise that Chase had already established and draw upon the source of strength now pretty well monopolized by Frémont. In securing delegations, Chase likewise continued his efforts. In his own state he pleaded his service in the cause and promised appointments, but could get only local and partial assurances. Bingham told him that sixteen of the Michigan delegates were for him, the rest for Seward. Personally he would make Chase president, if he could. He was going to Washington for interviews before the convention.[28] In Wisconsin all the delegates but two were approached and twelve of the fifteen were for Chase. The Republican convention had instructed for him, but a clerical error put Seward's name first in the report.[29] There were a number of Chase men in the Illinois delegation, but availability ruled there.[30] Friends who had tried to call attention to him in the East, felt that their case did not "look good" when committed to paper, and that the only hope was "sober second thought".[31] From the West had already come the assurance that Frémont would be nominated.[32] His friend who gave him this assurance said that Chase was the best man "but", he continued, "the very qualifications which entitle you to superior regard are those which are thought to diminish your availability. Posterity will do justice to the leaders of the anti-slavery enterprise, but the men of this generation do not recognize the prophets sent unto them".

The elimination of Chase explains also that of Seward. However, Chase stood nearer the goal on the basis of availability than he. Seward had been an uncompromising enemy of Americanism from the first. He had refused to give it quarter as Chase had done, for which, Dr. Bailey, speaking the mind of the true free-soiler, had constantly insisted on Seward's superior strength in their cause. The North Americans who had revolted at Philadelphia in February were to

be reached in a program of building an extensive party, and
with them Seward was impossible. Furthermore, it might
be possible that the Americans of New York, stimulated by
having a presidential candidate, would turn his own state
against him. Yet, Seward was a logical leader. He had
a long anti-slavery record, and his leadership in the Senate
for the admission of Kansas with a free constitution gave
him as great an opportunity to maneuver as Chase had as
governor of Ohio. Like Chase, he did not need to enhance
a record which was already too strong. He was doubly impossible. In fact, he never was a candidate.

Seward was withheld by his friends. From the time Weed
was approached on the Frémont candidacy in December[3]
until the nomination, he was consistent in the position that
he was not for Seward until the right time, and that time
was not yet.[34] He fell in with availability. "In May", he
wrote, "the way opened too bright and clear to mislead any
political Pathfinder." Then he "became convinced that Fré
mont was the best man to put in nomination."[35] Though th
public did not know it until four years later, Greeley was no
Seward's friend.[36] He praised him highly while seeking th
best candidate and passed him by. Seward wanted the nom
ination, and apparently did not give up hope until the end
His letters to his wife indicate his disappointment.[37] Ther
was a harsh irony in the situation, for it was given out as ac
cording to his own wishes. "The nomination", he wrote jus
three days before the convention, "of either the Californi
candidate or the Ohio judge, is regarded as a foregone con
clusion, and as a conclusion arrived at with my own approv
and consent."[38]

Little need be said of Sumner, the other member of th
trio of great anti-slavery leaders. He had made a record i
the Senate and in the making of a new party had lent a han
—he desired a "Back-bone Party". In the spring of 185
he was in New York "Making speeches on slavery, makin
good speeches and some money."[39] In the summer he mad
a speaking tour in the West. His Faneuil Hall speech, de
nouncing Know-Nothings, had a wide vogue in the Germa
press.[40] He was circulating his speeches widely, and by
indicated that he may have had some thought of being non
inated.

On the test of availability he was less acceptable than Chase or Seward. He had all Seward's defects and no wide political support for a background. His state was in the hands of Know-Nothings and his return to the Senate in doubt. Massachusetts endorsed her anti-slavery champion as such, while he denounced the ruling party in the State. He was mentioned at various times as a candidate, but no constructive king-maker ever took up his name. He proved one of the most valuable men in the ensuing campaign, but in the capacity of a martyr, not a candidate.

The Man on Middle Ground

Anti-slavery leaders were not available because of their antecedents. Almost anyone who was placed in nomination could secure the votes of those who would vote for anti-Nebraska principles for their own sake. The most satisfactory candidate would be just strong enough to hold these, and have qualities to include others. It would be a great advantage to incorporate the Jacksonian antecedents which Blair had recently brought to the party. Deference must also be paid to the North Americans. In the personality of what man could these best be united?

A very practical suggestion in answer to the question came from Philadelphia in the summer of 1855.[41] A number of conservative merchants of that city met privately with Morton McMichael of the *North American* to contrive a movement more inclusive and less radical than the one current promised to be. Among them was E.M.Davis, son-in-law of Lucretia Mott. He was an "abolitionist of the dilettante school", had had some experience in the romantic beginning of California, and now suggested Frémont, a Californian adventurer, as a possible candidate. Bigelow of the *New York Evening Post* and Nathaniel P. Banks, of Massachusetts, were both approached and committed to the new project. These early connections without doubt purposely included Bigelow, who was of Democratic, "Barn-Burner" ancestry, and Banks who was an anti-slavery American. Frémont was in the East at the time, seeing about the last phases of the litigation that secured his title to the Mariposa estate,[42] and was available for political machination. Out of this small beginning came the first Republican candidacy.

The idea of Frémont for candidate had made its debut at just about the time the "anti-conventionists" gave up Houston and were in need of a "new man". They were also restless because nothing had been accomplished; were planning a meeting to secure action, and Welles was still making good political capital by attacking conventions.[43] He had also prepared a ticket for publication and put Benton's name at the head as their strongest man in spite of his Nebraska error of the preceding winter.[44] Bigelow intercepted his proposed move and introduced the new idea. Their friends were "talking about the availability of Frémont". He recommended him to Welles: "Personally, I feel that Frémont possesses points of strength which could not be combined in any other man; whether they are sufficient for the exigency will depend. Weed says he is contented with Frémont, and if so, of course Seward is."[45] He had wished to talk the matter over with Welles the last time he was in New York, but had failed to meet him. King was in Washington, and returned with new ideas. He was converted to holding a convention that friends were considering for next March, was convinced that Benton was impossible, and had gone so far as to advise Bigelow not to print Welles' proposed ticket. He found also that Seward was not a candidate, and that nothing could be done for those that were considered until after the speaker was elected.[46]

While the speakership fight was in progress, the enthusiasm for a "new man" which had captivated King was being generated in Washington. It is hard to ascertain the extent of happenings there where men talked with Banks and with other bearers of the new creed, and did not have to write. Benton went on a silent hunt for Judge Wayne whom Blair pronounced so new that nobody ever heard of him.[47] Blair was more fortunate in his choice. He thought of "Frémont as a *new man*", because "he is brave, firm, has a history of romantic heroism, has rendered services as a man of honor—always democratic, and has no bad political connections, nor ever had—no train of hungry, corrupt hangers-on like Buchanan, who will I think be the outstanding (Democratic) candidate."[48] A man with such a back-ground—a son-in-law of Benton, a friend of Blair—was a real find and politicians soon recognized it. Frémont reciprocated Banks' partiality for him by making a record as a staunch supporter in the speakership fight.[49] The outcome of this contest was another step towards assurance that Frémont would be the "new man." A movement was started to organize a press ostensibly for liberal ideas, but in reality to support him.[50] The scheme was baffled by the refusal of Blair to take the editorship.[51] He did consent, however, to go to Pittsburgh. He had had Frémont in mind for some time before he went, and so also had Greeley, Hall of Massachusetts, and other "recent brethren."[52] Although an unadulterated Republican sentiment dominated the utterance of the convention the force that was to name the candidate was well defined there. A few days later Bailey expounded the new creed to Julian, lamenting its influence upon the straight-laced, anti-slavery principle: "The mania of mere success has seized the majority of the members here, and to accomplish it, they are already talking about taking up some *new* man, Mr. Availability. The people must look to themselves and not take counsel of their representatives. I want a man clearly and unmistakably representing our movement."[53]

From the time of the convention forward, the progress of the party was pretty largely usurped by the newcomers and managed from Washington. Bailey and his free-soil thoroughbreds might protest, but they had little choice but acceptance. Welles when he learned the nature of the movement, bolted, as did a number of his associates,[54] but they did not change the course of events. The Garrisonians would not accept it at all.[55] Nor did Blair's friends follow him, generally, into his new venture. The merchants of Baltimore held a public meeting to deny that he represented them in his "Southern Address" at Pittsburgh. Blair replied in his letter to the editor of the *Baltimore Democrat*. He pointed out that he had not said that all the merchants of that place supported him, and that he committed himself to nothing more radical than a restoration of the compromises with their attendant tranquillity.[56] Nothing could persuade Benton to support his son-in-law. Blair accounted for this only on the ground that he believed the country would soon need a God and there was but one.[57] Report was current for a while that Blair's own family repudiated his new position.[58] VanBuren kept far away. A final attempt was made to get him to attend the nominating convention to be held in June, but without avail.[59] Blair knew the hopelessness of it, although he made the attempt; and then, in terms of their old friendship, asked VanBuren to come to his home, Silver Spring, and visit a "Black Republican." The lot of his old companions was cast with the Democracy where they gave it a very valuable northern quality.

During the month after the convention at Pittsburgh, the Frémont enthusiasm was spreading, and those who were working for other men felt its growing strength. By the close of March he was pronounced most formidable, and many were manufacturing public sentiment for him.[60] His prospects had assumed such proportions that men outside who were interested in Kansas and free-soil began to inquire about the guarantees of the "new man."[61] But the Frémont promoters had the stage set when it should be time. Early in February Governor Robinson of Kansas, probably through instigation, wrote Frémont a letter. Robinson's position as the leader of the Free State Party, his former connection with a supposedly similar situation in California, and associations with Frémont there, made the necessary connecting link. Frémont's answer bore the date, March 17, and in due time it made its appearance. The Lawrence *Herald of Freedom* was the first to publish it. The editor explained that he had it by the kindness of a friend and although it was not for publication, he saw no harm in giving it to the world. He was pleased with the stand Frémont had taken, in fact he had long looked and hoped for it. He had complete confidence, and placed Frémont's name at the head of his column for the next president. The other two Free State papers of Lawrence did the same. April 23 the *New York Tribune* copied the letter with the *Herald's* explanation of its source, and the Robinson Letter was the property "of the millions."

It was an ingenious document.[62] Frémont was pleased that Robinson remembered him, but association during periods of stress always registers in memory. The Kansas struggle and the recent balloting in Congress reminded him of the time when they had stood firm on a hundred odd ballots in California.[63] As Robinson had stood by him then, he would reciprocate now, but success depends greatly on the Governor's own prudence and perseverance. His position was difficult "for it is to be

feared from the Proclamation of the President that he intends
to recognize the usurpation in Kansas as the legitimate government, and that its sedition law, the test oath, and the means
to be taken to expel its people as aliens, will all, directly or
indirectly, be supported by the army of the United States."
This was opportune for it committed Frémont on the efforts
going on in Congress to smash the administrative party over
the Kansas question. It was subtle, for Greeley and his following were preaching that the fate of Kansas depended on
the coming election. Because of his antecedents Frémont had
a fellow feeling for the Kansas leader in his "struggle for
liberty." As for the inquiry in the letter about him in connection with the presidency, modestly, this was the solicitude
of friends who thought of him more flatteringly than he did of
himself.

Frémont was safe on Kansas, but he was a Southerner, and a
Democrat. Some might want further assurances of his position on slavery in the abstract. Fears were soon allayed. He
found the proper occasion in declining an invitation to a Republican meeting in New York, April 29.[64] Engagements, he
said, prevented his accepting the invitation, but he approved
their efforts as he did all movements to undo "the mischief
arising from the violations of good faith in the repeal of the
Missouri Compromise." He was opposed to slavery in the
abstract and upon principle, "sustained and made habitual by
long settled convictions." He was "inflexible in the belief that
it ought not to be interfered with where it exists under the
shield of state sovereignty," and was "as inflexibily opposed
to its extension on this continent beyond its present limits."
He took Republican ground in his statement and was well
squared with their Pittsburgh platform.

The New York meeting of April 29 to which Frémont's
letter was addressed, was a land mark in Republican progress
as well as in his candidacy. Schemes had been on foot for
some time to entrench the party in that "city of trading men"
which was a *"bad soil for free soil."*[65] By April 15 Blair had
prepared his "Letter to the New York Democrats," Bigelow
had printed an edition of three thousand copies and congressmen had been approached relative to circulating it.[66] This
document was presented as a part of the proceedings of the
"great" New York meeting. It was made up of letters of the

later days of Jackson's life in which he protested against the "intrigue" that defeated VanBuren's renomination and turned Blair out of the editorship of the *Globe*.[67] It showed the Democratic party an imposter, its leaders, especially Buchanan, enemies of Jackson. Jackson's blessing was given to the new party that would restore his principles. B. F. Butler, his Attorney General, was president of the meeting and made an appropriate speech. Welles wrote a satisfactory letter which was too late for the meeting but was published in the report.[68] It was quite a reunion of the old school, capable of conferring a blessing, and of impressing the fitness of the young counterpart of "Old Hickory."

With the receiving of the blessing of Jackson, the Frémont movement was at flood tide. May 3, E. L. Pierce, scouting for Chase, pronounced the Pathfinder's nomination sure.[69] In Iowa the Burlington and Keokuk papers were for Frémont, so was Grimes and so the state delegation, though not instructed. In Chicago Wentworth supported him, though Vaughn clung to Chase, and Medill was for Seward. In Iowa the Germans were for him. In Illinois they pronounced him the man.[70] Remelin on accepting Chase's commission said that he could go for Frémont. Gustave Koerner, influential German of Illinois, making a tour of the East just prior to the convention found those Germans who were Republicans at all enthusiastic for him. Dorsheimer of Buffalo was very much in favor of his nomination, and Koerner himself was introduced while in New York, and pledged.[71] The grip he would have on the Germans had not been miscalculated.[72] New England papers also began to place his name at the head of the political column. This was as it should be; for they were supposed to lead the country in anti-slavery sentiment. The work of Banks, Wilson, Hall, and other politicians had been thoroughly done, and New England was considered a unit for Frémont. Bigelow committed the *New York Evening Post* on April 10, and May 18 began to publish his biography.[73]

April 29 the Tribune moved a little nearer to naming the right man by being more elaborate on the object of the search it was conducting. In the first place; their purpose in nominating was to elect. They did not intend, as some desired, to put up their brightest leader and go down with colors flying. Anti-Nebraska sentiment had sufficient power to elect, could

it be united. Second: those thinking that to be for free
Kansas was sufficient, were wrong. Men had prejudices and
a candidate must be secured for whom the ex-Americans, the
foreign born, the Whigs, Democrats, and Abolitionists could
vote without embarrassment. Who was he? Third: careful
computation showed that thirty-five votes must be secured
from the doubtful states, and they must have a man to carry
them. "No blind, vague confidence in the justice and strength
of the cause, no guess that ends will shape themselves without
the imposition of means, will answer the purpose. To be
beaten means to lose Kansas and all further territory." For
more than a month the *Tribune* held this position while merits
of candidates still passed its columns. June 3 the Democrats
put their platform and nominee before the country. June 6
Greeley committed the *Tribune* on Frémont. The convention
was to pick the candidate best fitted to win. Could anyone
they chose be elected, Seward, Chase, and Sumner were the
ones to consider. Of them, the *Tribune* preferred Seward.
Many of his friends considered him not the strongest man, but
it would support him if the convention considered him strongest. But considering the anti-Nebraska sentiment not strong
enough to elect anyone, there were four possibilities: Banks,
Bissell, Frémont, and McLean. Banks was eliminated because of his own support of Frémont. Bissel had a signal
service to perform in beating the Douglasites in Illinois.[74] This
left Frémont and McLean. He preferred the former for many
reasons, and disapproved the latter for as many more. The
Frémont movement had reached a climax a little too early and
one for McLean was threatening it. Greeley took up arms
and fought for his candidate until the convention of June 17
settled the question.

A Conservative Afterthought

Availability had crowded the anti-slavery champions aside.
Frémont would broaden the party to include the North
Americans and he would hold the foreign vote in so far as that
was possible. He gave satisfaction to the mass of anti-
Nebraska sentiment. He was a young man of the "school of
Old Hickory," ready to lead a new party on its hunt for re-
stored democracy. But he was not the man to get the vote

of the "Old Conservatives." There was a whole stratum of votes that might be reached by a more conservative candidate, which otherwise would stay by the "old Whigs" or else swing to Fillmore or even Buchanan. If a movement had come to trim down from anti-slavery leaders to one who could include a wider scope, it was only natural that there should be one to trim still further and include this conservative stratum.

Justice McLean of the Supreme Court became the central figure in the endeavor of the more conservative to place a candidate. He was an old man with a long record of public service. He had been a Democrat in earlier times, but in later years had acted with the Whigs. He had joined the Americans as had so many from the Whig party. When the new creed promised to sweep the country, he, with Houston and Stockton, was talked of as a national leader, and ground was broken for his candidacy in the lodges of Michigan and Ohio.

McLean responded readily to any suggestion,[75] and a well defined movement was on foot when the split at Philadelphia Council in June, 1855, paralyzed action for a time. Although it checked progress, it left possibilities. Reconciliation on national grounds would mean more chances than ever for a northern man with a conservative record. If this failed and the North continued apart, there was still hope of giving a candidate to the Republican party that was fusing all others on the anti-slavery principle.

McLean's candidacy was taken up again soon after Chase's election to the governorship of Ohio. The Republican-Know-Nothing divergence which began to show immediately after their victory was closely associated with the insurgence of the endeavor to make McLean president. Late in October Judge Truesdale clipped from an old issue of the *State Journal* and published a letter of McLean's in which he declared his belief in the local nature of slavery. Some of McLean's decisions in fugitive slave cases were believed to injure his strength in the North, and Truesdale thought it was time to put him right by restating them.[76] Before the month was out politicians in the East were considering him as the man to unite the Americans and Republicans, and were making plans to do something for him at the Seceders' national council at Cincinnati in November. When this body elected Lieutenant Governor Ford national president and made overtures to the regular council, it greatly enhanced McLean's chances for the nomination. Ford reported that prospects were good.[77] The Order had received his name well, and it was thought that under proper management he could be nominated and elected. Ford believed that the steps taken towards unity were necessary, and that they must prepare to unite all conservatives. There was danger, he admitted, from all "Old Hunkerdom;" but "Young America" must "wait for years and its brawlings must be put down with a prudent hand."

The assembling of Congress which shifted the center of political affairs to Washington found a group ready to take care of McLean's interests. L. D. Campbell smarting from his recent discomfiture at the hands of Chase, was a logical leader, while Samuel Galloway, likewise a member of Congress, Ford, Judge Spaulding, and Judge Truesdale added to the number of his Ohio backing and made it seem respectable. They were ready to dispute with Chase the national preferment he claimed on the strength of the Ohio victory. To do this Galloway gave out the remarkable news that Chase had pledged the Whigs of Ohio that he would not use the governorship as a stepping stone to the presidency, and in doing it, started the rift that furnished useful argument for politicians to discard any Ohio candidate. To the necessary support from his home state an eastern contingency rallied to McLean. This was led by John Allison of Pennsylvania, a doubtful and conservative state, and added great strength to the Judge's prospects. Imbued with the idea of the all importance of Pennsylvania, Allison approached Giddings on the subject of choosing McLean as the only man to carry it.[78] To his support came further strength from Pennsylvania—this time from the eastern part which was more conservative still. Early in January a meeting of Philadelphia business men had directed Samuel S. Rea to inquire concerning McLean's susceptibility to a nomination. McLean replied that he was not a candidate; but his response was not so couched as to check efforts in his behalf.[79] Even the double grip on Pennsylvania did not enable McLean's friends to make progress rapidly. The Republican convention at Pittsburgh had practically ignored the Americans, though prominent Free-Soilers mentioned McLean's name, and even Greeley was reported as favorable.[80] The American

convention at Philadelphia was a great disappointment. Fillmore was nominated and the party split anew. This undoing
was laid at the door of the New York delegation. The South
was willing to accept McLean, so his friends thought, but
New York was there to nominate her man or ruin the party,
and had done both.[81] It was also believed that many Republicans would have taken him without a nomination. Now the
only possibility for McLean lay with those Republicans who
had maintained an utter independence of the Americans and
who were rapidly drifting to Frémont as a leader.

There was still hope. A representation on the Ohio delegation to the Philadelphia convention of June 17 was necessary.
As it became obvious that Chase could not be nominated, Mc-
Lean's friends doubled their energy to secure delegates. They
even attempted reconciliation with Chase.[82] Chase's friends
would not give an inch to what was considered the machina-
tions of his old Whig enemies; even after the Frémont move
had "taken like tinder" in Ohio, Chase was not satisfied that
it was not their work.[83] The best McLean's friends could do
was to secure a few delegates and take strong grounds against
the "packing system"[84] used by Chase. The free-soil partisans
of the state responded by making war on the Judge. The
Salem *Anti-Slavery Bugle* attacked him as a slave-owner.[85]
This was overstressing the point, but McLean took occasion to
get a little nearer to anti-Nebraska ground. Questionnaires
were coming in from many places, asking for his true position.
A committee took up the matter of his influence in the Gaines
case, and published a statement by Judge Leavitt exonerating
him.[86] An opportunity for a personal statement soon presented
itself. May 12, Senator Cass made a speech relative to slavery in the territories and based it on an opinion of McLean's
of December 22, 1847. The opinion on which it was based,
along with McLean's position in 1850 appeared in the *National Intelligencer* the same day. The following day he published
a note to Cass to explain it. He said that he never doubted
that Congress had power to prohibit slavery in the territories
and could never have expressed any doubt on the subject.[87]
It left the affair in an unsatisfactory condition, inviting further efforts on the part of McLean.

While friends were trying to secure at least a share of the
Ohio delegation, and the Judge was putting himself constitu-

tionally right on free Kansas, the thunder was being loosed at
Washington that put him under way for the nomination. The
Frémont move had come prematurely to a climax, and its
measure had been taken. It was whispered about that a
certain southern man of wide political experience had been
through North Carolina, Tennessee, and Kentucky, Know-
Nothing strongholds, and was of the opinion that if the anti-
Nebraska men selected such a candidate as McLean, and
added Bell or Houston, the South would accept it, and they
might avoid the stigma of sectionalism. This would also
annihilate Fillmore. Such a nomination was pronounced feasible for the large interests in the North which were opposed
to the Nebraska affair in all its phases, and which were "essentially conservative and must be addressed through a candidate
of tried character and acknowledged weight with the country"[88]
The Cass note was putting him in the proper light on slavery
and Kansas. There came to be much talk about a "tried man."
This was the argument that the supporters of Buchanan were
using against Pierce, and it would work against Frémont. It
was noised around that most of the members of Congress were
for McLean,[89] and he was pronounced in the ascendency. The
tide had come in with a rush. Stockton of New Jersey had
moved in his favor; Pennsylvania and Illinois were setting
strongly to him.[90] J. S. Pike went to Washington, was caught
up in the boom, and was ridiculed for trying to convert his
colleagues.[91] May 30, Rea, who held a position on the *Philadelphia Times* swung it from Fillmore to McLean.[92] Pennsylvania was declared a unit for him, save some radicals. He
alone was believed able to carry New Jersey and Delaware,
and the opposition in Ohio was softening and looked promising.[93]

As the movement began passing from words to deeds, it
confronted the entrenched Frémont supporters. They controlled
the party machinery, and would not give up New England,
New York, and the places of which they felt sure with their
candidate, for the assurity of a "doubtful middle."[94] It was
supposed that they might shift from Frémont to Banks and
annex Bell or Houston. It was this supposition plus the
Democratic nomination that brought Greeley into the open
on June 6 and caused him to fight for his man until the day
of the convention. However, it seemed worth while to attempt

to oust the Frémont group. On the night of May 31, J. E. Harvey dined with James Watson Webb of the *Courier and Enquirer*, friend of Seward and Weed. Together they concocted a scheme whereby the nomination might be secured. With an agreement struck, Harvey elaborated a plan of action and Webb immediately communicated it to McLean.[95] The vital point in breaking up the Frémont support was the alienation of Seward's friends, which as a matter of course meant gaining an alliance with Weed. They had stood aloof when McLean was boomed on the ground that once elected he would be unfriendly to them. The plan was that McLean write a letter putting his attitude in unmistakable terms, and giving assurance that Seward, Weed, and Company would be cared for by his administration. The letter was to be held absolutely confidential, save to use it at the right time. Webb was also in touch with Stockton, and had assigned him the Navy department. Stockton had given his assent and could be relied upon in securing New Jersey and Pennsylvania. He could also do much in postponing action at the New York convention when it was feared the Frémonters would carry the day. McLean's letter was to contain a specific paragraph for Stockton. At the same time, A. M. C. Pennington was planning to get the Judge's record on anti-slavery decisions a more satisfactory presentation to the public than the Cass note had made. The venerable Judge Hornblower of New Jersey had addressed a letter to McLean on seeing his Cass note, and in it asked his opinion about Kansas and expressed a desire to live to see it free.[96] Allison, urged by Pennington, insisted that McLean answer Hornblower's note.[97]

Buchanan's nomination gave McLean an added impetus. "Old Buck" was admittedly the Democrats' strongest man, and the securing of Pennsylvania was now a more potent argument than ever. The "Voice of Pennsylvania" called McLean. New Jersey had a solid delegation for him; but its leaders despaired of securing the convention from the radicals.[98] McLean wrote the letter for Seward and his friends entirely to Webb's satisfaction, who armed with it, and supported by Pennington and Schenck, went to Philadelphia.[99] Further pressure was put on McLean to answer the Hornblower letter.[100] June 11 the reply was in the hands of Pennington and he and Allison doctored it up for publication. It would secure the doubting and hush those who referred to the Judge's silence.[101] In the letter McLean aptly referred to the Missouri Case (Dred Scott) which was held over to be reargued: it went on to assert his belief in the power of Congress over slavery in the territories, and then added sundry patriotic gushings.[102] Israel Washburn and Fessenden of Maine became identified with the movement, although Maine had instructed for Frémont. They were to do what they could for it, and Washburn was to give a tip to E. B. Washburne to bring in the Illinois delegation already partly favorable.[103] McLean's cause at the convention was assigned to Judge Spaulding whose guiding star was to be the "voice of Pennsylvania," and his own judgment.[104]

McLean's case went to the convention with possibilities, but the odds were still against him. Greeley, who had said he would support anyone the convention saw fit to nominate, refused to promise his support in the event it should nominate McLean.[105] He had met the enhanced Pennsylvania argument when Buchanan was nominated with a powerful editorial.[106] He featured Frémont's points of availability and stressed the arguments against McLean. None can summarize better than Greeley: (1) A Supreme Court Judge should not look for nomination, the Court was getting bad enough without becoming a nursery for presidents. (2) McLean must either resign and have his place filled by a *genius* like Pugh,[107] or else campaign and dispense justice at the same time, which did not look well. (3) Anti-slavery men of ten years standing thought they had "felt his shoulder pressing against them in the late cycle of depression and disorder." This came from Ohio where he would lose more anti-slavery votes than any other man. (4) "Some of his decisions in slave cases—the VanZant especially—leaned very hard against the rights of humanity, and would be used against him in canvass." These were no doubt according to his sense of constitutional obligation, but they indicated "a strong bias towards pro-slavery interpretation of the Federal Pact." (5) There is no "professedly anti-Nebraska man of consequence who was unsound or shaky in the long contest for speaker who is not now for McLean." Greeley clung to the young man to lead the young party.

On June 17 the battle would be fought out at Philadelphia. Availability on middle ground had overthrown the anti-slavery champions.   Conservative afterthought with an American backing, had called out McLean to question its right-of-way. The rise of this threat to break Frémont, loosed scattering talk in favor of Bissell, Banks, and even Seward.   What might the Philadelphia convention have in store?

1. Grimes to Chase, March 28, in Slater, *Life of Grimes,* pp. 85-86. Remelin of Cincinnati and Dorsheimer of Buffalo were the leading political figures among the Germans.
2. H.Kreissman to Sumner, Dec. 28. Sumner MSS. H.L.
3. Latta to Chase, Dec. 18. Chase MSS. L.C.
4. Thos. Spooner to Chase, Feb. 5. Chase MSS. L.C.
5. B. F. Williams to Chase, Feb. 7. Chase MSS. L.C.
6. F.D.Kimball to Chase, Feb. 28. Chase MSS. L.C.
7. John Heaton to Chase, Feb. 25. Chase MSS. L.C.
8. F.D.Kimball to Chase, Feb. 28. Chase MSS. L.C.
9. S.Moliter to Chase, March 27. Chase MSS. L.C.
10. Remelin to Chase, April 29. Chase MSS. L.C. In the same letter Remelin declared that he could support Frémont.
11. Chase to Hoadly, March 16. Chase MSS. L. C.
12. G.Bailey to Chase, Jan.20. ChaseMSS. L.C. Bailey could not believe that Chase ever made such a promise and wished to set it right.
13. *New York Tribune,* April 5.
14. C.F.Cleveland to Chase, April 21. Chase MSS. L.C.
15. Bailey to Chase, April 18. Chase MSS. P.H.S.
16. Quoted from letter to Chase, April 18. *National Era,* April 10.
17. *Pittsburgh Gazette,* April 22. Clipping in Chase MSS. L.C.
18. Chase to Hamlin,April 23. Chase MSS. L.C.
19. Grimes to Chase, March 28, in Slater's *Life of Grimes,* pp. 85-86.
20. Kimball to Chase, April 29. Chase MSS. L.C.
21. E.L.Pierce to Sumner, May 3. Sumner MSS. L.C.
22. The movements of the Tribune are treated in connection with the Frémont movement. See below *The Man on Middle Ground.*
23. Editorials, "Presidential", *New York Tribune,* April 21 and 23.
24. *New York Tribune,* April 23.
25. Editorial "Politics in New England", *New York Tribune,* April 25.
26. Chase to Hoadley, May 7. Chase MSS. P.H.S.
27. They were presented in Congress May 21.
28. Bingham to Chase, June 7. Chase MSS. L.C.
29. D.McBride to Chase, June 7. Chase MSS. L.C.
30. J.Cady to Chase, June 10. Chase MSS. L.C.
31. Joshua Leavitt to Chase, June 12. Chase MSS. P.H.S.
32. E.L.Pierce to Chase, May 3. Chase MSS. L.C. Pierce had recently moved to Chicago.
33. Bigelow to Welles cited below.
34. Practically every letter that touches the political situation states this in regard to Seward as a candidate.
35. Barnes,T.W., *Life of Thurlow Weed,* vol. II. p. 245.
36. Seward's friends in 1860 forced Greeley to publish a letter of

1854 in which he declared "Seward, Weed, Greeley and Company" dissolved.

37. Bancroft, *Life of Seward*, vol.I, pp. 421-422.

38. Seward to his wife, June 14, in Bancroft, *Life of Seward*, vol. I, p. 421.

39. Henry Wilson to Chase, April 16. Chase MSS. P.H.S.

40. H.Kreissman to Sumner, Dec. 28, '55. Sumner MSS. H.L.

41. G.Bailey to Chase, April 18, '56. Chase MSS. P.H.S. The story of origin is based on Bailey's account which came from the political talk of the time. Subsequent events bear it out well.

42. See Chapter IX.

43. Preston King to Welles Nov. 17. Bigelow to Welles, Dec.27. Welles MSS. L.C.

44. Welles to Bigelow, Dec. 28. Welles MSS. L.C.

45. Bigelow to Welles, Dec. 27, cited above.

46. Preston King to Welles, Jan.3,Jan.9. Welles MSS. L.C. They were talking of Frémont, Blair, and Chase.

47. Blair toVanBuren,Jan.25.VanBurenMSS. L.C.

48. Blair to VanBuren, Jan.25, cited above.

49. Bailey to Chase cited above. This was a general impression among politicians and the basis of an attack on him later. See Chapter XI.

50. Richard Mott to Chase, Feb. 21. Chase MSS. L.C.

51. Blair to Van Buren, Feb. 13. Van Buren MSS. L.C. Blair said VanBuren's last letter kept him from accepting. He felt that an honest man must do something, even if the new combination was as bad as those in the Democratic party.

52. G.Bailey to Chase, Feb. 21 Chase MSS. L.C.

53. Bailey to Julian, March 9. Julian MSS. L.C.

54. C.F.Cleveland to Welles, Jan. 9. Welles MSS. L.C.

55. See Chapter VII, *Minor Parties.*

56. Text of Blair's letter, *New York Tribune*, March 7.

57. Blair to VanBuren, May 17. VanBuren MSS. L.C.

58. This impression was based on a letter of F.P.Blair Jr. in the Philadelphia *Times*, and a statement by Montgomery relative to his father's former relations with VanBuren.

59. E.D.Morgan to Blair, May 14, Blair to VanBuren,May17. Van Buren MSS. L.C.

60. A. P. Stone to Chase, March 30-31. Chase MSS. L.C.

61. C.F.Adams to Sumner, April 1, E.G.Loring to Sumner, April 9. Sumner MSS. H.L.

62. Text, Bigelow, *Life of Frémont*, pp. 447-448.

63. On this incident, Frémont's anti-slavery record was based. See Chapter IX.

64. Text in Bigelow's *Life of Frémont*, p. 449.

65. E.D.Morgan to Niles, March 18. Welles MSS. L.C.

66. Blair to Washburn, April 15. I.Washburn MSS. L.C.

67. Pamphlets—*Blair's Letter to the New York Democrats*, "*A Voice from the Grave of Jackson*". *New York Tribune* editorial, May 6, "*Wolves in the Fold.*"

68. E.D.Morgan to Welles, May 1. Welles MSS. L.C.

69. Pierce to Chase, May 3, cited above. Pierce to Sumner, May 3.

Sumner MSS.H.L.

70. H. Kreissman to Sumner, May 21. Sumner MSS. H.L.
71. Koerner,Gustave, *Memoirs,* vol.II,pp. 10-14.
72. For basis of account of Frémont's hold on the Germans, see Chapter IX.
73. Bigelow,John, *Life and Public Services of Colonel Charles Frémont;* Nevins, *New York Evening Post p.* 251.
74. Bissell had been nominated for Governor and was very strong.
75. McLean to Hector Orr, Nov.25,1854, McLean to Prettyman,Nov. 25, 1854, McLean to R.A.Parrish, March 31, 1855. McLean MSS. L.C.
76. Truesdale to McLean, Oct. 25. McLean MSS. L.C.
77. Ford to McLean, Nov. 27. McLean MSS. L.C.
78. Bailey to Chase, Feb. 21. Chase Mss. L.C.
79. Samuel S. Rea to McLean, Jan. 11, May 30. McLean MSS. L.C.
80. Judge Truesdale to McLean, Feb. 24. McLean MSS. L.C.
81. R.M.Corwin to McLean, March 30. McLean MSS. L.C.
82. T. Jewett to McLean, March 6. McLean MSS. L.C.
83. C.W.Elliott to Chase, May 16. Chase MSS. L.C.
84. R.M.Corwin to McLean,May 16. McLean MSS. L.C.
85. S.Horton to McLean, April 16, May 17. McLean MSS. L.C.
86. *National Intelligencer,* May 12. The committee's inquiry and Leavitt's reply bear the dates April 22 and 26 respectively.
87. Cass to McLean, Jan. 31. McLean MSS. L.C. *National Intelligencer,* May 12,13. *New York Tribune,* May 20.
88. *New York Tribune,* April 24; "Index" correspondent, April 22.
89. Wade to Chase, May 5. Chase MSS. L.C.
90. *New York Tribune,* May 7.
91. C.A.Dana to Pike, May 21, H.Greeley to Pike, May 21, *First Blows of the Civil War,* pp. 337-338.
92. Rea to McLean, May 30. McLean MSS. L.C.
93. J.E.Harvey to McLean, May 30, John Allison to McLean, June 21. McLean MSS. L.C.
94. J.EHarvey to McLean, May 30. McLean MSS. L.C.
95. J.E.Harvey to McLean, June 1, J.W.Webb to McLean, June 2. McLean MSS. L.C.
96. Hornblower,Letter in *Newark Daily Advertiser,* June 14. *New York Tribune,* June 16.
97. J.Allison to McLean, June 2, McLean to Hornblower,June 6. McLean MSS. L.C.
98. Pennington to McLean, June 7. McLean MSS. L.C.
99. Webb to McLean June 11 and 12. McLean MSS. L.C.
100. J. A. Bingham to McLean, June 9. McLean MSS.L.C.
101. Pennington to McLean, June 12. McLean MSS. L.C.
102. Text, *Newark Daily Advertiser,* June 14, *New York Tribune,* June 20.
103. Pennington to I.Washburn. I.Washburn MSS. L.C.
104. Spaulding to McLean, June 9, two letters in response to McLean's of June 6. McLean MSS. L.C.
105. H.Greeley to I.Washburn, June 13. I.Washburn MSS. L.C.
106. *New York Tribune,* June 12. "A Democrat for President."
107. Pugh was elected to succeed Chase in the Senate.

CHAPTER IX

CANDIDATE AND PLATFORM

The preliminary convention at Pittsburgh, February 22, had named Philadelphia as the place and June 17 as the date for a nominating convention. The method of calling the delegates together and the work necessary to complete the party organization were left in the hands of a committee. The service of Henry J. Raymond of the *New York Times* was at their disposal, and his presence was a guarantee against rashness. The long and educative address which became one of the important Republican campaign documents was the work of the committee. It also fell to its lot to issue the call that would make the nominating convention a reality.

On March 27 this committee assembled at Washington where it might have the ready advice of members of Congress. From the first there was bitterness among congressmen as well as the committee members themselves. To facilitate matters it was decided to have the anti-Nebraska congressmen meet with the committee and air their views and state their wishes.[1] On the third session some thirty were present from both branches of Congress who represented all shades of opinion—"Republicans, North Americans proper, and Americans who were more Republican than American."[2] In general, they wished to unite and make a call, but the North Americans objected to using the name Republican. Stone of Ohio, who was spokesman for the Pittsburgh Platform with its Republican principles was willing to address a call to the people of the United States as coming from "the committee appointed by the Pittsburgh Convention" without using the word Republican. Also, there was a variety of opinion as to the ground that should be taken on slavery extension and Kansas. Seward's friends wanted the admission of Kansas as a free state made a distinct issue. Some wanted merely the restoration of the Missouri Compromise; and some wanted restriction confined to territory that had once been closed to it. Several

177

styles of call were offered.³ Stone stood firm on complete restriction in the territories, but would allow a dual interpretation of what was meant by territories. After the discussion the committee met, as such, drafted the call, and sent it for publication.

March 30 the New York papers printed the call and it was different from the wording originally agreed to.⁴ Stone called at the office of the *Evening Post* to ascertain the source of the new version, and concluded that Morgan, their chairman, had altered it on his own responsibility. He sent an original form to Chase, and asked the feasibility of publishing it so in Ohio. The call that appeared for the Philadelphia Convention was a much different document from that which had been issued for the one at Pittsburgh. It showed the influence of the movement to trim down from the dominant principle in order to include more elements and make a larger party. The Republicans—those opposed to the extension of slavery into the territories—were asked to cooperate with the others.

> The people of the United States without regard to past political differences or division, who are opposed to the repeal of the Missouri Compromise, to the policy of the present administration, to the extension of slavery into the territories, in favor of the admission of Kansas as a free state, and of restoring the action of the Federal government to the principles of Washington and Jefferson are invited by the National Committee, appointed by the Pittsburgh Convention, February 22, 1856, to send from each state three delegates from every congressional district, and six delegates at large, to meet in Philadelphia on the seventeenth day of June next, for the purpose of nominating candidates to be supported for the offices of President and Vice-President of the United States.
>
> Signed,
>   National Committee ⁵

Although Stone objected to the wording of the call, as well might any full blood Republican, it succeeded well in including every type and degree of anti-Nebraska sentiment. The non-extension men could scarcely refuse to cooperate because theirs was not the only ground stated. Seward partisans found themselves favored in the clause on the admission of Kansas, and those who went no further than to wish a restoration of the Missouri Compromise were especially favored. The North Americans could have no objection to the proposed basis of cooperation and their convention which was to convene June 12 would put them on record before the Philadelphia convention met.

Choice of Candidate

On June 12, the very day that Fillmore's acceptance of the nomination of the Philadelphia Convention of the Americans was given to the public, the North American seceders from that convention assembled in New York.[6] Their meeting was attended by a large crowd which gathered outside the hall to shout for Fillmore. It was only a few days before the Republican convention was to assemble at Philadelphia, and New York was full of its delegates *en route*. The presence of both these outside groups might prove a moral support for some factions of the Convention that would make the last effort of the Know-Nothings to swing the North. The delegations from the Eastern states, especially from New England, were large. They came from the states where Know-Nothingism was still dominant and were unwilling to abandon their purpose in favor of the ensuing Philadelphia convention. This eastern bloc was led by the Connecticut delegation and threatened secession, if it could not make a nomination. What was more dangerous still, they intended to nominate Frémont who would be without doubt the choice of the convention at Philadelphia. If they did this, they would kill him as a Republican candidate; and friends began to be alarmed. They insisted that such a course would embarrass him at Philadelphia, that he would not accept an American nomination, and Greeley warned them not to try to dictate to the Philadelphia Convention.[7] Pitted against a formidable East were delegates from the West who worked to block their purpose, and to leave the naming of the anti-Nebraska candidate entirely to the Republican Convention.[8]

There was uncertainty and, for some, forbodings of evil when the North American delegations were called to order by Ex-Governor Colby of New Hampshire. Ex-Governor Johnston of Pennsylvania who had recently re-seceded from his state council because it endorsed Fillmore, was made President. The force that was to work out a solution of their relation to the Philadelphia Convention was soon discernible. An anti-Fillmore convention had met at Albany May 29 and had elected a delegation to go to New York.[9] At the head of the delegation was George Law, and Law proved as enthusiastic for Banks as the New Englanders were for Frémont. Chauncey Schaffer of the New York delegation raised the anti-slavery war-whoop and the convention was under way. A communication from E. D. Morgan, Republican national chairman, was read, which invited the cooperation of the Americans at Philadelphia. A special committee was appointed to consider this proposition, and Law was made Chairman. The discussion occasioned by the invitation from Morgan consumed the entire day with the exception of an abortive attempt to send some Fillmore enthusiasts to jail.

The next morning Law's committee reported, and tendered four resolutions to the convention. The convention would conduct a series of ballots for candidates for president and vice-president, and the one who received the majority would be considered their choice. When this was done a committee of one from each state was to confer with the candidates selected and then with the Philadelphia convention in regard to them. Their convention was to continue in session until the result of the conference was known. The proposition which Law offered really amounted to a compromise, and its unanimous adoption settled all question as to whether they would nominate or not. Immediately the convention listened to a discussion of the winning points of various favorites. A majority of the Pennsylvania delegation was in favor of McLean in spite of the fact that Fillmore's acceptance had injured him. It was figured that the latter would hold some votes in Pennsylvania that otherwise might have been reached by the Ohio Judge. New Jersey was for Stockton, the "Jackson of the Sea." New England had a large vote for Frémont, but New York joined the western delegations and gave Banks a numerous support. The first vote totalled: Banks, 43; Frémont, 39; McLean, 19; Stockton, 14; Johnston, 6; and Chase, 6.[10] Three more ballots were taken, and tremendous enthusiasm was shown for Frémont. The enthusiasm was all right so long as he did not receive votes enough to be declared their choice.

Voting was resumed the next day. Stockton's name was withdrawn and the New Jersey delegates walked out amid the cheers of the Fillmorites outside. As the balloting proceeded, the Frémont vote gradually decreased and on the tenth the count stood: Banks, 53; Frémont, 18; and McLean, 24. A Pennsylvania delegate then moved that Banks be given an unanimous vote and that Johnston be chosen as candidate for vice-president. The motion prevailed, and a real piece of political *finesse* was thereby accomplished. They had nominated and those who wished to maintain their independence had that fact for a satisfaction. Still they had not dictated to the Philadelphia convention. The position of Banks as a promoter of the Frémont candidacy made it impossible for him to do otherwise than withdraw, should the Pathfinder be nominated. Johnston then spoke and though not explicit, the import of his speech was to laud qualities that were accredited to Frémont. A platform was adopted that also looked towards unity with the Republicans. They stood for the Union after the fashion that Webster had described. They stood for "free" everything. Their only hint at Nativism was in the form of "the freedom of the ballot box from foreign influence." They stood for the improvement of rivers and of the harbors of the Great Lakes. They stood for the immediate construction of a Pacific railroad by such aid of the Federal government as might be necessary. There was nothing in the way of uniting with the Republicans; the vice-presidency was all the North Americans asked on the Philadelphia ticket. Whether or no this would be conceded remained to be seen, and in accordance with their resolutions the convention adjourned over until the 17th. The New Jersey seceders nominated Stockton for president and Kenneth Raynor for vice-president.[11]

On June 17, the anniversary of the day the fathers hallowed by their fight for liberty at Bunker Hill, the Republican convention assembled at Philadelphia.[12] The committee chairman, E. D. Morgan, called it to order. In his opening remarks he declared that their presence was not for the purpose of determining whether the North would rule or whether the South would rule, but whether the principle of freedom established by the fathers would be maintained. Robert Emmett, son of the Irish martyr, Thomas Addis Emmet, was made temporary chairman. He had formerly been a Democrat, and in light of their recent nominations, his presence and speech were fitting. He reviewed the Cincinnati Platform of his late party and lamented the fate of Buchanan who had "allowed himself to be chained to the Juggernaut of slavery." They would now merge the isms in patriotism,[13] he declared. The delegations were uneven, but there was little trouble over seating in the show of formality that was carried out. A group of one hundred Silas Wright Democrats came from New York, and the New England delegations offered to give up their seats that so welcome guests might be accommodated.

The second day's work completed the organization and displayed the temperament of the body. Henry S. Lane of Indiana was made chairman. He was a born orator, and spoke effectively. He came as a Whig, convinced by the times that Henry Clay was dead and that it was time for Democrats to unite with them on the great principle. The cry of disunion which everybody was hearing was raised by South Carolina— "by the unhung nullifiers who still had the halter of General Jackson about their necks." When he had finished, he took his seat, leaned back, and propped a pair of well-grown feet upon the table. There was a tremor among the New England delegation as if a secession might be contemplated; but harmony was soon restored.[14] Owen Lovejoy delivered an evangelical speech and Henry Wilson followed with something more practical. He was convinced that the old parties were unable to check slavery. All should unite in a new one standing for "free speech, free press, free soil, free Kansas"—and somebody shouted "Frémont." Upon this suggestion he surveyed the field for prospective candidates. He called Seward the greatest statesman in America whereon the convention rose with cheers. There had been cheers for others in turn.

Some homely details were next cared for. The report of the committee on credentials was accepted. A national committee was then appointed. Wilmot, chairman of the committee on resolutions, reported next. With an exception of a quarrel over the wording of the last resolve, which might or might not be construed to discountenance American principles, the platform was accepted without trouble. This, like its predecessor of the Pittsburgh Convention, was the work of anti-slavery men and it was distinctly on Republican grounds.

It was time now to name a candidate, and J. E. Seely of New York made a motion that they begin. James Watson Webb moved to block it; for he had not yet despaired of outdoing the Frémont men. It was evident that they controlled the convention, and the contingency for which Webb stood, alone had strength enough to make a fight. In spite of any overtures he may have made to Weed, the Albany editor was unwavering in his support of Frémont, and some thought he showed a little of the demagogue in his attitude.[15] Webb pleaded for deliberation, as the fathers had deliberated when a momentous decision was to be made. He knew, he said that he opposed one whom most members approved, but Seward, the greatest representative of their principles, had been turned down because he could not carry Pennsylvania. That being the case, why put in another man who was equally uncertain? He wanted a conference, and many delegates were willing to grant it. G. W. Patterson of New York took advantage of the suggestion to withdraw Seward's name. Webb insisted that this was not at Seward's behest, and forced Patterson to admit that his authority came from a committee representing Seward. Judge Spaulding almost immediately withdrew the name of McLean. Thaddeus Stevens then came to Webb's support and insisted that they must have a conference, that the withdrawal of McLean meant the loss of Pennsylvania by fifty thousand votes. Chase's showing had been so small from the first that it was believed his friends would meet and withdraw his name.[16] At this juncture, Mitchell after commenting on the fitness of Chase as a leader, read a letter of withdrawal. Though somewhat irregular, Stevens' request for a conference was granted.

Before the question of nomination was again taken up a communication from the New York North American Convention signed by George Law was read. He accepted the spirit of the invitation Morgan had sent them to unite as "friends of freedom." Littlejohn moved that it be submitted to a proper committee, for the Americans were true friends and were entitled to a candidate. Giddings objected, because the Republican Convention had similar proffers from bodies of foreign citizens. The motion for the acceptance of Law's communication was tabled.

Judge Spaulding then placed McLean's name again before the

convention, and an informal ballot was taken. Frémont had 359 votes; McLean, 170; Banks, 1; Sumner, 2; and Seward, 1. Seeing the inevitable, Webb then moved that an unanimous vote be cast for Frémont. A formal ballot was taken, and thirty-seven votes held to McLean, twenty-three of which were from Pennsylvania. Webb moved for an unanimous vote, the convention rose with a roar, and a big Frémont banner made its appearance on the platform. Allison of Pennsylvania voiced a protest at the loss of McLean; but the next day he presented resolutions from the Pennsylvania delegation accepting it. This was only a feint, however, for with the failure of McLean went something that was necessary to make Pennsylvania Republican. Some members of the delegation wept, and Philadelphia, in gloom, refused to turn out for a ratification meeting.[17] Although he supported the nominee Allison never forgot or forgave the loss of his candidate, and when the Pennsylvania election finally registered the results he felt it would convince, "Greeley, Weed, and Company, that they could not make a president, even if they could nominate one." [18]

Balloting for vice-president was intermingled with discussion over the acceptance of the overtures from New York. The name of Dayton of New Jersey was presented, and a speech he had delivered before the New Jersey Republican Convention was read. Many other names were put before the convention. Among them was that of Abraham Lincoln. Judge Palmer of Illinois made a speech in his favor, and it was concluded that he had the proper fighting qualities for a candidate. An informal ballot gave Dayton 253 votes; Banks 46; Lincoln, 110; Wilmot, 43; Sumner, 35; and ten others a small recognition. Elliot of Massachusetts withdrew Banks name on authority of a telegram and positive instructions. After a series of withdrawals, a final ballot was called. Dayton was nominated, though there was much feeling in the Pennsylvania delegation. The occasion for it arose from an old feud. Some of the anti-slavery men of the group would not accept Johnston, nor would Johnston's friends sustain Wilmot. They would not unite on a candidate; yet imbued with the conviction of Pennsylvania's importance in the campaign, insisted that one be taken from their statesmen. Dayton, who was from an adjoining state and who was respected by Pennsylvania's citizens, was nominated as the best choice. In this alone was he preferred over Lincoln.[19] Dayton had been a Whig, was a man with a substantial record, and Whigs and conservatives as a rule commented favorably on his nomination. Besides being the best possible selection in view of the Pennsylvania situation, he also stood a good show to carry New Jersey, likewise a doubtful state. He was born at Morristown, reared in Monmouth, and now lived at Trenton.

The brethren from New York were still outside awaiting an answer. Giddings yielded to the opinion of friends and the convention voted to hear them. A great many were in favor of accepting their cooperation; but Lovejoy held out. They might accept them as individuals but if they received them as an organized body, that "Demagogue Stephen A. Douglas would tickle the sense of the foreign-born citizens of Illinois, and Illinois would be lost." Since they had been invited as a party, it was rather a trying question, and was referred to the committee on platform. From this Wilmot soon reported that a conference with the New York committee had done nothing. It was decided to call upon all other parties to cooperate, and the matter of arranging terms was left in the hands of a committee of three. This was really advantageous to the Republican cause. They had put a ticket into the field without reference to the North Americans, and they had not cooperated with them as a party.

The last hours of the Convention were spent in speeches, and in getting expression from the Germans. Schneider and Grimm, newspaper men from Illinois, were well pleased. A letter was read from Remelin approving Frémont. Dorsheimer felt sure that Frémont could carry Pennsylvania.[20] The shouting died, the convention adjourned, and the Republicans went before the country with candidates and a platform. So also had the North Americans.

On June 20 the American Convention resumed its session at New York, and the Fillmore enthusiasts again collected outside the hall. The report of the liaison committee was now to be heard. It put in succinct form what had happened at Philadelphia. At first they had been scorned utterly until the Republicans had nominated for the presidency. Then, on reconsideration a committee had been chosen to confer with them. The conference lasted from nine o'clock until two in the morning. The vice-presidency alone remained for consideration. The Pennsylvania delegate from the Republicans had refused to support Johnston, and Banks was not satisfactory. Failing to agree, the settlement was then turned over to sub-committees, and the Republicans enjoined to make a satisfactory nomination and to pass no resolution against American principles. The American sub-committee named Johnston as satisfactory for candidate for vice-president. Regardless of this, the Republicans had nominated Dayton. The whole transaction was pronounced an indignity.

There was trouble at once in the convention. One extreme struck out in the direction of supporting Fillmore, and another led by Chauncy Schaffer moved towards the Republicans. Allen of Massachusetts acting on authority withdrew Banks' name, since he was for Frémont in case of any disagreement. He then moved for Frémont for President, and Johnston for vice-president. After much discussion, his motion was carried by acclamation. The *finesse* for the presidential candidate had worked, but the dual candidacy for vice-president forboded mischief. Dayton had accepted with a public speech and considerable ostentation, and could not well back down, had he been so inclined. Frémont accepted the nomination with a well-worded conciliatory letter, and promised further statement.[21] The Republicans made overtures through a public letter from Giddings declaring that their action contained no motive of hostility.[22] The vice-presidency embroglio remained open for settlement, and friends of the cause were greatly exercised.[23]

The first test of the tenacity of the Americans came in the Massachusetts State Council when it assembled at Springfield, July 1. There had been a constructive effort to get an endorsement of the Republican ticket. Allen made a trip to New York to interview Morgan, and sent a representative to Trenton to see Dayton.[24] The general agreement was that the Republicans stand firm, and Allen went to Springfield to see what he could do by way of securing an endorsement. At the same time Francis H. Ruggles, Secretary of the North American National Committee, directed a note to the Republican Chairman. Since they had withdrawn Banks, he wished a statement from the Republicans in regard to their withdrawing Dayton which he might put before the Council. He never received a reply.[25] The Council stood by the American ticket, and adopted resolution for Frémont and Johnston.[26]

This made the affair more serious than ever. The Republicans felt that they could not give way, and that the popularity of their candidate and cause had better be risked to sweep all before them regardless.[27] Connecticut and Rhode Island both followed Massachusetts in endorsing the American ticket, and in Connecticut Frémont's security was felt to be endangered.[28] The Americans still attempted to get an agreement of some kind, and finally on August 4 Chairman Ruggles tried without results to secure a convention on the basis of the withdrawal of both Johnston and Dayton.[29] Finally Johnston had an interview with Colonel Frémont, who, though he made no promises, agreed to remember Johnston's friends, and Johnston wrote a letter to Ruggles withdrawing his candidacy.[30] The letter was given to the public, and Frémont and Dayton stood alone.[31] New England was out of danger, the last Know-Nothing barrier was down; but Pennsylvania was still disgruntled.

The disappointment in Pennsylvania was keen. The loss of McLean was resented in the eastern part of the state. That of Johnston rankled with men of the western part. They had telegraphed the second session of the New York convention, urging firmness, and Thomas Williams, the Pennsylvania member of the Republican National Committee, felt it of sufficient importance to act upon.[32] Nothing, however, could be done for Pennsylvania save that the National Committee began to plan a thorough canvass there.

The Candidate

The Republican nomination, looked at as a solution to the problem of availability, was well made. The personality of of John C. Frémont was an important factor in the campaign of 1856. His subsequent career no doubt casts a reflection on the judgment of the politicians who chose him to lead in a crisis; but they were not greatly in error when they chose him as a candidate who would be most acceptable to all parties. Frémont, the Pathfinder of the Rockies, was a well-known figure in the fifties, and one that had not ceased to interest the American people.[33]

Frémont's father was a French refugee; his mother was of an

old Virginia family, kindred of the Washingtons.[34] The father possessed the wanderlust the son inherited. In his travels in the South-west he chanced to be in the Nashville Hotel when the brawl occurred between Jackson and the Bentons in which Jackson was shot. This was the first Jacksonian antecedent of his son, though the son was not yet born. In Savannah on January 21, 1813, John Charles Frémont Junior first saw the light of day. Five years later his father died, and as a widow's eldest son the path to the status of a self-made man lay open. In his childhood and early education his campaign biographers found many instances of precocity which gave promise of a remarkable future. He entered Charleston College in 1828 and was expelled in 1830 just before graduation. The degrees held from this institution, both A. B. and A. M., came later and were honorary.

After his college days were over, young Frémont worked as librarian, taught Mathematics, dabbled in politics, instructed in Mathematics on the sloop *Natchez*, and finally joined Captain G. W. Williams of the United States topographical engineers in some surveying enterprises. This made a point in his apprenticeship that was similar to that of Washington, and it gave him training in work where he was to gain fame. His next employment was with Nicollet in two expeditions into the region of the upper Mississippi from which he emerged with a commission as second lieutenant in the topographical engineers. While at Washington helping to reduce to usable form the data taken on these expeditions he began a romance with the daughter of Senator Benton. Benton looked with disfavor of the suit of the young soldier of fortune; but the daughter possessed her father's strenuous temper; Frémont did not habitually take no for an answer, and in the end the old senator was defeated. In spite of a period of absence while on a dangerous expedition in the Sioux country, and the refusal of Protestant ministers to perform the ceremony, Frémont and Jessie Benton were married by a Catholic priest on October 19, 1841. With this event Frémont rose to national fame. Benton was considered an authority in the art of killing, both in rules and in practice. He had "killed his man," and had credit for shooting General Jackson himself; so the young adventurer who dared to scorn his wrath for the hand of his accomplished daughter completely caught the public eye.

As a member of the family of Benton, one of the greatest of Western expansionists, Frémont was ready to become famous as a pathfinder. His first noted expedition came in the summer of 1842. Associated with this as well as with subsequent excursions was the German topographer Preuss and the far-famed Kit Carson. This expedition covered no unexplored territory; but it furnished data on parts of the Oregon Trail, especially the South Pass, and thereby identified itself with the public interest in the Oregon country. The spectacular things that Frémont did made the basis for the notoriety gained. He showed a hardihood equal to that of "Old Hickory" by eating dog at an Indian banquet. He braved dangers which the indomitable Kit Carson refused to face without making a will; and the ingenious mending of a barometer bore witness of resourcefulness and determination. Though beyond the scope of his orders, he penetrated the Wind River Range and placed the stars and stripes on what was supposed to be the highest peak of the Rockies. It was hard climbing, but Frémont finally reached the top where one step more would have precipitated him "into the snow-field a thousand feet below"—and all this while he was ill. Then, lest something be left undone, just as they started their homeward journey, he chiseled the Christian emblem on Rock Independence, a landmark of the far west.

A second expedition was the logical sequence of the first. This was much more extensive than its predecessor and added several rungs to the ladder of fame. It was unique in that it was conducted in violation of orders from Washington.[35] This time Frémont went as far west as Vancouver and then projected his explorations into the Great Basin. Finding this region uninhabitable he was compelled to seek relief in Mexican California by effecting a dangerous passage over the Sierras. He made his return to American soil by a more southern route and in August, 1844, reached St. Louis. A captain's commission instead of a court martial awaited him at Washington. His report on the expedition along with that of the first was printed by order of Congress in 1845.[36] It was an elaborate account, 693 pages in length; went through several printings, and was widely copied. The style of the report, the human touches that it contained added to the popularity which the subject itself commanded. This report made Frémont a famous man. The public both at home and abroad was interested in exploration. It was the age of Baron von Humboldt and Sir John Franklin. The American people seized upon it because of their hunger for knowledge of the great region beyond the Rockies. This, and the power which Frémont possessed to appeal to human interest gave the reports their hold on the public mind.[37] No one knew better how to achieve the spectacular and none could tell it better. His writings still speak for themselves. The press took account and continued doing so. *Niles Register*, never trivial, devoted quite half its columns during September, 1845, to this report. He was a popular hero, a true explorer, and an exemplar of the strenuous life. He was already in the public eye, and on the ground floor when California burst in like a meteor.

The third expedition, the one that took him opportunely to California, was even more extensive in design than the previous. It identified him with the interest in a Pacific railroad just then taking hold of the public, and he reported a suitable route directly across the Great Basin.[38] It added a full quota of spectacular episodes and reached a climax in making him "the conqueror of California." [39] He led the Bear Flag Revolt, conquered the North, then went to Monterey where Stockton received his work as part of the American operations although it had started as an independent filibustering enterprise. He received a commission as lieutenant colonel in a rifle regiment and had left Monterey on a recruiting expedition when the Californians, supposedly subdued, rose in revolt. The actual fighting done by Frémont in this second lap was small; but he made several grandstand plays. His pardon of Don Pico bespoke humanity. His "ride of one hundred" eclipsed a similar performance he had done while leading the Bears and put him in a class with Paul Revere. He appeared at the eleventh hour to capture the glory of the capitulation which ended the revolt and which should have fallen to either General Kearney or Commodore Stockton. Whatever the worth of his service, there is no question as to its renown. It was not necessary to prove that his work in the North was not a buccaneering enterprise to establish the fame of Frémont in the public mind. He had saved the Americans from butchery and the province from Mexican mis-rule. Whether or no he grabbed the country just in time to save it from the British matters much

less than the fact that there were many of his abettors ready
to say that he did and thousands of Americans ready to believe it true. In the second phase of the conquest he had
shone, but better still, he remained on the scene destined to
become a martyr.

Frémont became a factor in the contest between General
Kearney and Commodore Stockton for control of the new
province. When he had established his authority Kearney
brought Frémont back to "the states" in disgrace, arrested
him on reaching the frontier, and handed him over to a court
martial. Benton made it an occasion to attack the West-
Pointers on a charge of jealousy and to break with the administration.[40] There was popular response to the attack on
the regulars, and the time was to come when a breach with
the Polk administration had political value. The trial was
well reported. Niles started to publish it completely, but
found it too copious. To add to the dramatic effect, Frémont
was called to the bedside of his mother just before the verdict
was rendered. He failed to see her alive, but received from
the city of Charleston a sword and a declaration of public
sentiment in his approval. The court found him guilty of a
long list of charges. President Polk accepted the verdict,
except the charge of mutiny, and also accepted the recommendation of restraining the sentence. This made way for a
master stroke. Frémont refused to admit guilt by accepting
clemency. He resigned. The great explorer and conqueror of
California was now a martyr. Like Columbus of old he had
been brought back in chains from the field of his glory.

Though now in private life there was no occasion to drop
from sight. There was California still. He had laid the basis
to his claim to a great estate, the Mariposa, and could look
forward to a career in the new ElDorado. Then came the
gold rush when so many, interested in travel, would acquaint
themselves with the work of the great pathfinder. With the
acquisition of California the interest in a Pacific railroad became more intense and the work of the finder of mountain
passes and routes thereby gained in importance. Frémont
planned an expedition to explore the upper waters of the Del-
Norte for suitable passes for a central route. This expedition
proved tragic, but Frémont still rendered it spectacular. He finally reached California by way of the Gila and reported no

suitable passes in that region except on Mexican territory.[41] Although in California Frémont was still a railroad man. Benton featured his son-in-law's report in his first Pacific railroad bill.[42] Railroad conventions at St. Louis in the fall of 1849 and one at Philadelphia in the spring of 1850 gave due consideration to Frémont's work.[43] He was identified with the project of a Pacific railroad on a central route although Benton in his second bill introduced the following December went beyond Frémont's survey and followed the buffaloes as pathfinders.

While in California Frémont entered politics. In the Snyder Letter,[44] he announced his political creed and explained some things relative to his career. He pronounced himself a Democrat, endorsed a Pacific railroad on a central route, and explained his claim to Mariposa, his relation to Weller in regard to a commission to survey the Mexican boundary, and the purchase of some cattle made while officially connected with the California government. He was elected senator from the new state on the first ballot and reached his post of duty when only twenty-one days of the session were left. Illness prevented his return for the short session, and since he had drawn the short term in casting lots with his colleague Gwinn, his senatorial career came to an end with only seventeen working days. His vote on subjects touching the slavery question put him on record as opposing slavery but not strongly enough to please abolitionists. He introduced a number of bills that had a bearing on the development of the new state. Remarks from Senator Foote of Mississippi on one of these led to an affair of honor. Though amicably settled, and not an unique event, it had political value later. Foote was a southerner and the affair was construed as an attempt to brow-beat Frémont—part of a greater move that defeated Benton for re-election in Missouri, and Frémont himself in California. On his fight for re-election Frémont won his reputation as an anti-slavery champion. His credit lay in holding the balance of power between Whigs and Democrats whose candidates both favored a division of California, thus delaying election until there was sufficient dissenting sentiment to elect Weller of Ohio. It was from this event that the Robinson letter took its rise.[45]

Though out of public service, private affairs again took

Frémont to the East.　The title to his estate had met the law's delay.　Business affairs took him to England where Mrs. Frémont was presented at court and her husband arrested for debt contracted as governor of California.　On his return Frémont conducted a successful expedition through the Del-Norte passes,[46] and added more points of interest to his record as an explorer.

In the spring of 1855 Frémont was again in the East and took up his residence in New York.　One of his motives was the preparation of a complete account of his expeditions.[47] Here Koerner found him a year later employing a German scientist to classify his plants, and being talked of for the presidency.　Politics intervened and two years later the work was still incomplete.[48] The Mariposa title having had a long and tortuous career was again before the Supreme Court on a new application.[49] Palmer, Cook, and Company financed the suit for a half interest.　In February, 1856, the title was finally granted.[50] Coming at this time it made ground for accusing him as an associate in shady financial schemes.　It gave him the stigma of being a rich man.　He was a "rich man without a dollar," and his brilliant wife was now the "Duchess of Mariposa."

The career of the man politicians began to consider as "Mr. Availability," fitted him well for their purpose.　He was a popular hero, associated with romance and adventure.　He was young and active—just the man to lead in the new and militant cause.　Every detail of his background seemed to fit exactly.　In political antecedents, so far as he had any, he was of the school of Jackson.　The North Americans would accept him, in fact had supported him to the point of endangering his political usefulness.　In spite of this, he had a grip on the German vote.　He was an associate of Preuss, his topographer, and other German scientists.　He was called the American Humboldt, and that namesake had presented him a medal in behalf of the King of Prussia for progress in the sciences.　It must be remembered that many of the leading Germans, forty-eighters especially, were interested in science as well as liberal political ideas.　His power among them was found with little sounding.　In the convention that nominated him Dorsheimer spoke their sentiment in regard to him.　According to Koerner he rose and in his broken language said:

"I am a plain old German, no politician; but I can
tell this Assembly that I know my countrymen
and they will vote for no one more cheerfully
than for John C. Frémont who is well known to
them as the Pathfinder and the one who first
planted the Stars and Stripes on the face of
Mexican California." [51]

He seemed the proper man to assimilate the various factions
necessary to make a large party.

Greeley when driven to the open by the power of the boom
for McLean, gave a good summary of his many points.[52]
He preferred Frémont for the following reasons:—

"(1) He is a young man and the struggle for Free Kansas
must devolve mainly on those of our countrymen who
have never yet been actively or prominently engaged in
political contests. These will naturally be attached to and
sympathized with one of themselves. (2) Though young
and born poor, he has done more service, braved more
peril, and achieved more reputation than any man of his
years now living. That must be a very dark and squat log
cabin into which the fame of Colonel Frémont had not
penetrated ere this. (3) Though never a partisan Colonel
Frémont has hitherto ranked with the Democratic Party
which we consider desirable in our candidate. We want
the issue of Slavery Extension or Restriction presented as
fairly as possible. If the demagogues can persuade the
most stupid and besotted of their habitual devotees to
believe 'anti-Nebraskaism' a 'Whig trick,' they will make
some votes to which they have no more right. Let the
rival candidates both be Democrats—one for Free
Kansas and the other for the Border Ruffians—and the
case will be pretty clear. (4) Colonel Frémont's name is
the spontaneous suggestion and first choice of Francis
P. Blair, N. P. Banks, Jr., and John Wentworth, with the
great mass of old Jackson and VanBuren Democrats now
cooperating in the movement. We have great faith in the
sagacity of these men and their knowledge of the political
art of war. (5) Colonel Frémont was one of the men who
by prompt and determined action at the critical moment
made California a free state. For so doing the Chivalry
promptly ejected him from the state. He was among the

first to sympathize actively with Free Kansas in her trials and perils and is the choice of her leaders and her journals —leaders now fugitive or in prison, and journals now crushed under the feet of Border Ruffians. Their preference is, however, none the less significant. (6) He has done nothing to render himself justly abnoxious either to Americans or adopted citizens. (7) We believe he can carry California and make a good fight for Missouri and Delaware. We shall need all the votes we can get. (8) We have intimations that should he be nominated, he will be assailed by the journals in sympathy with the Border Ruffians, as incompetent, unqualified, underserving, etc. Candidates thus assailed have rarely failed of an election. And besides against a man whose life has been one of action and shining achievement and whose name is known and honored in every school district of the Union such arrows are sure to fall pointless or rebound into the faces of the bowmen."

The Platform

The platform was all that any Republican could desire. The principle of non-extension was kept secure in it, while the personality of the candidate was being used to attract a variety of less radical voters. The first two resolves were used for orientation. They placed the party on the ground which of necessity it took in defense against the accusation of being sectional and unconstitutional. "Freedom was national; slavery, sectional," and under the constitution Congress had no power to legalize it in any territory.

"*Resolved* That the maintenance of the principles promulgated in the Declaration of Independence and embodied in the federal constitution is essential to the preservation of our Republican institutions, and that the federal constitution, the rights of the states, and the union of the states should be preserved.

"*Resolved* That with our republican fathers we hold it to be a self-evident truth, that all men are endowed with the inalienable rights of life, liberty, and pursuit of happiness, and that the primary object and designs of our federal government were to secure these rights to all persons within its exclusive jurisdiction; that as our republican

fathers, when they had abolished slavery in all our
national territory, ordained that no person should be
deprived of life, liberty, or property without due process
of law, it becomes our duty to maintain this provision of
the constitution against all attempts to violate it for the
purpose of establishing slavery in any territory of the
United States, by positive legislation prohibiting its existence or extension therein; that we deny the authority of
Congress, of a territorial legislature, of any individual or
association of individuals to give legal existence to slavery in any territory of the United States while the present
constitution shall be maintained."

The next division was devoted to the principle of the squatter
sovereignty.

"*Resolved* That the Constitution confers upon Congress
sovereign power over the Territories of the United States,
for their government, and that in the exercise of this
power it is both the right and duty of Congress to prohibit
in the territories those twin relics of barbarism—polygamy and slavery."

There was an element of subtlety in this. Under the "squatter
sovereignty" theory, a state might name polygamy as one of
its local institutions, and a recent tilt the administration had
had with Brigham Young seemed to give emphasis to the point.

Next came a review of all the Kansas thunder to date.

"*Resolved* That while the constitution of the United
States was ordained and established by the people in order
to form a more perfect union, establish justice, insure
domestic tranquillity, provide for the common defence,
and secure the blessings of liberty, and contains ample
provision for the protection of life, liberty, the property
of every citizen, the dearest constitutional rights of the
people of Kansas have been fraudulently and violently
taken from them. Their territory has been invaded by
an armed force, spurious and pretended legislative, judicial and executive officers have been set over them by
whose usurped authority sustained by the military power
of the government, tyrannical and unconstitutional laws
have been enacted and enforced. The rights of the citizens to keep and bear arms have been infringed. Test

oaths of an extraordinary and entangling nature have been imposed as a condition of exercising the rights of suffrage and holding office; the right of an accused person to a speedy and public trial by an impartial jury has been denied; the right of the people to be secure in their persons, lives, papers and effects against unreasonable searches and seizures has been violated; they have been deprived of life, liberty and property without due process of law; the freedom of speech and the press has been abridged; the right to choose their representatives has been of no effect; murders, robberies, and arsons have been instigated and encouraged; and the offenders have been allowed to go unpunished;—that all these things have been done with knowledge, sanction, and procurement of the present administration; and that for this high crime against the constitution, the Union, and Humanity, we arraign the administration, the President, his advisers, agents, supporters, apologists, and accessories, either before or after the facts before the country and before the world, and that it is our fixed purpose to bring the actual perpetrators of these atrocious outrages, and their accomplices to a sure and condign punishment hereafter."

Then the remedy is prescribed—the grounds the Republicans had taken in Congress:

"*Resolved* That Kansas should be immediately admitted as a state of the Union, with her present free constitution, as at once the most effectual way of securing to her citizens the enjoyment of the rights and privileges to which they are entitled, and of ending the civil strife now raging in her territory."

The Ostend Manifesto which fell within the scope of the sectional fight was denounced in strong language.

"*Resolved* That the highwayman's plea, that "might makes right" embodied in the Ostend circular, was in every respect unworthy of American diplomacy, and would bring shame and dishonor upon any government or people that gave it their sanction."

The remainder of the platform was devoted to endorsement of things that could be incorporated with assurance of added votes.[53] The seventh article declared the Republicans in favor of a Pacific railroad.

"*Resolved* That a railroad to the Pacific ocean by the most
sensible and practicable route is imperatively demanded
by the interests of the whole country, and that the federal
government ought to render immediate and efficient aid
in its construction, and as an auxiliary thereto, the immediate construction of an emigrant route on the line of
the railroad."

Next they endorsed river and harbor improvement.

"*Resolved* That appropriations by Congress for the improvement of rivers and harbors of a national character,
required for the accommodation and security of our existing commerce, are authorized by the constitution and
justified by the obligation of government to protect lives
and property of its citizens."

In conclusion they invited cooperation and made a faint suggestion of disapproval of Know-Nothing principles.[54]

"*Resolved*   That we invite the affiliation and cooperation
of the men of all parties, however differing from us in
other respects, in support of the purposes herein declared;
and believing that the spirit of our institutions as well as
the constitution of our country guarantees liberty of conscience and equality of rights among citizens, we oppose
all legislation impairing their security."

It was a well-made platform.[55] It was strong enough to hold
the anti-Nebraska sentiment at the front.   It accepted the
gauge of battle for Kansas that the anti-Nebraska forces had
laid down in the House.   It included only declarations of economic principles that were safe vote getters in the North.   It
reached out for California in the Pacific railroad endorsement.
The Platform, the political value of the Kansas embroglio,
and last but not least, the personality of the nominee made
the composite upon which Republican strength was based.

1. A.P Stone to Chase, March 30.   Chase MSS L.C. An extensive
   report of the work of the committee.
2. Stone to Chase cited above.
3. Blair offered one that was generally unacceptable. It doubtlessly
   contained many elements of his New York address which he
   printed about two weeks later.
4. A.P.Stone to Chase, March 31. Chase MSS. L.C.
5. National Committee: E.D.Morgan,NY.(Chairman); F.P.Blair,Md.;
   John M. Niles, Ct.; DavidWilmot,Pa.;A.P.Stone,Ohio;Wm.M.Chase,
   R.I.;JohnZ.Goodrich,Mass.; Geo.Rye,Va.;Oliver R.Hollowell,Me.;

E.S.Leland,Ill.;Chas.Dickey,Mich.;Geo.G.Fogg,N. H.; A. J.Stevens, Ia.;A.Cole,Cal.;Lawrence Brainard,Vt.; Wm. Grose, Ind.; Wyman Spooner,Wis.;C.M.K.Paulison,N.J.;E. D. Williams, Del.; Jno. G, Fee, Ky.; James Redpath,Mo.; Lewis Clephane,D.C.

6. Statements of facts based on reports in *Springfield Republican, New York Tribune,* and *National Intelligencer.*
7. *Springfield Republican,* June 14. *New York Tribune,* June 14. Greeley was careful to call the Philadelphia convention the "Peoples' anti-Nebraska Convention."
8. James F. Baker to Chase, June 14. Chase MSS. L. C.
9. *National Intelligencer,* May 31.
10. The vote for Chase came from the Michigan delegation. The Ohio vote in part might have been swung for him, but dare not be without authorization. Baker to Chase, cited above.
11. Stockton later withdrew in favor of Fillmore and Raynor refused to accept.
12. Despite the nature of the call, it was regularly referred to as "Republican" or "Black Republican."
13. Douglas had been making much of the allied isms. See Chapter XI.
14. Errett in *Western Magazine of History,* vol. X, p. 263.
15. Errett in *Western Magazine of History,* vol. X, p. 262.
16. J.S.Pike to *New York Tribune,*June 16, in *First Blows,* pps. 344-345.
17. Allison to McLean, June 20. McLean MSS. L.C.
18. Allison to McLean, July 14, Oct. 17. McLean MSS. L.C.
19. *New York Tribune,* June 21.
20. Dorsheimer's speech in support of Frémont. See below.
21. Fremont's letter, June 20, text, Bigelow's *Life of Frémont,* pp. 459-460. His general letter of acceptance was dated July 8. See Chapter X.
22. Giddings Letter, *New York Tribune,* June 21.
23. An account of the settlement of this breach is found in Nichols, R.F., "Some Problems of the First Republican Presidential Campaign", *American Historical Review,* vol. XXVIII, pp. 492-496.
24. E.D.Morgan to Welles, June 28. Welles MSS. L.C. William L. Dayton to I. Washburn, July 12. I.Washburn MSS. L.C.
25. F.H.Ruggles to Executive Committee of Republican party, June 30. Welles MSS. L.C. E.D. Morgan to Welles, July 9. Welles MSS. L.C.
26 *Springfield Republican,* July 2.
27. E.D.Morgan to Welles, July 9. Welles MSS. L.C. Greeley to Thomas Williams, July 7., Konkle, *Life of Williams,* vol. I, p. 299.
28. F.D.Baldwin to Welles, July 11. Welles MSS. L.C. *New York Tribune,* July 26.
29. E.D. Morgan to Welles, Aug. 8, Wm.L.Dayton to E.D. Morgan (private), Aug.12. Welles MSS. L.C.
30. E. D. Morgan to Welles (private), Sept. 1. Welles MSS. L.C.
31. *New York Tribune,* Sept. 16.
32. Thomas Williams wrote to Greeley on the subject. Konkle, *Life of Williams,* vol. I, p.299. Greeley's reply, July 7, cited above.

33. R.L. Duffus, "Frémont and Jessie" in *American Mercury*, vol. V, pp. 289-297, gives an interesting interpretation. Bashford and Wagner, *John C. Frémont the Man Unafraid*, 1927, is a popular account of little historical value. Allen Nevins, *John C. Frémont, the West's Greatest Adventurer*, 2 vols., 1928, gives a satisfactory account of Frémont's life and work. R.D.Bartlett, *The Political Career of John C. Frémont*, a recent doctoral dissertation at Ohio University, covers Frémont's political career.
34. Bigelow,John, *Life and Public Services of John C. Frémont*, a campaign biography gives documentary proof of this in Chapter I.
35. Mrs. Frémont held the countermanding order at St.Louis until after the expedition had started.
36. Senate Document 174, 29th Congress.
37. Cleland, R.G.,in his recent *History of California* gives this interpretation to the popularity achieved by the report.
38. Letter in *Niles' Register*, May 16, 1846.
39. There is still disagreement as to the value of his service. H.H. Bancroft has presented him as a villain of no small mien, and as careful a scholar as Justin Smith reaches a similar conclusion. Cleland and Schafer present him as an ordinary man responding normally to the situation. Nevins does not accept the interpretation of Bancroft.
40. Quaife, M.M., *Polk's Diary*, entries Oct.26;Nov.22 and 23, 1847.
41. Report in Bigelow's *Life of Frémont*, pp.359-360; 365-376; and 394-407. Pamphlet, *Report of the National Railroad Convention at Philadelphia, 1850*.
42. *Globe*, Thirtieth Congress, 2d Session p. 472.
43. Cotterell,Robert,"National Railroad Convention in St.Louis", *Missouri Historical Review*, vol.XII; report in *Philadelphia Inquirer*, Oct.16,1849; Pamphlet, *Report of the Philadelphia Convention*.
44. Letter in Bigelow's *Life of Frémont*, pp. 389-396.
45. Robinson,Charles,*Kansas Conflict*, p. 63.
46. Letter to Benton, Feb. 9; Bigelow,*Life of Frémont*, pp.443-445.
47. Bigelow's *Life of Frémont, p. 446*.
48. His complete works were advertised in 1858 as on the press and to appear in two volumes. These never saw the light of day and evidently perished in the fires that destroyed so much Frémont material.
49. A review of this case dated Jan.6,1856, is found in the Crittenden Papers. Crittenden was one of his attorneys.
50. *New York Tribune*, Jan.28, Feb. 16, and 27.
51. Koerner,Gustav, *Memoirs*, vol. II, p.16.
52. *New York Tribune*, June 6.
53. See Chapter IV, "Accumulating Issues."
54. The word "prescriptive" before "legislation" was struck out of the original draft of the platform. It was this that caused the only wrangle on the adoption of Wilmot's report.
55. David Wilmot was chairman of the committee and the nature of the platform reflected his influence.

PART IV

THE VERDICT OF THE PEOPLE

CHAPTER X

THE APPEAL TO THE PEOPLE

The people must decide the issue. There were three candidates in the field, all sanguine of victory. Each claimed to be there by the spontaneous wish of the people. Each claimed, in his own way, to be a conserver and protector of the constitution and the Union. Each stood for principles widely divergent from the others upon which the people must pass judgment. The skill and the effectiveness with which the men and issues were presented would largely determine the response of the voting masses. In consequence, each party would do its best.

Presentation

Buchanan was the first of the prospective chief magistrates to be put before the public. After the Cincinnati Convention, "Wheatland near Lancaster" became the mecca of the Democracy. Politicians came for conference before going home. The Keystone Club returning with a large buck which had been presented them by the citizens of Cincinnati stopped at Wheatland, and to them Buchanan made his first utterance of public importance. Ordinarily, he would have made a longer speech under the circumstances, he said, but the platform made it unnecessary now. "Being the representative of the great Democratic Party, and not simply James Buchanan, I must square my conduct according to the platform and insert no new planks nor take any from it."[1] The official letter of acceptance bore the date of June 16.[2] He had not sought the honor bestowed; but since it came thus, he accepted it gladly. He would abide by the platform and not put it in a new light by answering interrogations. He stood with the party for civil and religious liberty. The slavery issue he predicted would soon reach a "finality." The principle of letting the people decide on it in the territories was "demonstrated by the fact that any territory when it became a state had the right to keep or abolish." The present agitation was leading to a dangerous questioning of our national stability abroad. It would be his duty to restore tranquillity. He agreed furthermore, that foreign affairs should be "conducted with wisdom and firmness."

The nomination was received with great demonstrations by the Democracy. Cannons were fired and bonfires lit throughout the country. In Washington a crowd went to the White House, called for the President, and listened to an endorsement speech.[3] Cass and Douglas were also called upon and both responded. Douglas could, on the basis of the platform, endorse Buchanan as a "squatter sovereignty man," and as such he recommended the support of all to help to stay the flood of isms.[4] June 10 Philadelphia which had refused the use of Independence Hall for a Buchanan reception in April, now held a meeting to give expression on the nominations of the "favorite son." Cass, Douglas, Cobb, and William B. Reed spoke.[5] The cannons fired, the crowd drank, and "old Buck" was officially started for the presidency.

The nomination of Frémont received its salvos at numerous endorsement meetings throughout the North. One held at the Tabernacle in New York City on the evening of June 25 was the official welcomer of the "Pathfinder." A large crowd gathered to "shriek for freedom." They listened to speeches by Robert Emmett, William A. Howard, who had just returned from service on the committee investigating in Kansas, Senator Trumbull, and others; they listened to letters from Seward, Preston King, and B. F. Butler.[6] Robert Emmett made the leading speech and directed his efforts to showing why Frémont was just a man. Somebody in the audience asked what he had ever done. Emmett retorted that he had not aided in the Repeal of the Compromise; and a friend in the audience added the Ostend Conference. Frémont had "conquered California with sixty-two men," explored the Rockies, stood with his fellows, married Jessie Benton, and trained in the political school of her father. After Emmett's speech resolutions were presented. They were five in number and the last accepted the issue "as between freedom and thraldom." When the gauntlet was thrown down to slavery, the assembly rose with a roar and sang their new rallying song to the tune of the Marsellaise.

"Behold the furious storm is rolling
Which border fiends, confederate rise.
The dogs of war, let loose, are howling
And lo, our infant cities blaze.
And shall we calmly view the ruin
While lawless force with giant stride
Spreads desolation far and wide
In guiltless blood his hands imbuing?
    Arise, arise, ye brave
    And let your war cry be
Free-speech, free-press, free-soil, free-men,
Frémont and victory."

This proved to be a typical performance. It came to be a usual thing at exciting points in a political meeting for the assemblage to rise spontaneously and sing this song.

A procession was formed to go and wait upon the nominee at his residence.[7] The throng of admirers reached their destination and clamored for a word from Frémont. They packed the street and the open spaces about the house. Some gained access and poured out upon the front balcony. They pressed upon a stone balustrade which was displaced to fall upon the heads of the crowd below. The report of no serious injury was given just as the hero appeared. His talk was short; for all his utterances were guarded. Then a shout rose for Jessie. She, too, appeared and the crowd was frantic. The cheering finally ceased, and the assemblage dispersed. It was a sample of the enthusiasm that could be invoked for the candidate, and it was a fair gauge of the ardor of the campaign.

In his letter of acceptance Frémont had as delicate a task as Buchanan. While "Old Buck" was troubled by being one thing to the North and another thing to the South, the "Pathfinder" was forced to use tact in being nothing to either the Americans or the foreign born. In his letter of acceptance he declared that were he elected, he would administer the government for the benefit of the whole nation.[8] He agreed heartily with the principles of the platform. He felt that the United States had no right to take the dominions of another nation simply because it wanted them, and that open, not secret diplomacy should characterize its foreign relations. As for slavery, the founders of the country did not countenance it. A few intriguing to extend it had "reversed the principles of Revolution," and had thereby brought on the trouble in Kansas. The solution he found in the admission of Kansas as a free state which the South would sanction to vindicate her good faith and correct her mistake of the repeal. It must be saved to free labor, to the immigrant, and as a safe-guard for the interest of non-slave holding whites. If elected, he would execute the laws of Congress in relation to the territories. This he felt would result in the establishment of free labor there. Another letter from Governor Robinson put him nearer the Kansas situation.[9] The free state governor expressed his desire for a president who would not persecute the citizens of an infant state because they did not agree with him. Beecher soon discovered the hand of Providence in the nomination, and that Frémont was like Washington, his illustrious proto-type.[10]

Fillmore had been nominated in February; but his presentation did not come until after that of the other candidates. It had been properly timed and occurred just as the second of the "sectional" parties took the field. Fillmore had not been in the country for a long while, and there was a general rumor that he might not accept the nomination unless there should be a manifest need for a Union saver when he returned. To make such a need apparent, and to emphasize it by an enthusiastic reception was part of a well-ordered program. While the National Convention was assembled at Philadelphia, the New York State Council was in session at Canandaigua. On receiving the report of the nominations, they adopted resolutions of thanks for the selection of the native of New York and also the statesman of the Jacksonian school, who, in the words of his predecessor, "by the powers of Sam," they would elect.[11] Then came the Law insurgency which was used in behalf of the Republicans and had sent a delegation to the North American convention at New York.[12] A purged state council met in New York City June 3 and repeated the endorsement of candidates. Following the recommendation in the national platform, the oath of secrecy was abolished, a pledge of honor substituted, and the order declared a political party. This action, coming from the New York council, was considered nationally significant.[13] The Democrats had just made their nominations, in a few days the Republicans would make theirs and Fillmore was on his way home. Quite fittingly the New York Council resolved that:

"the extreme partisan measures of the administration, Democracy on one side and the Black Republicans on the other, driving the country with a frenzied zeal into the most dangerous sectional strife, not only requires a prompt and signal rebuke, but abundantly proves that neither party can be trusted."

June 12 Fillmore's letter of acceptance was given to the world. It had been dated at Paris May 21, and was a response to the committee communication dated February 26.[14] His delay in answering had been due to his absence in Italy. When he left the White House he never dreamed of returning; but he accepted the candidacy as a duty without inquiring of its likelihood of success. He yielded to the wishes of his "fellow citizens in every part of the Union, who, like himself, were sincerely anxious to see the administration of our government restored to that original simplicity and purity which marked the first years of its existence, and if possible, to quiet that alarming sectional agitation, which, while it delights the monarchs of Europe, causes every true friend of our country to mourn." He spoke of his record—he was the compriser. It was only ten days from the time that the acceptance was published until the steamer *Atlantic* put into New York harbor with the "Union-saver" on board. The reception committee took charge.

It was never difficult for the Know-Nothings to secure a demonstrative gathering. The crowd and also Alderman Briggs greeted him. He was aroused in the small hours of the morning to address a "multitude." The next day a committee from Philadelphia—city of Independence and Union—waited on him, and the Whig General Committee of New York interviewed him. The following day he was carried off to Brooklyn for like ceremonies; but he gave no political utterance—it was all so sudden. Then he left for Albany by boat. While on board, he had time to collect his political thoughts, and at Albany began a series of speeches which finally terminated by one at Buffalo, his native city.

The political thunder Fillmore collected on the way to Albany and released in this speaking tour started the campaign. He opened on the Republicans:—

"We see a political party presenting candidates for the presidency and vice-presidency selected for the first time from the free states alone, with the avowed purpose of electing those candidates by suffrages of one part of the Union only to rule over the whole United States. Can it be possible that those who are engaged in such a measure can have seriously reflected on the consequences which must inevitably flow in case of success? (Cheers) Can they have the madness or the folly to believe that our southern brethren would submit to be governed by such a chief magistrate? (Cheers) Would he be required to follow the same rule prescribed by those who elected him in making his appointments? . . . . . Therefore, you must see that if this sectional party succeeds, it leads inevitably to the destruction of this beautiful Union, reared by our forefathers, consecrated by their blood, and bequeathed to us as a priceless heritage."

Fillmore had "opened the ball."

It was the beginning of our most dramatic campaign, making a reluctant exception for that of 1840. The mass of memoirs of the period bears witness to the impression it left on the minds of men. Julian, who had occasion to remember it with unkind feelings, leaves a typical statement:—

"The canvass has no parallel in the history of American politics. No such mass meetings had ever assembled. They were not only immense in numbers, but seemed to come together spontaneously and wholly independent of machinery. The processions, banners, and devices were admirable in all their appointments, and no political campaign has ever been inspired by such charming and soul-stirring music."[15]

All the political methods of the times were used to the utmost—mass meetings, stump oratory, processions with transparencies, riots, and whiskey. The records of the period, whatever their source, tell the same story. There were the meetings in the country school house and the country church. There were the open air assemblies when people came for miles to listen to the orators, and shout their approval or dissent. There were great processions—"thirty thousand people in line." Costume, pantomime, and pageantry emphasized the winning points of candidates and platforms. The outcry for freedom gave the Republicans an advantage in mottoes and designs for floats and transparencies, while the pioneer characteristics of their candidate had all the popular appeal that had been so forceful in the canvass for "Old Tip." The Path-finder's brilliant wife was also featured, and "give 'em Jessie" was shouted throughout the North. Democratic papers com-plained that even Jessie's baby was an active campaigner. In addition, hickory poles of tremendous length were raised by all the parties, for all claimed kinship to the spirit of Jackson. At the top the Democrats floated banners inscribed for Union and at the base was characteristically the wreathed antlers of a buck. The Republicans inscribed their banners for freedom. The general nature of the entire campaign was to appeal to the emotions—to enlist those who acted rather than those who thought.

In music and song making the nature of their attack and the personality of their candidate gave the Republicans an advantage. Everyone seemed to join in parodying old songs and in writing new. Papers and clubs offered prizes, and the best productions were collected into "Songsters." The rallying song to the tune of the Marseillaise mentioned above had a rival in the "Three F's."

> "Hark the long roll of battle has sounded
> The Standards of Freedom's unfurled;
> The chart which our forefathers founded,
> Our banner we've spread o'er the world.
> The Spirits of old hover o'er us
> We are baptized in Liberty's fount,
> Our watchword, our war cry, our chorus,
> Is Freedom, Freemen, and Frémont." [16]

Or,

> "All hail to Frémont swells the lofty acclaim
> Like winds from the mountain, like prairies aflame,
> Once more the pathfinder is forth on his hunt,
> Clear away for Free soil, for Free men, and Frémont." [17]

Jessie was also an object of poetic expression:

> "Thy "horn" poor old Buck it were vain to "exalt"
> You were born a mean dough-face, so 'tis not your fault.
> Not a "Buck" but a "Buckler" for freedom we want,
> So we turn to thy husband, dear Jessie Frémont.
> A poor "Broken ridge" is poor Buck's only stay
> From the *Free-Mont*-ain summits, our free banners play,
> And the garland of freedom henceforth we will twine
> With the olive, the laurel, and sweet *Jessie* mine." [18]

One of the most usable songs was "The White House Race" which had a catchy chorus and a numerous array of verses. It went:—

> "There's an old gray horse whose name is Buck
>   du da, du da,
> His dam was folly and his sire bad luck
>   du da, du da, day.
>   We're bound to work all night,
>   We're bound to work all day,
>   I'll bet my money on the mustang colt,
>   Will anybody bet on the gray?" [19]

The Americans and the Democrats sang songs and published "Songsters;" but the new "party of freedom" with its adventurer candidate had every advantage. It literally sang the North, particularly the young men of the North, into a new, radical, and sectional party.

War of Personalities

In none of our national campaigns has the personality of candidates played a larger role. The attempt on the part of the Republicans to harmonize so many factions through the personality of their leader, made him a special object of attack. Frémont had no political background, and his record in politics was not very usable as evidence against him. The lack of such a record, and the romance that surrounded him as an adventurer, magnified the effort expended on his personal character.

A second edition of "Old Hickory" presented in the person of a Rocky Mountain explorer was provocative of attack. The "mustang colt" which the Republicans pitted against the "old gray hoss" and regarded as emblematical of their new and vigorous party, became, in the hands of their enemies, the "wooly horse." The Democrats said that "Old Wooly" had not a drop of mustang blood but was a freak from Barnum's menagerie—a wooly coat and a rocky mountain origin were considered fitting. Instances of dash and adventure were held up to ridicule. The engaging eye and leonine hair and whiskers of the man who had eaten dog at a Cheyenne council, were set upon by caricaturists, and their owner converted into a very plausible savage. A special menu attributed to a banquet of his political friends was typical.

> Soup—mutton, sheep, lamb
> Roast—black mutton, sheep
> Boiled—sheep's head
> Fried—mutton chops (wool on), Frémont stew

> Side dishes—cold "horse meat" (From Barnum's
> wooly horse)
> Dessert—plucked goose, niggar hash[20]

Through all the bandinage with which his opponents discussed his qualifications ran the ironic assumption that such were not proper qualities for the chief magistrate of the nation.

When the adventurer was thrown into contrast with the mature statesmanship of Buchanan, and the current disrepute of "presidents on trial" invoked, he was at a disadvantage. He was a man without a public record—what evidence was there of his capacity?[21] His brief record in the Senate was raked for advantages, for either party, but with neutral results. His fight with Senator Foote in the lobby, and the affair of honor that followed were valuable politically. His enemies pronounced him a dualist.[22] This was used to counteract the capital the Republicans were making of the "slave driver's" violence, and Frémont was pronounced the inventor of the methods used by "Bully" Brooks.

Is He Honest? is he capable? was Jefferson's measure of an official.[23] Frémont's opponents not only insisted that his career showed lack of capacity, they endeavored to show that it disclosed lack of honesty. The settlement of the obligations contracted as governor of California had already been the object of an investigation, and a renewal would have political value. Early in August, Bigler of Pennsylvania introduced a resolution in the Senate to call upon the President for the accounts and to inquire why "if not arraigned upon the charges, it was not done."[24] The resolution passed after striking out the clause assuming his guilt. The President complied, and the Democrats had a document for the public.[25] They claimed to prove much but established little damaging evidence save that he was careless.[26] His recently established claim to the Mariposa estate furnished ground for still more accusation and insinuation. Being reported a rich man was not in his favor, and styling Jessie "dutchess of Mariposa" had its point. Palmer, Cook, and Company had financed the litigation for half interest in the estate, and connection with a large banking firm was rather unbecoming a popular candidate. It also happened that a California branch of the firm had misappropriated some funds it had in charge to pay the interest on state bonds. This, with the relation to Frémont, led to a widely circulated story that the funds had been used to buy the speakership and were now being used to buy the presidency.[27] G. W. Wright, a partner in the firm, spoiled a good story by publishing a statement to the effect that Frémont was not and never had been a member,[28] and Joseph Palmer supported Buchanan for the presidency.   There was also a tendency to accredit Frémont with support from railroad interests, but so great was the enthusiasm for a Pacific railroad that very little was made of the argument.   Larkin, an old associate wrote a letter to exonerate him in his financial affairs in California.[29] On all points specific evidence was given to clear his reputation, but the very necessity of giving evidence left a stigma upon it.

The most vexing charge Frémont had to face was that of being a Roman Catholic.   This started with his nomination and did not cease until after the campaign when he made a public denial over his signature.   His campaign managers out of deference to the Catholic vote which they hoped to secure would not let him make the denial during the canvass, although his friends disproved the charge and took special pains to give his religious history in all campaign biographies. They were making an offensive for Catholic votes[30] and so long as this continued, the opponents were enthusiastic in identifying Frémont with "popery" thereby to lose to him the American vote.   The Democrats were skeptical of the results of the attack on the ground that it might persuade Catholics to support him and still not alienate Know-Nothings who would vote for anything.[31] The Fillmore partisans led by Brooks of the *New York Express* launched the story and never let it die until the election returns were in.

Frémont's early supporters were confronted with the general impression that he was a Catholic;[32] but the fact that they took him up as a candidate who could secure the North Americans is proof of their satisfaction that he was not.   His name, antecedents, and some points in his career made plausible evidence that he was of Romanist faith.   His enemies used all these against him, added new ones, and wove the whole into a tale of conspiracy.   Seward, Weed, and Bishop Hughes had consummated a popish plot.[33] The evidences of his Catholicism were that his father was a Catholic from France, that he was educated in a Catholic school by Catholic charity, that he was married by a priest who did not join heretics, that his adopted daughter had attended a Catholic school, and that on his first western expedition he had inscribed a large cross on Rock Independence. It was a good background and all that was needed was something to keep the subject alive. Quotations were found to prove that Catholics claimed him before his nomination. Witnesses were found to testify to his attending mass in St. Louis, and Alderman Fulmer of New York, a man of reputed veracity, declared that he had seen him at mass in Washington. An instance was brought to light wherein he refused to accept an Episcopal prayer book which was presented to him while on a visit to West Point. Colonel Russell, an old associate in the West, was quoted as believing him a Catholic. There were witnesses that Father Olivetti of New York supported him as a fellow-believer, and Bishop Hughes and the Catholic press were said to claim their own. He had even been named by a priest.

As this series of accusations, ever refreshed by the animus of the Fillmore Americans, persisted throughout the campaign, the Republicans were forced to meet it. They proved that Frémont was an Episcopalian, that he was not educated by Catholic charity, and that his children were all baptized in the Episcopal faith.[34] That he was married by a priest could not be denied: circumstances explained it. An adopted daughter had gone to a Catholic school, but so had many Protestants, even Fillmore's daughter. But records and reason did not squelch the opposition, and the Republicans turned to personal testimony and direct proof. The *Cincinnati Gazette* of August 5 contained a letter from Lieutenant-Governor Henry J. Raymond of New York in which he vouched for the Protestant convictions of Frémont, cited his family records, and explained the undeniable charges. He took up Fulmer's story of having seen Frémont at mass in Washington and proved that at the alleged time he was in mid-Atlantic. Since Fulmer was a reliable man, it was concluded that he must have confused him with another Frémont, an army man who was a Catholic. The *Rochester American* accused Raymond of indefiniteness, and August 9 he wrote the editor a letter asserting that in personal conversation Frémont had declared himself to be Protestant. The testimony of Raymond failed to silence the stories and a group of divines thinking that their testimony might have more weight than that of Raymond, waited upon Frémont and published the result.[35] The Fulmer story was the most effective, for politicians hesitated to give it the lie directly. The *Ithaca Citizen* weakened it by too liberal use. It came out with the startling news that Chauncey Schaffer, prominent American bolter of New York and supporter of Frémont, had been convinced by Fulmer's story and had renounced his political allegiance. This gave Schaffer opportunity to deny it flatly and to write a long document on the subject.[36] He vented his fury on the *New York Express*, the source of the popish stories. Regardless of efforts, the story persisted.

The process of counter testimony was applied to every old as well as new piece of evidence of Frémont's Romanism. To meet the statement of Colonel Russell, an old associate, J. M. Welch replied to a letter from R. F. Livingstone.[37] He stated that during their twenty years of association, Frémont had been an Episcopalian and had really been religious. He also added a little touch to his anti-slavery record. A published letter of J. C. Gray refuted the West Point story,[38] and direct hits were made on other proofs of Frémont's Catholicism. Greeley at last attempted a master stroke by proving that there were two Frémonts.[39] But this was not an end to the matter. Just before the election the Democratic papers published a letter from the other Frémont declaring that he was not a Catholic. Greeley had admitted that one of the Frémonts was Romanist, and the Republican candidate alone refused to deny the charge.

Ridicule proved more effective than argument and documents. Receiving the stories as propaganda to make Frémont a Catholic against his will and in spite of the facts in the case for a political purpose, was a good antidote.[40] Beecher's Dog Noble story did much to counteract the influence of the *Express*.[41] That paper reminded him of a dog he once had—the dog Noble. One summer he took Noble out to Lenox with him, and here the intelligent animal busied himself chasing red squirrels. Once a squirrel hard pressed, ran through a hole in a stone fence and scaled a tree beyond. Noble had found what he wanted. "The enthusiasm of the dog at the hole can hardly be described. He filled it full of barking. He pawed and scratched as if undermining a bastion. Standing off at a little distance, he would peruse the hole with a gaze as intense and fixed as if he were trying magnetism on it. Then with tail extended and every hair as though electrified, he would rush at the hole with tremendous onslaught." The squirrel sitting on the tree overhead could not distract him. When tired of mischief and sleep, he would return to bark. Now the action of the *Express* called it all vividly to mind again. The Catholic business was a lie; but Brooks, like Noble, having opened at the empty hole, could not desist.

Ridicule, reason, and records made a good case for Frémont; but the fact that such a controversy existed, and that a case had to be made, injured him. His friends admitted that it was harmful to their cause. The assaults upon his career and character made an added impression. An attack upon his parentage and the legitimacy of his birth took the originality out of a similar charge later applied to Lincoln.[42] Although the charge was met,[43] it was needless effort; for it could do him little harm in the North. It was also necessary to nail a story that he was a slave-owner.[44] Such personalities as these were used ruthlessly, shamelessly, even though many were not backed by a grain of truth. Although convinced of this, one cannot read the accounts without feeling that there was something very doubtful about Frémont.

The attack on Buchanan was much less effective, in spite of the fact that many counts were against him. The Republicans were desirous of accepting him at first with expression of respect. They had reasons for wishing peace in this quarter, but there could be no peace. Could their own friends have been restrained in taking the offensive, the Democrats certainly would have forced it.

Buchanan's antecedents were soon attacked. In early life he had been a Federalist. In a Fourth of July speech in 1818 he was reputed to have said that had he a drop of democratic blood in his veins, he would open them and let it out. On another occasion he had said that ten cents a day was sufficient pay for mechanics. His relation to Jackson and Clay in the corrupt bargain affair of 1824 was used against him. Blair released some letters from Jackson concerning Buchanan's conduct in this affair with intent to damage him politically.[45] Blair also associated him with the questionable financing of the *Globe* when it was taken away from himself. Things that grew out of his position more than his personality were objects of attack. He was a "doughface," a double-faced Janus, and after the address to the Keystone Club, he was "platform James." He was presented as a political hack, and an old man whom the slave drivers could handle. His being a bachelor and the sinister carriage of his head were often objects of comment. A Republican song summed up his personal attributes thus:—

> "Oh, if I thought that I had got
> One drop of Democrat's blood
> My jugglar vein I'd rip in twain
> And spill the filthy flood.
>   Chorus of "loafers"
>
> I think those vile mechanics
> Get ten times too much pay.
> With a federal screw I'd put them through
> At just "ten cents a day."
>
> I don't believe in marriage
> A curse on wives and weans
> I love myself too much to share
> With them my pork and beans.
>
> No more I'm Jim Buchanan
> I sold myself down south
> Henceforth I'll do what my masters please
> And speak what they put in my mouth."

The Democrats met these assaults with documents and arguments as they came out. The sum total they rounded into a satisfactory defence.[46] The "low wage doctrine" was met by a widely published list of quotations from Buchanan's speeches. The age and tried statesmanship of their candidate was the main point in his nomination, and spurious attacks could not injure him greatly.

Fillmore enjoyed a fair degree of personal immunity. He, too, was a seasoned statesman. A discussion of whether or not he was a member of the Know-Nothing Order still caused him some embarrassment.[47] He was attacked in the North as a signer of the "kidnapping act," and as the running mate of "hundred nigger Donelson." In the South he was accused of abolitionist sentiment and finally published a letter to give assurances.[48] Several personal attacks were made, with special purpose during the course of the campaign; but bitterness was poured out on the party position and only indirectly on the man that led it.

Special Appeals

Within the conglomerate population of the country were various groups of people who might be reached by special appeals. The Catholic Irish were fit subjects for such procedure. They were regularly aligned with the Democratic party, and were not generally friendly to the idea of freedom for the black. Still, there were a number of points at which this vote might be approached, and the attempt seemed worth while to the Republicans.

Among the recent stirring events was the killing of Keating. This furnished a hold on the Irish vote and the Republicans made the incident count for as much as possible.[49] They gave wide circulation to a letter written by the dead man's brother in order to refute the story that Herbert had given a large wergild to the widow.[50] The killing of Keating was interpreted for the Irish as a proof of the slave driver's attitude towards the working man. The *American Celt,* a leading Irish newspaper, denounced Herbert, but the *Boston Pilot* took a more characteristic attitude by pronouncing him a Know-Nothing.[51] To reach the Irish as a laboring class, there were approaches other than that furnished by the death of Keating. The working class appeal made by the Republicans could be readily applied to them.

The nominal kinship between the agitation for freedom in Ireland and that in America, made another way of access to Irish support. The activity of Robert Emmett at Republican meetings was testimony to the public that the two enterprises were closely related. It also happened that just at this time Bishop Hughes gave a widely noticed lecture on Daniel O'Connell,[52] the late apostle of Irish liberty, and it happened equally opportunely that material to commit him on the slavery question was brought to light. In 1843, stimulated by free-soil activities in the Democratic party, the Repeal Association of Cincinnati had published a defence of slavery which brought out a condemnatory reply from O'Connell.[53] At the same time that O'Connell's views were given to his countrymen in America, a papal bull condemning slavery was also circulated among them. A widely circulated pamphlet, *The Pope's Bull and the Words of Daniel O'Connell,* was based on these two documents. The cover page showed the negro before His Holiness with his chains struck asunder. The contents made the case. The South American party, it argued, set up a religious distinction and could they prove Colonel Frémont a Catholic, would oppose him for that reason. The Democrats made no such distinction; but they were in favor of extending slavery into Kansas which was against "the teachings of the Catholic Church." A true Catholic could not oppress the poor and extend slavery to territory that justly belonged to the free-working man. The Pope's Bull against slavery was quoted as proof of the case. Thus, the Republican party which stood for "freedom in religion, in politics, in speech, and in labor" was their only recourse. Its candidate, Mr. Frémont, was a friend of labor and would build a Pacific railroad which would employ it and open the wealth of California to it. Were Daniel O'Connell living and an American citizen, he would vote for Frémont. In his appeal to Irishmen in America, he had said: "Once again and for the last time, *we call upon you to come out of the councils of the slave owners and at all events to free yourselves from participating in their guilt.* Irishmen! I call on you to join in crushing slavery, and in giving liberty to every man of every cast, creed, or color."

The German vote was nearer the Republicans, had been a consideration in the process of constructing the party, and was less an object of special appeal. A vigorous canvass was carried on among them. Men like Koerner, Schurz, Dorsheimer, and Remelin were active. Many of their leading papers were Republican and the young Henry Villard got his first training on a newly established German paper.[54]

Special appeals were made to groups and factions in various states; but this was part of the process of carrying the states and not of the campaign in its national aspects. It was an open field for all parties. An appeal to the Pennsylvania Dutch used by the Democrats might be included to indicate the extremes that were indulged in.[55] This peculiar rural population dwelling in the southeastern part of Pennsylvania was told that Republican success meant civil war and the results vividly pictured to them. Their state would become the seat of the war. Their barns and homes would be burned and their crops destroyed. Their men and boys would be away in the war, and their wives and daughters outraged "especially by niggers."

1. Pamphlet, *Address to Keystone Club.*
2. Moore, John Bassett, *Works of Buchanan,* vol.X, pp.81-85. Also Pamphlet.
3. Republican papers reported it a very weak endorsement.
4. Letter June 5 stated this and called all to aid in the fight on the isms. *National Intelligencer,* June 9.
5. *Pennsylvanian,* June 11.
6. Reported in the *New York Tribune,* June 26. Pamphlet, *Republican Grand Ratification Meeting at New York.*
7. Abbott, Lyman, in his *Reminiscences* gives a good account of this meeting, and also shows the impression it and others made on the mind of a young man.
8. Letter of acceptance, July 8. Text in Bigelow's *Life of Frémont,* pp.456-459.
9. Robinson to Frémont, June 3, in *New York Tribune,*June 18.
10. Article in *New York Independent* reprinted in pamphlet form.
11. Resolutions in pamphlet, *Fillmore at Home.*
12. See Chapter VII.
13. *Daily American Organ,* June 5, 6.
14. *National Intelligencer,* June 13. Pamphlet, *Fillmore at Home.*
15. Julian,G.W.,*Political Recollections,* p. 153-154.
16. *Republican Prize Songster.*
17. *Republican Campaign Songster;* published first in *National Era.*
18. *Ibid.*
19. This was found in practically every "Songster".
20. From *Madison Argus and Democrat* (w), July 20.
21. Pamphlet, *Frémont Only Seventeen Working Days in the Senate.*
22. Frémont was sensitive on this point and tried to get Bigelow to leave any account of his duals out of the biography.
23. Pamphlets both for and against Frémont bore this title.
24. Senate Journal, Second Session, 34th Congress, Aug. 9, Aug. 11.
25. *Ibid.* Aug. 18. Senate Ex. Document. No. 63.
26. Bigler to Buchanan, Aug.13., Buchanan MSS. P.H.S., explains it as a political move and not a questioning of Frémont's honesty.
27. Pamphlet, *John C. Frémont, Is He Honest, Is He Capable?*
28. *New York Tribune,* September 3.
29. Larkin's Letter, pamphlet.
30. See below, "Special Appeals".
31. J.Glancy Jones to Buchanan, June 27. Buchanan MSS. P.H.S.
32. Bailey to Chase, Feb. 21. Chase MSS. L.C.
33. Typical pamphlets were: *Frémont's Romanism Established,* and *To the Americans of Pennsylvania.*
34. Material in Bigelow's *Life of Frémont.* Pamphlets: *Colonel Frémont not a Catholic, Republican Pocket Pistol; Letters of Livingston,Schaffer,Raymond.*
35. *Evangelist,*Sept. 13. *New York Tribune* (w), Sept. 27.
36. Letter dated August 14 in Pamphlet cited above.
37. Letter dated August 30 in Pamphlet: *Letters of Livingston, Schaffer,Raymond.*
38. *New York Tribune,* Sept. 8, letter dated Sept. 6.

39. *New York Tribune*,Oct.11, gave notice that a supply of pamphlets settling the difficulty had been printed.
40. Beecher's *Must a Man be a Catholic against his Will*. The Raymond letter also took up these tactics.
41. Published in *New York Independent*, August 7, widely copied and circulated in pamphlet form.
42. Pamphlets: *John C. Frémont by One Who has Long Known Him; Letter of Geo.Wm.Gordon,John C.Frémont,His Character, Achievements, and Qualifications for the presidency*, by Charles E. Puckett.
43. Letter of Col. J. D. Stephenson, *New York Tribune* (w), Sept. 9.
44. *New York Tribune*,July 9, reply to Letter of J.D.Miller to Greeley,July 2.
45. The Lewis Letter and Buchanan's letter to the *Washington Telegraph*. See Chapter XI.
46. Pamphlet, *Short answers to Reckless Fabrications against the Democratic Candidate for President, James Buchanan*. Horton's *Life of James Buchanan*, the authorized campaign biography, meets these attacks.
47. See chapter VII, "The Americans".
48. Fillmore to J.W.M.Berrien, Sept. 29. *Fillmore Papers*, vol.II,pp. 354-357.
49. Pamphlet,*The Killing of Thomas Keating, Tribune* editorial, "A Democrat has a Right to Kill an Irishman".
50. Letter of P.M.Keating, June 24.
51. *Boston Pilot*, May 24.
52. *Boston Pilot*, June 21, clipped from *New York Herald*.
53. Letter of Daniel O'Connell on American Slavery, Dublin, Oct. 11,1834, and Letter of SalmonP.Chase, Cincinnati, Nov.30,1843. The O'Connell letter with Chase's answer was printed again in 1863 for political purposes.
54. Villard, Henry, *Memoirs*, vol. I, pp. 61-63.
55. Pamphlet, *Warrende Stimme eines alten peenselvani deutschen Bauren aus Beiten der Revolutshion und Washington*.

CHAPTER XI

THE FIGHT FOR THE AUGUST AND SEPTEMBER STATES

The state elections which preceded the general election in November were used as trials of strength in the individual states. Through this means the result would be pretty well ascertained before the fateful day in November. The spring elections in New England were the first installment of this preliminary.[1] In August, Kentucky, Arkansas, Texas, Missouri, and Iowa held elections. Early in September Vermont, North Carolina, Tennessee, and Maine followed. This group of states included the border slave states where Know-Nothingism was strong and the outcome would indicate how nearly the Democrats would have a solid South. Enough northern states would be on record to indicate how many more could be spared to the Republicans and still give Buchanan the victory.[2]

Further Events

The nominating conventions of early June had withdrawn attention momentarily from the series of events which were being used for political propaganda, and which had reached a dramatic climax late in May. With the candidates in the field the battle in Washington and in Kansas Territory was renewed. The assault on Sumner proved so useful politically as to class it as one of the most important events of our political history. It served as a final incentive to action and came at a very opportune time to round out Republican organization. Indignation meetings became a means to this end. An audience could be assembled to denounce the assault and once together it was used as a political gathering. Denouncing the assault as an attack on the freedom of speech and the privileges of a senator did not add to the sum of transgressions attributed to the South. Its value lay in interpreting it as an insult to the manhood of the North.

221

"What are you going to do about it?" was the inquiry made.[3]
Several New England States sent resolutions to Congress.[4]
Newspapers and public meetings made the most of it. Health
bulletins were issued and many conjectures about Sumner's
recovery and the effect on his mind, indulged in. His seat
in the Senate was left vacant as a witness of his martyrdom.
An attempt at inquiry into the affair by the Senate resulted in
the conclusion that the Senate had no power to discipline
Brooks. An uproar was made at this—the Senate had no
power to punish a violation of its privileges when the senator
struck was "for freedom" and his assailant a member of "the
chivalry of the lash." The House appointed a committee
which took a different view of the affair.[5] Douglas, Toombs,
and Slidell who chanced to be near the affray, were questioned.
Slidell said he had heard without any particular emotion that
Sumner was being beaten. Douglas said that he went immediately, but withdrew fearing that his "motives might be
misunderstood;" Toombs stated that when he heard what was
happening he "approved it." These responses furnished press
material for many days and Douglas finally made a defence
that was given to the public.[6] A resolution for the expulsion
of Brooks failed for lack of the necessary two-thirds majority.
A resolution to censure him carried. A resolution to censure
Keitt of South Carolina and Edmundson of Virginia as accomplices carried in the case of Keitt but failed in that of
Edmundson. Brooks and Keitt both resigned and their seats
were placed at the disposal of their constituencies.[7]

There were other and exciting ramifications of the affair.
Wade of Ohio blustered and wanted to fight. Wilson, Sumner's
colleague, denounced the assault, and was challenged by its
author. He refused to fight on the ground of barbarity and
illegality; but asserted his belief in the doctrine of self-defense.
This appeal to the principles of self-defence ushered in an
episode of arming. If "Ruffianism" had come to Washington,
it must be met, was the assumption. A few days later when
Wilson went to the railroad station on his way to address a
political meeting in New Jersey, he was escorted by a body-
guard of friends whose belts bulged with pistols and bowie-
knives.[8] Burlingame took the affair under personal charge in
the House, produced a good campaign document,[9] and was
likewise challengened. There was quite a bit of parleying

about this affair of honor; but finally, Burlingame named rifles as weapons and the Clifton House, Canada, as the place of meeting. He left in the night to avoid arrest, but Brooks tarried, and gave out that he feared crossing the enemy's country to reach Canada. There was political subtlety in the circumstances. Choosing Canada was pronounced as necessary to prevent the "scions of chivalry" from hounding and unnerving him as they had done Cilley some years before.[10] Burlingame's willingness to fight seemed to compromise the position that only "slave driving" society retained the barbarous relic, and his reputed expertness with the rifle gave concern to many. A duel might be fought, he might kill Brooks; and then the value of the whole affray would perish. As it stood, a letter from James Watson Webb, using the assault as a climax of a series of similar violences that had occurred, made another useful document.[11]

The response of the South added to the political usefulness of the affair at the North. To the conservative view of Robert Winthrop, the statement of Toombs and the support of some papers, did not mean the whole South;[12] but the Republican press took a different view. The reelection of Brooks by overwhelming numbers, his speeches, and the presentation of new canes inscribed "hit him again" made the finest kind of electioneering material for the Republicans.

Legislation for Kansas which had been placed in abeyance in the House until after the nominating convention, was soon doing its share in politics again. The admission bill was taken up June 25 and debated until July 2. That day the select committee brought in its report. The findings were all that could be desired. It made a sort of culmination to all the Republicans had been arguing for and it made the leading political document of the campaign.[14] The minority report did not come until a few days later, in fact not until Oliver saw the political use made of the finding of the majority. July 3 came the notice that the Senate had passed an enabling act for Kansas,[15] and forthwith the House passed its admission bill. The plank in the Republican platform to admit Kansas as a free state had been under-written so far as the action of Congress could do it.

As soon as the Cincinnati Convention was over, the Senate had begun to fortify the Democratic position on the continued

working of squatter sovereignty.   June 10 Trumbull introduced a bill[16] to erase all the territorial machinery in Kansas,
and to attach it to Nebraska.   Douglas had pointed out peaceful Nebraska as an example of applied squatter sovereignty
when no attempt had been made to abolitionize, and the resolution to attach Kansas to it was designed to embarrass him.
Clayton and Geyer both offered bills on Kansas.[17] All these
were recommitted along with the original bill and Seward's
and Toomb's amendments.   June 30 Douglas' committee reported.[18] July 2 the new bill was reported and after attempts
to block it on the part of the Republicans, was passed.   This
was the Toombs bill, following the lines of his amendment,
and was the official position of the Democrats on Kansas for
the campaign.   According to its provisions, five commissioners
were to take a census of Kansas and register the legal voters.
In November, delegates were to be elected to a constitutional
convention.   All persons who were residents July 4 would be
qualified to vote.   December 1 the Convention should meet
and draw up a constitution.   There was to be no interference
from any quarter.   The citizens should decide on their local
institutions, when the constitution was drafted, and that would
be done soon.

The Toombs Bill secured several advantages for the Democrats.   It promised peace to Kansas and a continued application of the principle of squatter sovereignty which at the
North might easily mean the making of a free state.   The
Republican members of the Senate attacked the bill and the
"Buchaniers" founded a strong argument on their refusal to
accept the proposed measure for Kansas.   They argued that
the Republicans did not want peace; that they had stirred up
the Kansas embroglio for political purposes and wanted it
continued.[19] As a counter stroke the editor of the *New York
Evening Post* directed an inquiry to Roberts of Kansas, asking
his opinion of the Toombs Bill, both as a Democrat and as a
man on the ground.   Roberts' reply opposed it for many
reasons.[20] The bill acknowledged the "Bogus Legislature" and
at the same time enacted election laws for the territory which
were against democratic principles.   It refused to submit the
proposed constitution to the people for ratification, and at the
same time put the delegates in control of the press and the
commissioners.   This, as a matter of course, was expedient

for the Democrats; for to submit the constitution to the people
would make it necessary for them to retain an armed force
in Kansas all winter. They had a further advantage in enum-
erating the voters at a time when most of the *bona fide* citizens
who were now driven from home would still be away. As a
Democrat he wished for no meddling on the part of Congress,
but rather to leave their affairs to the majority of the "people."
"Congress cannot *give us back our dead*, but it can wipe out a
legislative government established by fraud and violence, and
institute another that shall reflect the will of the people."

The Democrats rested their case on the Toombs Bill; the
Republicans could not handily do so on their admission bill.
There was war in Kansas and they were accused of instigating
it. Pacification measures were thus in order. July 29 the
House acted. A bill that had lain on the table since the
early part of the session was recalled by Dunn of Indiana,
completely amended, and passed. The Dunn Bill provided
for the complete reorganization of Kansas. The territory included in Kansas and Nebraska was to be erected into one
territory. This might later be divided or parts attached to
any state not legalizing slavery. The details of organization
were worked out in a way to countermand the points in the
existing organization on which Republicans made war. The
Kansas-Nebraska Bill was to be repealed and the compromise
line restored. Slaves and children born of slave mothers were
not to be emancipated if they left the territory before January 1, 1858, and the fugitive slave law was to be enforced.
All cases for treason and violation of laws pending in the
Kansas court were to be suspended. The appointive officers
were to be temporarily retained. There were necessarily
many vulnerable points in a new organic law for a territory
which already had organization and population.

The passing of this bill by those who had failed to concur
in the Toombs Bill, re-opened attack.[21] The Republicans had
legalized slavery until 1858, and endorsed the fugitive slave
law which some of them declared unconstitutional. They had
retained in operation laws they were sending men and money
to combat—"all this that violence might continue and blood
might flow there; that they might make political capital out
of outrage and blood." The Senate, refusing to concur in the
Dunn Bill, gave the question a final review in a report from

the Committee on Territories.[22] In the majority report the boundaries defined in the Dunn Bill were attacked on technical points. The new pacification proposed by the Dunn Bill was described as insuring violence by stopping action under the only criminal laws in the territory, and by leaving it indefinitely in a territorial form. Furthermore, it gave no safeguards that there would not be further interference from the outside. The Democrats rested their case on their original position: to restore peace to Kansas by protecting the ballot box, and to bring it quickly to state-hood through the unimpeded application of squatter sovereignty.

The minority report stated the case for the Republicans. The ills of Kansas were reviewed to date and the New England Emigrant Aid Society again exonerated. To meet the Democrats' promise of peace and progress through a protected ballot box, it argued that progress depended on the condition of the territory, and that this one was in no condition to advance. The House, the report maintained, had proved the Kansas Legislation a fraud, and refused to seat Whitfield,[23] but the President had taken no action. The Senate declared the enactments in Kansas binding until repealed, but had taken no steps to repeal; for the Toombs Bill left most of the old order in force and slavery established. It could not mean a free Kansas; for the Senate had turned down the admission bill, and would leave it to a vote of such free-state people as would be left in the territory by November. The report concluded that squatter sovereignty had been a failure:—"The experiment may proceed, the people of Kansas may be *dragooned* into submission, and power may for a time continue that vassalage, which usurpation produced, but the end is not yet. Can it be expected that a slave-holding state made such by such activities can ever be admitted into this Union by any votes given by the representatives of a free people." The Republicans looked to the election for the final solution. Unless Kansas were admitted free, or the Compromise restored, or some like measure taken, the people would elect a President who would stop the execution of laws which "usurpation had produced."

Passing an appropriation for the army which was to "dragoon the people of Kansas into submission" was the last engagement between the Republican House and the Demo-

cratic Senate. August 18 had been set for the day of adjournment, and the close of that day found the two houses still far
apart. President Pierce issued a proclamation for an extra
session which convened the following day. August 30, the
final day of this session, found them still failing to concur,
and the Republicans insisting on a condition "that no part of
the military force of the United States for the support of
which appropriations are made by this act, shall be used in
the aid of the enforcement of any enactment heretofore passed
by the bodies claiming to be the Territorial Legislature of
Kansas." The crisis was at hand. Government arsenals were
closing, a war scare was abroad, and people began to take
alarm. Pressure was put on congressmen to cease blocking the
appropriation lest they ruin the cause. The contention that
the Republicans would ruin the country was already too strong,
and the House receded from its position.

In the long series of maneuvers in which the two houses had
indulged the Democrats secured a technical advantage both on
the solution of the Kansas situation and in forcing the appropriation bill. The influence of the work of the Republicans on
the masses of the North had certainly not been a failure.
Furthermore, any advantage lost in the parliamentary contest
might be offset by what was happening in Kansas.

The dramatic climax of late May in Kansas which produced
the "sack of Lawrence," did not exhaust the political usefulness of the trouble in the territory. The state of civil war
which immediately ensued was a real embarrassment to the
Democratic party which endorsed "squatter sovereignty" and
recommended its continued application. Another circumstance
that added to the reaction at the North was the appearance
among the "law and order" men of "Buford's cavalry" and
other distinct units from the southern states. Regardless of
what the motives of these groups may have been, the report
was circulated that they were there to claim Kansas for slavery, and that the South Carolina unit displayed its banner
inscribed "Southern rights" over the spot where the free-state
press had stood. Throughout the North the process of organizing Kansas aid societies, raising funds for the Kansas settlers,
and of sending men and arms to the territory increased
apace.

Three days after the Lawrence crisis, John Brown began a

series of murders in the neighborhood of Potawatomie. Captain Pate at the head of a retaliating band was captured at Black Jack on June 2, and two days later an attack was made on Franklin, a pro-slavery stronghold. Governor Shannon telegraphed to Colonel Sumner for troops to prevent the wiping out of the inhabitants of the Wakarusa Valley.[24] On June 7 Osawatomie, the home of John Brown, was sacked. This was sufficient to offset the fact that Brown and radicals had actually started the civil war, and "Latest from Kansas" remained a reeking column in northern papers. It was necessary to accept the situation and avoid damage from the fact that the free-state men had started the civil war.[25] It was contrary to the policy of the leading promoters of the Topeka movement and was not uniformly approved elsewhere. The Osawatomie affair and the presence of southern units proved a saving grace—it was necessary to fight to drive out the warring units sent by the South.

Shannon's action of June 4 brought results, and June 8 he reported quiet restored.[26] The brief lull in hostilities which ensued served to throw into relief another event of political significance. The Topeka Legislature had named July 4 as the day when it would re-convene, and much interest was evinced in the prospective meeting. The "treason prisoners" gave it their blessing.[27] Official action was taken to prevent it, and troops under Colonel Sumner were on the scene at Topeka on July 4. The acting Governor issued a proclamation for the dispersion of the legislature.[28] This was endorsed by Sumner who cited the President's proclamation of February 11 as a mandate for it. He appeared before the assembly in company with Marshal Donelson and ordered a dissolution. He was reported as stating that it was the most painful duty of his service. Since the legislature maintained that the right to assemble was a constitutional principle, it made a show of resistance. The speaker asked if the dispersion was done at the point of the bayonet. Being allowed to assume it, the legislature disbanded and put before the people a case of constitutional right violated by federal authority. To add to the effect of this, late in July Sumner was superseded by General Persifer Smith. This was interpreted as a move to relieve the man who protected the citizens and put in his stead one who would "dragoon" slavery into Kansas. This action of the military forces in Kansas furnished a good background for the army appropriation fight in Congress.

The product of the Kansas situation was unceasing. Civil war was renewed. The Free-state men set about driving their opponents out of the vicinity of Topeka, and in August carried out a series of captures of pro-slavery strongholds.[29] Also in August Lane appeared with an army, made a dash into the territory, liberated the "treason prisoners," and then withdrew towards the Nebraska border. Shannon's last official act was to effect a treaty and exchange of prisoners between the two parties. August 18 he resigned; he had had enough of Kansas.

The coming of Woodson to power again was sure to aggravate the situation. August 21 he issued orders to his militia generals to expel armed forces from other states, working in collusion with armed rebels who were resident.[30] On August 25 another proclamation called on law-abiding citizens for support.[31] This meant an invitation to Missouri Borderers. Woodson also issued a requisition on Colonel Cooke for troops to act as a marshal's posse, and ordered them to destroy Lawrence; but this Cooke declined to do and referred the request to General Smith.[32] These actions laid the basis for what is known as the "Invasion of the twenty-seven hundred." They again sacked Osawatomie and Frederick Brown, son of John Brown, was killed. The Free-State men were not remiss in retaliatory measures. Lane returned from the north with three hundred and fifty men, made several feints, and narrowly missed a clash with the troops at LeCompton under Colonel Cooke over the question of the surrender of prisoners. The free-states rallied to the number of two thousand to contest the territory with the "invaders." Kansas was an armed camp.

Response in the North

At the same time political capital was being made in Washington and in Kansas, battle was waged for the August and September states. The reaction in the South to the position taken by the Democrats in the North came nearly being serious. Radicals took umbrage at Buchanan's letter of acceptance. "His letter acknowledging that the *people* of a territory may pass what *laws they please* makes *much* mur-

muring here among many" wrote Henry Wise from Virginia.[33] "If there is a doubt excited in Virginia about squatter sovereignty he cannot carry this state. I will do all I can to correct the mischief from distrust; but it is *actively reacting here against us.*" The advice that had come to Buchanan was to commit himself to nothing, and that the Pennsylvania press should be checked.[34] A good many questionnaires were sent him on the subject, and in spite of his own tendency to give assurances, his friends kept him silent. Gradually the South quieted and the Democrats were free to turn to the North and to prevent the Republicans driving home their proposition that the election of Frémont meant freedom in Kansas, that of Buchanan, slavery. To meet the insistence of the Republicans that their program meant one thing in the North and another thing in the South, the Democrats attacked the new party as a group of derelict politicians, "sunk in the cess-pool of political ambition," and using sectional strife for personal ends.

Several minor adjustments had also to be made. The support of Benton, valuable at the North but dangerous at the South, was left to work itself out in the Missouri elections. There was the further problem of inducing the administration to pacify Kansas and thereby show that the Democratic program meant peace and progress. This involved approaching the chief magistrate in behalf of closer cooperation, and was in itself a problem. The administration was pronounced a two-edged sword. The best method of canvassing for Buchanan in the Northwest was to attack Pierce and his work, and resorting to it tended to counteract all efforts made to get the whole-hearted support of the President and the office-holders. There was also a problem of creating or subsidizing a larger press support in the North.

Fillmore's speaking tour which had opened the campaign and had struck the Republicans in the most vulnerable point, was viewed with delight by the Democracy. It aided them in launching in the North. July 4 was a gala day for all parties; for all were avowed savers of Union and liberty; and the country was full of political meetings. The second official gathering of the Democracy was held at Philadelphia. It was a large and noisy meeting, quite the thing to be expected in Buchanan's own state and on so friendly a terrain. Ex-

Governor Seymour of New York had refused an invitation to speak at Philadelphia in order to attack the enemy in his own camp. July 4 he delivered his great campaign speech at Springfield, Massachusetts, which probably did more to define the grounds on which the Democrats won the North than any other single effort.

Seymour was of the Soft Democracy of his state. The acceptance of the Hards at Cincinnati on equal terms, and the nomination of Buchanan had been a defeat for his faction. Regardless of this, the exigencies of the campaign threw Seymour, representative of the "free-soil end" of Democracy into leadership.[35] At Springfield he read the riot act to New England, and defined the position of the Democrats. His audience was small but he honored it:

"I honor those who have stood up manfully in this
state against the overwhelming number of the
adherents of the Alien and Sedition laws; against
those who preached and practiced treason in the
late war with Great Britain; against those who
prayed that our armies in Mexico might be met
with bloody hands and hospitable graves; against
those who have persecuted defenseless women for
their religious faith; against those whose chief
efforts at this time is to teach one-half of our
common country to hate the other." [36]

His chief points were the respect for the rights of states; the opposition to coercive temperance, and to Know-Nothingism on the basis that it was non-American in principle. He touched the all-absorbing Kansas issue under the topic, *Political Meddling with the Rights of Self-Government in States and Territories.* The consequence of *Political Meddling,* he said, was now seen in the form of a party engaged in inflaming one section against the other. Immigration had made the North strong; but the South had made no move to stop it.[37] The North had now the political control and sought to use it in a way the South ought to resist. There were two extremes, he pointed out, one insisting that Congress should prohibit slavery in the territories, and the other that it should protect it. The proper ground was to let the territories decide for themselves. States had abolished slavery; but now some did not want territories to have the same right. Too much attention

had been paid to Kansas. Neither extreme had let it alone:—
"Neither Missouri nor Massachusetts have learned the prag-
matic doctrine of the Democratic party." The Republicans,
he contended forgave all past offences, endorsed the coercive
liquor law, appealed to passion, and associated with abolitionists in order to interfere with sovereign states. There could be
no peace until press and political agitation ceased. Seymour's
position was in line with "squatter sovereignty" according to
the Toombs Bill, and in line with Buchanan for free Kansas.
Four days later Toombs gave the public his letter to a Virginia
friend. In this he declared that the British situation was not
the real danger but rather the victory of Frémont. The Republicans intended to conquer the South but they could not
own it until they did so.[38]

The Republican response was immediate. At the same time
Seymour was pleading the case of the Democrats at Springfield, the Republicans were holding a meeting in another part
of the town.[39] A typical concourse of speakers, including some
from Kansas, was present. In their resolutions they denounced
Fillmore's speech, and in their stand for the immediate admission of Kansas, they maintained the oft-asserted thesis that
Buchanan meant slavery in Kansas. The Maine Republican
convention which met July 8 was emphatic. In their resolutions, they conceded the South the right to speak and act as
they wished relative to the territories, and claimed the same
right themselves. Any attempt to stigmatize them or their
representatives for it would be "repelled as an unwarrantable
act of aggression."[40] The letters of acceptance of the candidates, just now to be given to the country, aided the Republicans in counteracting the charges of sectionalism and of endangering the Union.[41] Frémont's letter was dated July 8 and
contained the following promise:—

> "If I am elected to the high office to which your
> partiality has nominated me, I will endeavor to
> administer the government according to the true
> spirit of the constitution as it was understood
> by the great men who framed and adopted it,
> and in such a way as to preserve both liberty
> and union."

Dayton's letter a day earlier made a more elaborate statement:—

"I very much deprecate all sectional issues. I have not been in the past nor shall I be in the future instrumental in fostering such issues. But the repeal of the Missouri Compromise, and as a consequence the extension of slavery are no issues raised by us. They are issues forced upon us and we act but in self-defence when we repeal them. That section of the country which presents these issue is responsible for them, and it is this sectionalism which has subverted past compromises and now seeks to force slavery into Kansas."

Along with these special declarations the Republicans launched a general offensive on Fillmore whose performances had called attention enough to make it seem as if there were a boom for him. They nailed him as a "dough-face." It was known, they argued, that he could not carry a single state at the South. He had been put in the field to divide the North, while the Democracy was used to grab Kansas. They construed his portrayal of the results of Republican success as a threat of secession made in the name of the South. The Democrats who used the same tactics were alike classified as sectionalists who brandished the threat of secession as a political weapon. Weston, the champion pamphleteer of the Republicans, spoke out on the question of sectionalism.[42] Greeley replied to the Toombs Letter that Frémont, like all southern presidents, would be ready for the emergency.[43] The Republicans were forced back to their original thesis that slavery was sectional, freedom, national. They maintained that they were the only party which did not threaten a dissolution of the Union, in the event of failure. They argued further that when their young Jackson had control of the government, there would be no secession.

In August and early September the elections in three northern states indicated how much Republican chances of "sweeping the North" had been injured by the campaign tactics of their opponents. Iowa was the first of these northern states. The Republicans considered it of primary importance to hold it.[44] One of the two seats in Congress was still occupied by Hall, a Democrat, and his return was the crux of the contest. The election gave the Republicans both seats and a large

majority in the legislature.[45] Vermont was carried in the same
manner. All of the opposition had acted together as Republicans in convention at White River Junction, July 2. Only two
tickets were put into the field, and the Republicans literally
swept the state.[46] The only real gain in these two elections
was the influence they had on the general morale and the
securing of a tighter grip on the states—the Republicans already had them.

The situation in Maine was different. Here the Whig-
Democratic combination had defeated the Republicans the
year before. The Whigs of Maine were still independently
inclined—still "Webster Whigs"—and held a considerable
bloc of votes. The opposing forces were pretty evenly bal-
anced, and there was an opportunity for a spirited fight.
June 12 Senator Hamlin made a speech in the Senate withdrawing his allegiance from the Democratic party. This put
him forward for the governorship or for higher distinction.[47]
To add to this great gain, the Republicans had been pouring
documents into the state through the machinery they had
created for that purpose. J. L. Stevens, Chairman of the
State Committee, was sending lists of names to Israel
Washburn in Washington who responded with the desired
pamphlets.[48] A series of ratification meetings had been held
to generate enthusiasm. Prospects were bright for the Republicans when the campaign opened. July 1 the Democrats
re-nominated Wells. The Whigs nominated George E. Patton
for governor and endorsed part of the Democratic ticket.
July 8 the Republicans met, nominated Hamlin for governor
and adopted the spirited resolution occasioned by the recent
performances of Fillmore and Seymour.

The Republicans of Maine immediately caught up the idea
of the strategic importance of an early victory in a doubtful
state. Washburn convinced Weed on the subject, and secured
a promise of the proper funds. Cash was raised, and ground
was well broken when Hamlin returned to Maine late in July.[49]
Besides circulating documents, the Republicans stumped the
state well. Hamlin began August 4 and continued throughout
the canvass.[50] A wide variety of talent was employed. J. S.
Pike was in Maine and Greeley was joking him about keeping
Frémont's biography out of the Madawaska district and in-
troducing there some copies of the *Express* with the story of

Frémont's being French and Catholic.[51] The Democrats naturally put out every effort to carry the state. It was believed
that they had great resources in money and used them freely.
The amount was variously estimated.[52] Election day gave the
Republicans the victory. Governorship, legislature, and congressmen were theirs by large majorities.[53]

The Maine victory was a mile-stone for the Republicans.
It gave them prestige to face the election in the October states.
The coming over of Hamlin with his Jacksonian antecedents
was no mean addition in itself. William Pitt Fessenden, Lot
M. Morrill, Israel Washburn, and other prominent politicians
had been vindicated in entering a new political fold. It seemed
that the Republicans had made a good start to "sweep the
North." The Democrats doubled their energy in the free
states to be heard from in October.

Contest in the Border Slave States

While the Democrats were doing their best for Maine, and
making ready for a supreme effort in the October free-states,
they won a victory over the Americans in the Border Slave
States. The Americans had launched brilliantly at Fillmore's
return, and the Old Line Whigs had aroused to bid them God
speed. Their stronghold was in the Border Slave States, and
the result there would determine the magnitude of the role
they would play in the campaign.

The Missouri election was doubly important. Besides the
Americans, the Benton faction of the Democracy stood independently and was in a position to do damage in the North.
The Americans endorsed Fillmore and nominated Robert C.
Ewing for Governor. The Benton Democrats put Benton's
name at the head of their ticket. With complete independence
they had chosen a delegation to Cincinnati and also presidential electors. The Atchison Democrats nominated Thurston
Polk. The division in the Democratic ranks gave Know-
Nothingism a good chance, and their failure would be significant.

While engaged in candidate-hunting at Washington, Benton
rebuked any idea that any one might have had of making him
president.[54] Since politics had degenerated to strife over slavery, until even the Pacific railroad could not get a hearing,
he washed his hands of it all. He was going home, however,

to work for Democracy. Then came his nomination for governor, and the question of his acceptance. He did accept it; and in doing so, declared that Congress had power over slavery in the territories and that the repeal of the Missouri Compromise was wrong.[55] On this principle he was going back to stump the state. He attended the Cincinnati Convention *en route* to St. Louis, accepted the nomination of Buchanan as a victory,[56] and in St. Louis made a terrible assault upon the administration.[57] A three-cornered canvass was soon under way in Missouri, which created a wide interest. Here was Benton supporting Buchanan on his old free-soil principles, and contesting the control of the state with the other faction of the party that was supporting him on the Cincinnati Platform. It placed Buchanan in a sort of dilemma. Slidell and Cobb began an attack on Benton in the *Union.*[58] Buchanan ordered the attack stopped, and the *Lancastrian,* his official paper, endorsed Benton. Most of the Democratic press denounced it as authority on Buchanan,[59] and thus offset the influence it might have in the South. Benton's attack on the Democratic platform and on the party history at the same time he supported Buchanan had a good influence in the North and Northwest, though the South complained.[60] Some were fearful of the influence it would have on the elections in Kentucky, North Carolina, and Tennessee. Buchanan accepted Benton's support, and advised against attempts at reconciliation in Missouri where he knew the Benton electoral ticket would be withdrawn in the case its leader were defeated.[61] The Missouri election came August 4. It would soon be over, and he maintained his position.

The anti-Benton forces reached the goal they had set, and defeated both Bentonians and Americans, Polk was elected governor and all the other state offices went Democratic. The legislature was confused with no distinct majority for any one. F. P. Blair, Jr. was elected to Congress from St. Louis. Of the six remaining seats, the Democrats had four, and the Americans, two.[62] True to agreement, the Benton electors were withdrawn.[63] Though defeated, Benton did not recant his position on the platform and continued to support Buchanan.[64] Missouri was safe for November. With Benton out of the way it was both practicable and possible to secure a better understanding with the administration. Blair's election was received as a Republican victory—they had a member of Congress from a slave state.

Kentucky held its election on the same day as Missouri. The Bluegrass State was a special test since the Americans had carried it the preceding year by thorough victories and had taken the lead in making the "national" platform.   They took the initiative early; for they had a presidential candidate.[65] There was a great deal of hammering away at the old bugbears of the Know-Nothings—foreignism and popery.[66] The accusation that Buchanan had "vilified" Clay in the bargain story of 1824 was useful for the Know-Nothings. The Democrats hoped to gain many of the Old Line Whigs for Buchanan, but this bargain theory was thought by some to have power enough to "kill him off" with them.[67] The Democrats met it with proper documents.[68] The Old Line Whigs were not moved by the story and many were tinctured with Buchananism.[69] A few days after their Convention in July, James B. Clay, son of the great compromiser, came out with a letter that had weight not only in Kentucky but throughout the Union.[70] He approved Fillmore, felt that he was sound on slavery, but that he could not win. Buchanan was the man to save the Union, and it was the duty of Old Line Whigs to support him. He quoted letters to right the "calumny" about Buchanan and the "corrupt bargain."   When the results of the election were known, the Democrats had carried the state. Along with Kentucky and Missouri went victories in Arkansas and Texas.

The first group of the August states where Democracy was pitted against Know-Nothingism had resulted in a triumph for the former. A few days later Tennessee and North Carolina held elections.[71] In North Carolina the Democrats had to combat a statement that Buchanan was a member of Tammany Hall; but they carried the state and added another southern commonwealth as sure for Buchanan. The Tennessee campaign like that in Kentucky was an active one.   Ex-Governor, Aaron V. Brown, and Andrew Johnson led the Democracy.[72] They took the general ground that the American party had given up its principles, had no real place, and was merely helping to defeat Buchanan, the true "union and constitution" candidate. They attacked Fillmore's record on slavery and argued that he could not win in the national race.[73] They defended Buchanan against all stories in circulation about him.

They carried Tennessee when the election came.

With the exception of Maryland the doubtful slave states had gone Democratic.[74] This meant a solid South for Buchanan. Would there be a solid North for Frémont? The states that had voted thus far indicated it. Five of the states that had held elections, named their congressmen for the 35th congress. There were twelve Republicans, six Democrats, and two Americans.[75] The interest in the October elections became intense.

The defeat of Fillmore in the Know-Nothing strongholds, especially in Kentucky, gave a new turn to the national outlook. He had started with a boom; but now it seemed that the Republicans had predicted correctly, that he could not carry a single state in the South. With reasonable assurance of this, the Democrats were faced with the problem of "keeping alive" in the North the candidate whose prospects they had killed in the South. In Pennsylvania and New York, there was a good chance that he could take enough votes away from Frémont to defeat him.

Several things kept the defeats from killing Fillmore utterly. He stood a good chance to carry Maryland, and his American party leaders chose to think he could carry New York.[76] Could he make the Empire state a "bulwark against sectionalism" in the North, the southern states would fall in line. Such ample hopes were for argument's sake; but there was a chance of carrying a few electoral votes and of the election going to the House. In that event, the compromise candidate was felt to be the only recourse. Nor had the point of being a compromise party completely eclipsed the nativist principle. While the Democrats and Republicans were fighting in Congress over Kansas, the Americans had suggested means of peace, and a House committee had made a big find in regard to crime, lunacy, and indigency among the foreign born.[77] They produced lengthy documents to prove their candidate's worth as compared with his opponents,[78] and continued to bombard the Pope. With some chances still remaining to them, the Americans turned to renew the contest for their old strongholds in the border states, and to direct the Old Whig movement to their advantage.

The contest in Kentucky and Tennessee was resumed. The Know-Nothings in Tennessee secured delegations to the pending Old Line Whig Convention at Baltimore. These were to do what they could for Fillmore. At the same time Lewis, Donelson, and Blair were actively in correspondence as to bringing out private letters on the "corrupt bargain" story.[79] They hoped to make it a two-edged sword in order to alienate Clay Whigs of Kentucky and Jackson worshippers of Tennessee.[80] The series of letters published showed Buchanan the vilifier of Clay and also that Jackson questioned his veracity. The Democrats resorted to private correspondence, that of Polk in particular, and relied upon witnesses for refutation.[81] They did this with a fair degree of success. If Buchanan could carry Pennsylvania in the October election, they had no question as to the defeat of Fillmore in Kentucky and Tennessee.[82]

The Americans were reasonably sure of Maryland and set about to make the most of it. They had a good headquarters here for directing the Old Line Whig movement, since the Whig Convention at Baltimore July 10 had endorsed Fillmore,[83] and another convention was pending. But the Democrats did not concede even Maryland to the Nativists. Senators Pearce and Pratt both came publicly to the support of Buchanan.[84] Their letters were given wide circulation, and made the characteristic plea for the patriotic Whigs to support Buchanan and save the Union. Pearce pointed out that the only hope of the Americans lay in carrying Maryland, Kentucky, and Tennessee, thereby throwing the election into the House—the House that had elected Banks. The Democrats came loyally to the support of the Maryland senators, began a movement to have one of the members of their electoral ticket withdrawn to admit an Old Line Whig, and to cooperate in canvassing the state.[85] The Republicans were also heard from. The Baltimore Association which had sent Blair to Pittsburgh and which had shared with him the denunciation of the "Merchants Meeting," published a circular disclaiming abolitionism.[86] Furthermore, the Republicans had the temerity to attempt a meeting in Baltimore September 11, and some thirty or forty persons were bold enough to attend. A mob of at least two thousand collected outside and broke it up.[87] There was no danger from the Republicans, but the Democrats actually made the state insecure. The mayorality election in Baltimore in October, it was thought, would determine the fate of Fillmore in Maryland. The decision of the Old Line Whig convention to assemble in Baltimore on the third Wednesday in September would also have an influence on results.

The bringing to a focus of the Old Whig movement in the middle of September and committing it for Fillmore had a strong influence in the persistence of his candidacy. The national convention at Louisville July 4 had been a victim of dual influence. James B. Clay, an authority on Kentucky Whiggery was already identified with the Democrats.[88] Those who were like-minded prevented the adoption of a resolution to support Fillmore. The best that could be done was to resolve:

> "That we recommend the individual Whigs of this state and of the Union to support that candidate whose political opinions, past history, and present position are in nearest conformity to their own political views, but in all such action looking to the assertion of Whig Principles and the ultimate restoration of the Whig Party."

This might mean either Buchanan or Fillmore. Some asserted that it meant Buchanan, and James Brooks, Fillmore's squire, attempted to show that Buchanan could not be associated with the ambiguous recommendation.[89] With its schism and indefiniteness, the Louisville Convention had not been the national demonstration that some had hoped for, and another trial was soon under way. July 17 an Old Line Whig Convention at Richmond endorsed Fillmore and Donelson and issued a call for a national convention in Baltimore the third Wednesday in September.[90]

The response was general. That of New York came at once. The Old Line Whigs held a convention at Albany July 24, approved the project, called a state convention August 14 at Albany, and endorsed Fillmore as individuals.[91] The resulting convention declared Buchanan and Frémont unsatisfactory, endorsed Fillmore, but not the American platform, and elected delegates to the pending National Convention.[92] Edward Bates, out in the "Border Ruffian" state, declared his dissatisfaction with all parties as they were.[93] The Old Liners of Massachusetts with their illustrious personnel were already in line to give them support. On August 9 Choate had replied to a letter from the Whig committee of Maine.[94] He said that it was the first duty of Whigs to "unite with some organization to defeat the sectional party calling itself Republican." He approved Fillmore but declared that he could not win, and recommended Buchanan as the Union saver on whom to unite. This brought results from both Republicans and Old Liners.[95] The stand taken by Choate cast suspicion on those who were still silent.[96] They met the situation by declaring themselves unwilling to wait for expression until their Convention which "purported to decide between Frémont and Buchanan" put them on record. This declaration was signed by two hundred of their number. [97] September 1 at their convention in Boston the Old Liners of Massachusetts did their share towards the work to be consummated at Baltimore. Winthrop as President of the convention made a speech in defence of Fillmore which was considered of great influence for the campaign,[98] and resolutions sustaining him were adopted.[99] A state ticket was also nominated.

The Baltimore convention promised a *coup de grace* for Fillmore. The closest men to Buchanan admitted it an eminent body of men;[100] and even Greeley conceded that a party was all that was lacking of dignity. Twenty-one states sent delegates.[101] Although they did not endorse the American platform, they did endorse Fillmore and Donelson. The burden of their resolutions was the avoidance of sectional parties, and Fillmore was the only candidate who was not sectional. They called for a spontaneous rising, a prompt rally to the national interests, and appointed a national committee to restore the organization. If the defeats in the state elections had endangered Fillmore's candidacy, such a demonstration was sufficient to restore it.

1. See Chapter VI, "Early Results".
2. The Democrats fought in a sort of inner circle, and there is an advantage in viewing the marches and counter-marches of the campaign from their camp.
3. Headline used in Republican Papers.
4. Massachusetts, Rhode Island, Connecticut, and Maine.
5. House Report 182. *House Reports,* 34th Congress, vol. I.
6. Letter in *National Intelligencer,* July 28. In reply to a sermon by Rev.J.E.Roy preached at Chicago July 4. The sermon was circulated in pamphlet form.
7. *House Journal,* 1st Session, 34th Congress, July 14,15.
8. *New York Tribune,* May 28.

242   *The Early History of the Republican Party*

9. *Defense of Massachusetts,* Speech in the House, June 21. This had a wide circulation in pamphlet form. It was part of an interesting controversy as to the relative contribution of Mass. and S.C. in the Revolution. This feature of states' honor and patriotism was an important element in the Brooks-Sumner affair and in the discussions which followed it.
10. In the Cilley-Powers duel Cilley was killed. There was nothing in the fact of the duel to justify this use of it.
11. Pamphlet, *Letter of James Watson Webb.*
12. Winthrop to Clifford, June 7. Winthrop MSS. M.H.S.
14. One hundred thousand copies without the testimony were printed and twenty thousand of the copious reports containing the testimony. *House Journal,* July 23.
15. S. 356 discussed below.
16. S. 342.
17. Clayton, S. 343, June 16. Geyer, S. 351, June 24.
18. Senate Report, no. 198.
19. The best statement in pamphlet form was: *The Issue fairly Presented—Black Republicanism or Democracy, Law and Order, and the Will of the Majority of the Whole People against Usurpation, Anarchy, Revolution, and the Voice of a Meagre Minority of the People of Kansas.* This pamphlet was written by Senator Bigler of Pennsylvania, 500,000 copies of which were circulated by the Democratic Committee. T.I.McCammot to Buchanan, July 19. Buchanan MSS. P.H.S.
20. Roberts' Letter, July 11. Roberts was Lieutenant-Governor under the Topeka constitution.
21. Pamphlet, *"Dunn Bill—Hypocrisy of the Black Republicans."*
22. Senate Committee Report, no. 282, August 11.
23. Whitfield was unseated but Reeder was not seated. *House Journal,* First Session, 34th Congress, July 30, 31.
24. Minutes of Shannon's administration, *Kan.Hist.Soc.Pub.,*vol.I, p. 122.
25. Wilson,Hall P. in *John Brown Soldier of Fortune,* interprets Brown's action as a horse-stealing enterprise, and not political in nature.
26. Letter to Marcy, Robinson, *Kansas Conflict,* p. 295.
27. Letter to Free State Men, *ibid.* pp. 296-297.
28. *Minutes of Shannon's Administration, Kan.Hist.Soc.Pub.* vol.I, p. 128. Shannon was absent in St.Louis at this time.
29. Fort Titus, Franklin, and Fort Saunders were the three main captures.
30. Minutes of Shannon's administration, *Kan.Hist.Soc.Pub.* vol.I, pp. 132-133.
31. *Ibid.,p.* 138.
32. *Ibid.,*p. 138.
33. Wise to Robert Tyler,July 6, in Tyler,*Letters and Times of the Tylers,* vol. II, pp. 530-537.
34. Beverley Tucker to Buchanan, June 10. Buchanan MSS. P.H.S.
35. Alexander, DeA.S., *Political History of New York,* vol. II, p. 233.
36. Seymour's speech with notes in the Seymour papers. Also in

pamphlet form.

37. For this he cited a Speech of C.C.Clay in the Senate showing that the North had actually secured to freedom most of the common territory.
38. Toombs Letter to a Virginia Friend,*New York Tribune* (w), Aug. 16.
39. Reported *Springfield Republican,* July 5. The speakers were: Julius Rockwell, A.O.Brewster, Benjamin Stanton, Jas.Dixon, F.H.Warren,JohnWells, and Henry Wilson. Gen.Pomeroy and Wm.J.Patten represented Kansas.
40. *National Intelligencer,* July 14.
41. Frémont's Letter July 8 in *National Intelligencer,* July 11; Dayton's letter, July 7, *ibid.,*July 17.
42. Pamphlet, *Who are Sectional.*
43. *New York Tribune* (w), August 16.
44. Special Appeal, *New York Tribune* (w), July 19.
45. *Tribune Almanac,* 1857.
46. They secured the Governor, all three congressmen, and the legislature almost unanimously.
47. E.C.Hamlin, in *Life of Hannibal Hamlin,*p.297, says that the Maine delegation to the Philadelphia Convention had the idea of using him as a compromise between Frémont and McLean, and that he attended in person to block their effort.
48. I.Washburn to Stevens,June 29,July 5,July11,July 17. Wash.MSS. L.C. Washburn quit franking them directly, but sent them in bundles in sacks and sent the proper person orders to receive them at the Post Office.
49. I.Washburn to Stevens, July 12,July 17. I.Washburn MSS. L.C.
50. Hamlin, *Life of Hamlin,* p. 309.
51. Greeley to Pike, Aug. 6, Aug. 13, in *First Blows,* pp. 347-348.
52. Some money was subscribed from Boston. C.L.Woodbury to Buchanan, Aug. 6. The N.Y.Tribune charged the national committee of contributing $15,000., the *Evening Post* on the night before election, estimated the total at $100,000. See Hamlin, *Life of Hamlin,* p. 310.
53. *Tribune Almanac,* 1857.
54. Letter, March 12, *National Intelligencer,* March 31.
55. Letter of acceptance, *National Intelligencer,* May 27.
56. Telegram to *St. Louis Democrat.*
57. Pamphlet, *Benton's Speech at St. Louis.*
58. J.G.Jones to Buchanan, June 27,29. Buchanan MSS. P.H.S.
59. Jones to Buchanan, June 29,June 30., S.J.Treat to Buchanan, July 21. Buchanan MSS. P.H.S.
60. Treat to Buchanan, July 21, cited above.
61. Buchanan to William Cary Jones, July 22. Buch. MSS. P.H.S. Sterling Price had visited Wheatland after the Cincinnati Convention and made the arrangement.
62. *Tribune Almanac,* 1857. The Americans elected Akers to succeed Miller for the remainder of the 34th Congress.
63. *St. Louis Democrat,* Aug.14. Benton's letter to T.L.Price, Aug. 10, accepted the defeat without regret and felt the campaign had been a benefit. Letter in Buchanan MSS.

64. Benton's scheme evidently was to pull off enough votes from the other faction to ensure a legislature that would elect him and a Know-Nothing to the Senate. Treat to Buch.,July 21, cited above. W.A.Harris to Buch.Aug.18, Buch.MSS.P.H.S.
65. Frankfort Convention, June 23,24, recommended Garrett Davis for president.
66. *Footprints of Sam*—"*Put only Americans on Guard tonight*"; *The Catholic Question in politics, a series of letters addressed to Geo. D. Prentice esq. of the Louisville Journal by a Kentucky Catholic.*
67. This story involving Jackson was used later to injure him with the Democrats.
68. J.G.Jones to Buchanan, June 27. Buchanan MSS. P.H.S.
69. Breckenridge to Buchanan, July 1. Buchanan MSS. P.H.S.
70. Letter of James B. Clay, July 14, in *Terre Haute Journal*, also Pamphlet.
71. North Carolina also had a strong Know-Nothing vote, and they hoped to carry the state.
72. Pamphlets: *Address of Ex-Governor A.V.Brown at Nashville, June 24; Speech of Andrew Johnson before citizens of Nashville, July 15.*
73. A.V.Brown carried this doctrine to Philadelphia after the election in an address, Aug.15. Pamphlet.
74. Louisiana was considered in danger at one time and California also had the aspects of a border slave state.
75. The southern states did not elect congressman until the next year.
76. *Daily American Organ*, Sept. 10.
77. House Report no. 359, 1st Session, 34th Congress.
78. Pamphlets by Anna Ella Carroll: *Buchanan or Fillmore.*
79. Cave Johnson to Buchanan, Aug. 24. Buch. MSS. P.H.S.
80. Pamphlet: *The Democratic Party Repudiating the Memory of General Jackson—Issue Between Jackson and Buchanan—Read and circulate.* Nashville, Sept. 18. A Lithograph copy of Jackson's letter to Major Lewis was attached and its exactness sworn to by a Justice of Peace.
81. Cave Johnson to Buchanan, Sept. 7. Buch. MSS. P.H.S.
82. Cave Johnson to Buchanan, Sept. 16, Oct. 5. Buch. MSS. P.H.S.
83. *National Intelligencer*, July 12.
84. Pamphlet, *Letter of Hon.Jas.A.Pearce and Hon.Thos.G.Pratt.*
85. H.Cobb to Buchanan, Aug.14, Rev.W.Slicer to Buch.Aug.8,20. Robt.C.McLean to Buchanan, Aug.8,28. Buch. MSS. P.H.S.
86. Circular of the Republican Association of Baltimore.
87. Schmeckebier, *American Party in Maryland*, p. 37.
88. Breckenridge to Buchanan, January 1. Buch. MSS. P.H.S.
89. *New York Express*, July 6, clipped in *National Intelligencer*, July 11.
90. Reported in *National Intelligencer*, July 18,19.
91. *National Intelligencer*, July 26.
92. *Ibid.*, Aug. 15.
93. Speech at St.Louis, Aug.19, *National Intelligencer*, Aug. 30. Sept. 6 a meeting at St.Louis endorsed Fillmore.

94. Pamphlet, *Choate's Letter,* published in *Boston Courier,* Aug. 14.
95. See Chapter X.
96. Winthrop to Clifford, Aug. 17. Winthrop MSS. M.H.S.
97. *National Intelligencer* Aug.30. The list included such names as Everett, Wm. Appleton, L. V. Bell, R.C.Winthrop, Nathan Appleton, Thos.Aspinwall, Geo. Lunt, and Geo. S. Hillard.
98. Fillmore to Winthrop, Aug.29, Sept. 26. Winthrop MSS. M.H.S. Winthrop also corrected a statement in the *Boston Bee* accusing Fillmore in aiding in Webster's defeat for the nomination in 1852.
99. *National Intelligencer,* Sept. 14. A.A.Lawrence was nominated for governor but declined.
100. Beverley Tucker to Buchanan, Sept. 18. Buch. MSS. P.H.S.
101. *National Intelligencer,* Sept. 17,19.

CHAPTER XII

THE DRIVE NORTH

The elections in the August and September states left the Democrats practically assured of a solid South. Ultraism there which had demurred at accepting Buchanan's position, but which had never caused much uneasiness among politicians,[1] now became an asset useful in terrifying conservatives in the North. There also remained the work of taking Maryland from the Americans and of holding the gains made in the other Border States. This, however, might be made a minor concern, and a maximum energy be expended on the critical October elections in the North. The general plan of campaign adopted was that of contesting the whole North but at the same time to concentrate on the most vital point and carry it. It was generally agreed that Pennsylvania was the keystone state of the campaign.

Democratic Retrenchment in the North

The Democrats were well organized in the North and would adapt their machinery to the exigencies of the campaign. However, there were several things requiring special attention. They had to augment their press—a thing which seems strange for a party so well established. The *Union* representing the administration, could not under the circumstances be a wholehearted supporter. The *Sentinel* which was the chief reliance at Washington, became insolvent, and had to be reinstated by cash from the campaign fund. The great need was in New York where they had only a few minor sheets to combat the powerful press in control of their enemies. Reliance had usually been placed in Bennett's *Herald*; but that had gone with Law to Frémont's support. There were two ways to a solution; either restore the *Herald* to its former usefulness to the Democracy or else found a new paper outright.

The idea of a new "paper for the million" entitled *The Press* was indulged; and George Sanderson was sent to New York on the mission of establishment.[2] Robert J. Walker was thought to be the logical man for editor. He had been sulking in his tent for several years; but had lately been approached by the Buchanan forces and was thought to be amenable. He demurred, however, and the new paper never saw the light. Securing the *Herald* was the only recourse, and a regular program of wooing Bennett was opened. While Democrats were approaching him, the *Pennsylvanian* was making war on him in terms used by Greeley—"Satanic." Though he listened, Bennett still worked for Frémont. He based his opposition to Buchanan on a deceptive impression Buchanan had given him in regard to his candidacy. He had no personal animus, not even in the squibs he was running about Buchanan's dancing and making merry.[3] Buchanan was too fearful of his Southern support to open a public correspondence with a Frémont supporter.[4] The position of Bennett remained unchanged until after the result of the Indiana and Pennsylvania elections was known. Then he came out with an editorial indicating his belief that the contest was settled, and it was decided to approach him directly.[5] Although the crisis was past, it was considered best to have the support of the *Herald* again, and to save New York from becoming a Republican stronghold for 1860. Buchanan wrote a letter to be read to Bennett, who responded, and the prodigal thus returned although the fate of the election had already been determined.[6]

The Democrats had fences to mend in New York. There was some hope of carrying the state, and even without it, a constructive campaign was necessary for the value of its influence. It would not do to give up the Empire State uncontested. There had been a heavy loss of voting strength in the New York Democracy, especially in the Soft wing, which, of the two, was the stronger in numbers. When they "went south" for a platform to take to the Cincinnati Convention, voters who would follow the lead of men like Preston King, Abijah Mann, B. F. Butler, and William Cullen Bryant went to the Republicans. The bombardment by the *Tribune* on Kansas also had its influence. Out of this shift came a number of precedent bearing documents. Martin VanBuren gave a letter to the public denouncing the Republicans and pleading for the preservation of the Union.[7] "Prince John" VanBuren supported Buchanan and did so under a free-soil guise.[8] This same adjustment gave Seymour the party leadership in New York.

The Cincinnati convention had issued a dictum for a "union of shells" and politicians started to carry it out. The official news organs of the two wings of the party were united under one management.[9] Some were hopeful of an actual union; but Seymour doubted whether a practicable one could be effected. Late in June the two committees got together at Albany and tried to agree on a date for a convention. They succeeded in setting dates within a week of each other.[10] Then, after some wrangling, the Hards accepted July 31, the date set by the Softs.[11] The convention met at Syracuse and a joint ticket was nominated led by Parker who had hardly been of either faction. Nothing was said about the administration.[12] There was a great deal of dissatisfaction with the arrangement,[13] and a consequent loss of voting strength. The party leaders hoped to replenish the depleted numbers by recruits from Old Line Whigs who would act as soon as Pennsylvania held her election. They were sanguine of carrying the state. In the districts, the fusion of the factions did not always hold.[14] Except in these few districts, the Democracy was one; but its great voting strength had slipped away.

Besides the retrenchment necessary within their own ranks, something had to be done to check the Republican thunder on Kansas. The maneuvering in Congress had been to the advantage of the Democrats. They had promised peace and accused the Republicans of refusing it for the sake of the political value the embroilment had. It was now very necessary to show that they meant peace to Kansas, and a man was sent there with that object in view. This man was John W. Geary. He was essentially a soldier, well-fitted for the work; and what was very fitting, too, he was a Pennsylvanian. If Geary could give peace to the territory, he would thereby enact the first installment of the program promised by the election of Pennsylvania's favorite son to the presidency.

Geary reached Leavenworth on September 8, just in time for the best political results. The very day of his arrival he took some prisoners away from a band of Woodson's militia, and the next day ordered a prompt restoration of their property.[15] He respected neither the militia which he reported as capable of all that was accredited to it, nor the free state bands that he found in plenty. He decided on prompt measures against the militia that was blocking access to the territory. In this he would destroy a point of great value to the Republicans who had used the "blockade of Kansas" as proof that the exclusion of free-state citizens was part of a conspiracy which centered about the Toombs Bill with its proposed convention. Nor did he bear the olive branch to "Jim" Lane whom he found with an "army" near Lawrence. He declared his purpose to accept *bona fide* citizens of both parties and to use them in creating a new militia. On September 11 he reached Lecompton, and in his address asked for cooperation in "enforcing" squatter sovereignty. The same day he issued two proclamations. In one he ordered the militia disbanded and the armed bands to disperse. The commandant of the southern department offered him a thousand men but without results.[16] He proceeded to apply "squatter sovereignty" on the theory that trouble had been caused by interference on both sides.

His next step was to get in touch with the free-state men. The "treason prisoners" were admitted to bail and returned to their homes. A messenger was sent to see whether Lawrence was in danger, and September 12 he reported that there was every reason to believe an attack imminent. The messenger also reported that he had told the citizens there that the governor would not be harsh, if they were compelled to use their arms under the circumstances.[17] Soldiers were summoned, and Geary and Colonel Cooke went down to Lawrence. They prevented a collision, secured the promise of the citizens to enroll as militia, and made effective the proclamation for the disbandment of the armed forces in the vicinity. At the same time some soldiers under Captain Wood captured a well-equipped free-state band which had just taken part in the battle of Hickory Point. One hundred and one prisoners were taken to await trial on civil charges,[18] not treason. The régime of "justice to Kansas" had begun.

With the sources of civil war blocked, Geary at once set out on a program of sweeping from the country all armed plunderers and partisans, and in making it safe for citizens. Military force was necessary, and requisitions for detachments of troops to make arrests were numerous. Those identified with the Topeka Movement were not singled out. Any doer of violence was within the scope of the law, although the partisan tendencies of the judicial officers could not be completely hidden. During this stage of Geary's work an unoffending free-state citizen named Buffum was murdered. It was impossible to apprehend his murderers, although ample reward was offered for them. This was a sort of hold-over; for it was soon evident that there was a change. Geary found it necessary to check his militia generals in their zeal to stop invaders from the North; and he also found that the men of Lawrence were reluctant in forming the military company they had promised. Yet, a better day seemed in store for Kansas.

There was also an opportunity to show that an election could be carried on without help from Missouri. The House had declared Whitfield's seat vacant. September 21 Geary issued a proclamation for an election on the first Monday in October to fill the vacancy.[19] Besides this, the question of holding a constitutional convention was to be voted on. Geary politely declined proffers of aid from Missouri friends, and had plenty of military protection for the polls in certain exposed places. The election was accomplished in peace, 4276 votes cast for delegate, and 2670 in favor of a convention.[20]

With the country quieted and a demonstration election carried out, Geary was ready to declare Kansas in a state of peace. On October 10 he wrote Secretary Marcy to that effect. A tour of inspection followed the pacification—a sort of assumed era of good feeling. All this was just in time for the most critical elections in the canvass. The first action of the "new régime" was on record. The Republican thunder was stopped at its source, and in the rest of the campaign, they would have to pump for "latest from Kansas."

Republican Offensive

The elections on record to date gave every evidence that the Republicans would "sweep the North." New England would be a unit for Frémont, and every state in the group save Massachusetts was already on record. The way had been cleared for a Republican victory in New Hampshire by the March election. Connecticut and Rhode Island had given a victory in the anti-Nebraska cause in April. A Republican party had been formed in both states. In Connecticut, under the guidance of Gideon Welles, the Republicans refused to take a subordinate position and in a joint convention shared the electoral ticket with the American supporters of Frémont.[21]

The Vermont election in August and the Maine in September gave practical assurance of these states. In some there was a residue of Old Whigs still clinging. There was also a small faction of Americans who had bolted to support Fillmore, who had been recognized by the national president and who regularly put a Fillmore electoral ticket into the field. But all these could carry only a small vote. The lesser New England states would undoubtedly go for Frémont.

The Bay State held no election that would indicate its preference in advance, but as she was a champion of anti-slavery principles she was a maker of political precedent. Here the ambitions of Governor Gardner stood between the Republicans and a clear-cut victory. His henchmen had been influential in securing the compromise on the twelfth section at Philadelphia,[22] and he had gone so far in his bid for a place on the national ticket as to recommend in his January message the repeal of the personal liberty law of the state. But the Philadelphia Convention passed by his name with small notice and the nominations it made brought trouble in the state council. The *Boston Bee,* Gardner's official mouth-piece, endorsed Fillmore, and his forces were strong enough to prevent a denunciation in the state council at Boston, May 6.[23] It was the only New England state council that had not repudiated Fillmore, and further developments depended on the course Gardner saw fit to take. The *Bee* began to minimize the significance of the split at Philadelphia and to put itself in waiting for expression from Fillmore. At this juncture the Sumner assault came, and Gardner followed the trend of public sentiment without hesitation. The repeal of the "liberty bill" died on the verge of passing. The governor officiated at indignation meetings, relayed the Connecticut resolutions denouncing the act to the Massachusetts legislature, and recommend similar action.[24] When Gardner became conspicuous in the new role, the *Springfield Republican* which had been conducting a war on him, accused him of getting in line for the Republican vice-presidency which the North Americans hoped to secure.[25] The New York Convention named Johnston and not Gardner as their preference for vice-president, and a few days later the action of the Republican convention left the responsibility of solving the vice-presidency embroglio to the Americans of Massachusetts in their next state council.

There was scarcely a doubt but that Frémont would be endorsed by the council that assembled at Springfield July 1.
Gardner had indicated his position in a letter to a ratification
meeting late in June.[26] The first trial of strength found two-
thirds in favor of Frémont, but they stood firm on Johnston
for vice-president. The remainder bolted and made arrangements for a convention of their own.[27] An electoral ticket was
named and a futile attempt was made by Gardner's friends
to nominate a state ticket. The *Springfield Republican* objected to the action of the council in choosing the electoral
ticket, and took occasion to stress the point that all friends
of Frémont should have been invited to share in selecting it,[28]
since the Bolters could be strong only in conjunction with
Buchanan support; and a majority would have to cooperate
with other Frémont support to be effective.

The American nominating convention at Faneuil Hall, July
24, had a clarifying effect in that it completed the separation
of the factions.[29] The Frémont men elected the president and
the Fillmorites bolted. Gardner was nominated for governor
after some discussion as to whether or not he would support
Frémont. The Fillmore men decided to wait until the August
council, and if matters did not go right then, to nominate a
candidate of their own. July 28 Gardner accepted, endorsing
Frémont and the Springfield platform.[30] The Fillmore men
made good their threat. In council August 5 they possessed
an order from Bartlett, the national president, making them
orthodox and the Frémont majority of the council an outlaw.
August 20 they nominated a state ticket which the Whig
convention set for September 3 could accept.[31] This Whig convention did endorse Fillmore, but not the State ticket entirely.[32] There were now three tickets in the field, with the
Republicans as yet uncommitted.

The Republican convention was called for September 16 at
Worcester. September 4 the Frémont Americans issued a call
for a convention at Worcester at the same time.[33] They were in
position to give up their electoral ticket and by concession
there, to bid for Republican endorsement of their state ticket.
The call assigned as a reason for the action the receipt of a
letter from Johnston to the effect that he would withdraw.
The American convention accepted Dayton, and Johnston's
withdrawal was given to the public.[34] The Republicans hesi-

tated to endorse Gardner. Two-thirds were willing; but the remainder threatened to bolt. They agreed not to nominate at all which was satisfactory to Gardner who wanted to seem to carry the state "on his own hook," and for whom part of the Republicans would vote. An electoral ticket was agreed upon and the *Boston Journal* forthwith predicted a majority of fifty thousand.[35] A small group of the Republicans bolted, nominated Josiah Quincy for governor, and on its ticket appeared the name of John A. Andrew for attorney-general.[36] A victory was assured over the Democrats; but it would scarcely be a Republican triumph when attained.

In spite of the certainty of the result of the election in New England, the later phase of the canvass was not without interest and events that had a national significance. The illustrious Webster Whigs of whom Choate had gone to Buchanan and the remainder to Fillmore, had to be counterbalanced in kind. Late in May a letter from the venerable Josiah Quincy to E. R. Hoar was published, an address on slavery delivered at Quincy followed immediately, and this man of the Old Federalists was in line to make precedent for the new party.[37] Choate's letter to the Whig committee of Maine which came in August[38] was the signal for Quincy to act. He replied in a letter that was given wide circulation.[39] Before the campaign was over, the Old Line Whigs of Massachusetts were the objects of another effort.[40] The Fillmore American convention in August led to a response by Joel Parker which had a place in campaign literature.[41] Both Quincy and Parker endeavored to draw fire from Old Federalism of the time of the Louisiana Purchase and Hartford Convention. Parker was a little inconsistent when he identified Jefferson, the one to whose policies the Republican platform pledged a return, with the slavery conspiracy. The young G. W. Curtis made his debut in political life by a brilliant address at Middletown.[42] There was abundant material on slavery to accompany that which was distinctly political. There were also meetings and demonstrations. There were receptions for Wilson and Burlingame. Sumner, the martyr, did not return to Boston until the very day of the election.

To sweep the states of the middle Atlantic seaboard was patently a more difficult task. They were not so thoroughly dominated by the anti-slavery feeling as was New England,

were equally complicated with the presence of Know-Nothingism, and the Democratic party was much more powerful there.
Pennsylvania was the most important one and was an immediate objective because of the state election in October.[43] New
Jersey and New York did not hold their elections until November; but things of importance took place in both—especially
in New York whence came Fillmore's sponsorship in the
North.

Even before the Americans of New York had made straight
the way for Fillmore and launched him with a boom, they had
lent color to the gathering attack on the Republicans. They
agreed with Douglas as to the organic nature of the new party
on slavery and pronounced it similar to Lord Chatham's cabinet as described by Burke:—

> "He made an administration so checkered and
> speckled, he put together such a piece of diversi-
> fied mosaic, such a tasselated pavement without
> cement, here a bit of black stone, and there a bit
> of white, patriots and courtiers, kings' friends,
> and Republicans, Whigs and Tories, treacherous
> friends and open enemies, that it was indeed a
> curious show; but utterly unsafe to touch and
> unsure to stand on."[44]

They carried the defence of Fillmore into Ohio where Chase
had first subordinated Americanism.[45] Brooks of the *New York
Express* took up the task of proving Frémont a Catholic, and
doing any other public damage possible to the Republicans.[46]
A fight was soon on in New York that echoed throughout the
country.

The shift of the Law faction to the Republicans made good
material to use against Brooks. July 3 Law gave the public
a letter on his position.[47] For the presidency he passed by
Buchanan as a tool of the South. He said that he knew from
his personal experiences in the "Crescent City" affair that
Fillmore would not protect Americans; and that he was thrust
upon the convention by the "slave oligarchy." Although the
Republican convention was not as forward as it might have
been in effecting fusion, he wanted to vote for their candidate
who believed "freedom national and slavery sectional." He
wanted a man who had done something for national progress,
who was young and not "sold out." This from "Live Oak
George" was a Republican asset. Greeley thanked him for it,

and assured him that in calling their convention, they had invited all parties to attend.[48] This first letter was part of a controversy with Scroggs which continued and occassioned another letter from "Live Oak." This letter was designed to injure Fillmore with conservative Whigs. It declared him as subservient to the three hundred and fifty thousand slave owners as was Buchanan. It bore personal animus; for in it Law measured the breadth of Fillmore's statesmanship by his putting a clause in a reciprocity treaty to save the vegetable market of Buffalo. Chauncey Schaffer's letter arising from the contest over Frémont's religion was a product of the New York struggle.[49] Ephraim Marsh of New Jersey, President of the convention that nominated Fillmore, added to the group a letter denouncing him, and together they made a good political pamphlet.[50] Nor did the Republican counter-attack cease with public letters and denunciations. They managed to slip some anti-slavery delegates into the American convention at Syracuse, August 27. These delegates raised the embarrassing slavery question by a resolution to denounce congressman Brooks, and having failed, bolted to support Frémont.[51] "The Siamese Presidents," a sort of *Hudibras*, used the situation to ridicule both Americans and Republicans.[52]

The battle continued, led by the *Express* on one side and the *Tribune* on the other.[53] After the summer elections had taken the border states away from Fillmore, Greeley attacked his candidacy as a plot to elect Buchanan. On October 7, Brooks who had been nominated for governor[54] by the State convention at Rochester, Sept. 25, responded to the attack and defended his position in an open letter in the *Express*. In reply, Greeley marshalled the evidence against him.[55] Buchanan was a formidable candidate, yet Brooks said nothing against him; he had aided in putting Fillmore tickets in Vermont, New Hampshire, Connecticut, and Rhode Island where there was no hope of winning, and newspapers had been established in Iowa without cost. Brooks' attitude had changed, and must be so for a price; Governor Floyd in his recent speech in New York said that he could vote for Fillmore[56]— which was a statement to bridge the chasm. In two Connecticut town elections, Buchanan and Fillmore tickets had been combined, and the *Express* came out saying that the Republicans were defeated. A Fillmore man recently wanted to wager that New

York would not go for Frémont.   This was evidence of a
bargain already closed.   The Democrats had need to keep
Fillmore in the field in the North, and in the face of the exigency, Greeley's logic seemed convincing.[57] The whole situation was reduced to a conspiracy accusation against the
persistence of Fillmore.[58]

The Republicans took the field in good order and proceeded
with added numbers promised by every move.   Their convention at Syracuse May 28 which made ready for the national
convention at Philadelphia had also made several advantageous moves.   They denounced the Sumner assault and the
Herbert killing.   They endorsed the platform of the Softs
of the preceding September on the question of slavery extension.   Accepting a Soft platform drafted before that faction
"went south" in January, was no mean stroke.   July 24 a
convention of "radical" Democracy met at Syracuse.   They
endorsed Frémont as the leader to take them back to the original Republican party of Jefferson, who would now be driven
from his own state and not allowed to flee to Kansas.[59] The
State Republican convention was called for September 17 at
Syracuse.   Here John A. King was nominated for governor.
A resolution favorable to the North Americans was adopted
and Kauffman, a German, who supported this resolution, promised forty thousand German votes for Frémont.[60]   The Republicans were confident.   They could outvote either the
restored but depleted Democracy, or the Fillmore Americans
aided by the few Old Line Whigs who would drift to them
A letter from Senator Hamilton Fish to James A. Hamilton
son of the famous Federalist leader, was published for the
benefit of Old Liners.[61] It was a sop for conservatives everywhere.—

> "We find no assault upon a single Whig principle
> —no danger of an unsafe or belligerent foreign
> policy—no extreme or violent proposition in re-
> gard to slavery where it now exists, but only that
> resistance to its advance and spread over soil
> long since made free, which we have ever advo-
> cated."

John Cochrane began an attack on John VanBuren as a
doughface.   Late in October Seward who had been awfully
"grouty" took the field.   The Democrats kept steadily to

Seymour's position on the Kansas issue.[62]

A special feature in New York politics was the presence of the great metropolis whence both sides went for friends. Here Buchanan had brought friendly offerings to Tammany.[63] September 25 Banks made a speech to the merchants at the Exchange. The Democrats secured Governor Floyd of Virginia to reply just one week later. Their invitation was signed by one thousand, one hundred and four leading business men.[64] The president of the meeting in his address declared that it was his duty to say:—

> "to our countrymen and to the commercial world that we cannot consent to the going forth of the impression that the meeting which was held at this place on Thursday last and addressed by N. P. Banks, Jr., was a meeting of the merchants of the city of New York; nor that Mr. Banks in his public speech, embodies the aggregate sentiment of this mercantile community. That some of our merchants endorse such sentiment we may not deny; but that these are only a small minority of the whole we must sincerely believe. It therefore becomes an important duty to convene thus, to put forth the real sentiment of the great majority of the merchants of New York upon the political issues of the day."

The assemblage adopted resolutions and listened to a long speech by Floyd. Floyd praised everything except the Republicans who had disrupted their brotherhood and threatened to disrupt the Union for no greater purpose than securing office. He was claiming kinship to the Fillmore party on many points when an auditor injected, "the foreign vote." Floyd was not to be diverted and declared that could the Black Republican candidate be beaten by his vote and were Fillmore the only one that could defeat him, he would vote for Fillmore though the earth swallow him up. These fraternal lines in his speech were printed in italics for the benefit of Americans.

The Republicans pushed the work of organization as rapidly as possible in New Jersey and by the November election were in a situation to contest the state with the Democrats. Local meetings had heralded the coming of the party.[65] A call was circulated for an organizing convention at Trenton on May 28. It was to attend this that Senator Wilson left Washington under guard. The organizers had stimulating events associated with Kansas, Sumner, Greeley, and Keating, all to add color to their work. They created a state committee which was to select an electoral ticket that would unite all and care for other details of organization.[66] A nominating convention called by opposition members of the legislature met on June 4 at Trenton and nominated William N. Newell for Governor, Pennington and Frederick T. Frelinghuysen spoke.[67] They adopted a fusion platform which was endorsed by the Know-Nothing council on June 10.[68] The State Republican, or better named, Fusion convention, met at Trenton September 17. It was called to order by Ephraim Marsh who had been president of the convention that nominated Fillmore; but who had come out against him.[69] The convention gave due proportion on the electoral ticket to all elements represented. Its resolutions supported Frémont and thanked the party for the nomination of Dayton.[70] Dayton, however, had not harmonized all of New Jersey. Stockton who had been nominated for president independently by the bolters at New York withdrew and threw his support to Fillmore. A Fillmore electoral ticket was kept in the field and in two congressional districts, the Americans and Republicans ran different candidates.

Several other free states did not hold elections prior to November, and there too the Republicans prepared while the general election was yet afar off. Michigan and Wisconsin were part of the original stronghold, and although there were points of interest in the campaigns in both states, the outcome was forecast with accuracy and neither state was considered a turning point in the final result. Although more like a border state in sentiment than a free state, California was given an important place by political strategy. The Republicans talked much of carrying it and of the value of their candidate and railroad plank to that end; but their performance within the state made their promises seem like political gossip for eastern consumption. In keeping with its isolation, California's politics were primarily local and the great crisis in the older part of the nation was not vitally felt. In the election of 1855 the Know-Nothings backed by an enthusiasm for reform had swept the state and elected J. Neely Johnson governor. However, the original elements of the party remained so factional as to render concerted action difficult. In the summer of 1856 the Great Vigilance Committee of San Francisco entered the arena as a disturbing force. Governor Johnson outlawed it although it was closely in touch with the reform spirit of the Know-Nothings. The State convention at Sacramento September 2 which put their ticket into the field and adopted a reform platform, refused to denounce the "vigilantes."[71] Their failure to endorse the governor along with the inability of the party to use its majority to elect a senator broke its power. Though they endorsed Fillmore and Donelson, declared themselves a Pacific railroad party, and carried out a lively canvass in the state in which Senator Foote did a conspicuous share, their prospects were hopeless from the first.

Not until spring did the Republicans become active. Their first mass meeting which was held at Sacramento in April, was broken up.[72] On the last day of the month a state convention in the same city succeeded in organizing a party machine.[73] They met with violence at times but the work went steadily on under the leadership of such men as E. B. Crocker and George C. Bates. August 27 in Sacramento they held a convention and presented a ticket and platform to the people.[74] After the regular endorsements, they pronounced Frémont the only hope for a Pacific railroad, and declared for a general reform program calculated to disintegrate the Democrats and assimilate the Americans. They denounced Herbert and the failure of Congress to investigate his case, declared in favor of quick titles, free land for settlers, and free mining on public lands. The Democrats received them as a special charge since the Know-Nothings were "dead men" and at times acknowledged them as antagonists worthy of note.[75]

The Vigilantes at San Francisco created a special case. The Democrats made war on them and approved the Know-Nothing governor in the stand he had taken. Under these circumstances the leaders were in search of some vindicating force. A "Peoples Party" was initiated in July and consummated in August to supply this much needed support.[76] A Republican convention in October endorsed the local ticket of the Peoples convention and in spite of a minor bolt, gave the Vigilantes the backing they desired.[77] This combination had strength locally.

The position of greatest promise belonged to the Democrats. The torrent of sectionalism had not split the party—the Broderick and Gwin factions were cooperating in support of Buchanan. Their convention was held at Sacramento, September 9.[78] They congratulated themselves, endorsed the Cincinnati Platform, and denounced the Vigilantes. They wanted a Pacific railroad, recommended a homestead law, and economy in government. They knew no North and no South, and welcomed Old Line Whigs to their ranks. Being able to keep relatively immune from sectionalism, they had little to fear from the Republicans, and taking advantage of the embarrassment of the Americans, proceeded to grind them to pieces.

In the canvass all three parties carried the battle into the mining districts and stumped the state with relative thoroughness. All were agreed on a Pacific railroad as the most vital issue. The Republicans claimed an advantage here in both the national candidate and platform. American papers proved Fillmore a Pacific railroad man.[79] The unsatisfactory action on the issue at Cincinnati made further proof on part of the Democrats in order, in spite of their local endorsement. They had a *coup de main* in readiness. The Republicans had a doubtful advantage in their railroad plank and they had less than that in the personality of their candidate in spite of the fact of his being a Californian. The Democratic press took the nomination as a joke and raised the question as to whether he would carry a precinct or not.[80] There seemed to be some truth in their statement; for the greatest enthusiasm for Frémont came where he was least known personally. He had his supporters, especially among the native Californians; but there was not the burst of enthusiasm there as elsewhere. Although his private conduct was attacked and thereby an effort made to injure him by invoking the current sentiment against lawlessness, he suffered no such scathing assaults as were heaped upon him in the East. If the Republicans were expecting their railroad issue and their candidate to secure far-away California for them—a thing they had often referred to but done little to achieve—they were booked for disappointment.

October Elections

The several October states would tell the story of Republican success or failure to swing the North. The municipal election in Baltimore in which the Americans were making a last stand for the border states was the first in the October list. Then came the fateful elections in Pennsylvania, Indiana, and Ohio on the fourteenth. In Ohio an interesting contest was under way—the Democrats putting up a fight for the moral effect but generally conceding the state to the Republicans. Indiana and Pennsylvania furnished the real battle grounds. In them the fight for the control of the nation would be won and lost. Of them, Pennsylvania was considered the more important.

The Democrats felt that Maryland was safe for them, if the Baltimore election of October 8 could be won.[81] Know-Nothingism was rampant there, and if not checked, it was feared it would permeate the state.[82] Its rampant methods usually led to bloodshed; but the Democrats resolved to vote regardless of personal danger.[83] Their success in courting the Old Line Whigs was to a great extent nullified when Floyd's speech before the merchants of New York was published. They had been attacking Fillmore as vigorously as they denounced Frémont, and Floyd said that under certain circumstances a Democratic elector could vote for him.[84] A typical election day ensued in Baltimore. The "Plug Uglies" and "Rip Raps" fought the eighth ward "Blackguards." Four people were killed; fifty wounded; and the Know-Nothings carried the city.[85] The Democrats believed they lost because they were bullied from the polls, and placed the winning of Maryland in November as an objective still in the securing of a solid South.[86]

The great fight for Pennsylvania was the high-water mark of the "sweep of the North." In this the Democrats expended their greatest effort, and in it their arguments and methods of meeting the multiform attack of the Republicans were best developed. The importance of this election had been forecast in Buchanan's nomination. Both sides conceded its significance and made preparations accordingly.

The convention of March 4 that adopted the Pennsylvania platform and recommended "the favorite son" also nominated a state ticket. Malcolm Ives, nominee for attorney general, was put in through the action of a group in the convention; but was not a good selection. Not much was thought of this until Frémont proved a "tornado" instead of a "farce," and terror entered the ranks of the Democracy everywhere. Then, every attention was devoted to Pennsylvania for October on the belief that "to carry it would render all other efforts useless." "No other document for its sure and certain effects could be sent through all the states and all the classes as that one glad declaration—Pennsylvania has gone for Democracy by 20,000 votes in the majority——The whole North and Northwest looks bad, we must *work, work, work*."[87] With such convictions the first direct move was to substitute a stronger man for Ives. A re-assembly of the Democratic convention was called for August 6 at Chambersburg.[88] This Chambersburg meeting substituted John Rowe for Ives, and then indulged in a rousing political rally.[89] Forney outlined his program— Forney who wanted to be all things to all men at once, who had the enthusiasm of a school-boy, and who with every task "fell in love as easily as a sixteen-year old girl." He made the saving of the Union the key-note to his campaign.[90]

In July plans were being matured, especially for Wilmot's district, the West and Northwest, and Chester and Delaware counties.[91] In the "Northern Tier" it was necessary to control a newspaper,[92] and talent was employed to "do the school houses." John VanBuren, quondam political kinsman of the Wilmoters, was secured for September.[93] Campbell, administration favorite and a power with Catholic voters, pledged a silent influence.[94] Means were under consideration to reach the Germans. The land was mapped out and men and money at hand to meet the Republicans who would "come down like locusts and must be met." Forney, who was accused of wishing to get all the honor for the victory, was showing fastidiousness in accepting aid for Pennsylvania.[95] The National Committee was to give two entire weeks to the state, and Slidell went to New York to call upon the merchants.[96]

The Republicans had not found Pennsylvania a soil in which their organization flourished, although there was anti-slavery feeling to rely on. They were perhaps less than a faction among factions, as Errett had put it, they "were in the hands of the Philistins." The only hope of defeating the Democrats was in united action. Pursuant to this conviction, a call was issued from members of the legislature in February for a union state convention on March 26.[97] The convention was made up of Republicans, a few that might be termed Old Line Whigs, and Americans of a variety of degrees of anti-slavery sentiment. There was an argument between the Americans of East and West parts of the state; but finally a platform was agreed upon and nominations made.[98] Dawson Phelps, American, was nominated for attorney-general, Bartholomew LaPorte, Republican, surveyor general, and Thomas E. Cochran, Old Line Whig, canal commissioner. The Americans had occasion to show their factionalism in the convention of the Edie Branch at Harrisburg May 13. Fillmore and Donelson were endorsed, the administration and the repeal of the Missouri Compromise denounced. Ex-Governor Johnston and fourteen others bolted at this juncture. The convention refused a motion to reconsider in order to give Fillmore time to get right on slavery. The ticket nominated by the Union convention was ratified.[99] Combinations were formed in the districts to support Congressmen, although the Americans stood aloof on presidential electors. August 4 they met at Harrisburg, chose Fillmore electors, and adopted a resolution that the action could not be changed.[100] This looked towards independence in the presidential election. The October election occurred before that time, and for that they were in alliance with the Republicans to defeat the Democracy.

With the union ticket in the field, the Republicans began their fight for Pennsylvania. Carrying the state was considered of such importance that the national committee took charge. Henry B. Stanton was sent out to secure talent for the stump.[101] His field was to include Pennsylvania, New York, and New England. He was to employ speakers for a period of one to three weeks and to distribute them over the state. Talent directly from Kansas was used; Lieutenant-Governor Roberts, S. N. Wood, "Jim" Lane, and others were among the speakers. In all about two hundred orators of various types and varieties entered the field.[102] The Republicans also felt that their press should be strengthened although they had two important Philadelphia papers,[103] and the *New York Tribune* and *Herald* had a great influence in the state. Gibbons, the state chairman, secured the *Times*,[104] and Ford of Ohio after a time on the stump in central Pennsylvania, started a new effort by detecting a Fillmore bias in the press of that region.[105] He was commissioned by Morgan, committee chairman, to secure such papers as he could.[106] Although the Democrats believed the Republicans had obtained one hundred thousand dollars from New York to carry Pennsylvania,[107] in reality they were finding it difficult to finance their efforts at all. They faced the Pennsylvania canvass with an empty treasury.[108] Efforts were made in New York city, in fact, Speaker Banks was there on a financial mission when he addressed the merchants at the Exchange, and his mission took him also to Washington. Weed went to Philadelphia and he and Cameron undertook to secure funds there.[109] The first response came from Boston to the extent of two thousand dollars in cash and five thousand more in promises.[110] On the night of September 29, in the rain, Morgan and thirty or forty others succeeded in raising eight thousand dollars in New York.[111] Morgan was sure that they could get fifteen thousand dollars, and a week later he wrote to Welles telling that he had succeeded, and had apportioned the fund. Ford, however, embarrassed the treasurer by turning in a bill for eight thousand dollars. He had secured fifteeen or eighteen papers and had exceeded by three thousand his allowance for the purpose.[112] In spite of their financial handicap, the Republicans were able to stage an effective canvass.

The career of Reeder was an asset for the Republicans. For a while he demurred, refused to write a letter to a Republican convention in New York, and tried to identify himself with Buchanan and free Kansas. This was considered a little too radical, he was thrown over, and into the arms of the Republicans.[113] His letter to the editor of the *Evening Post* in which he came out for Frémont was a dangerous one for his former party.[114] He had always been an enthusiastic Democrat, he said, but in his letter he renounced these ties and his regard for Buchanan on the ground that it could not mean a free Kansas, and that the South was already demanding protection for slavery in the Territories. Should Buchanan's administration prove otherwise, he would support it; but, he continued:—"As I believe now, I must regard the Democratic party as fully committed to southern sectionalism, towards which for some time past it has been rapidly tending, and I quit it, well assured that my country demands at my hands the sacrifice of my personal feelings." Identifying Buchanan with slavery for Kansas was dangerous indeed. To offset it, B. F. Hallett of Massachusetts conducted a joint discussion with Reeder, and a phamplet attacking the Republicans for religious heterodoxy made its appearance among the clergymen of the state.[115]

Besides Reeder the Republicans added precedent by a letter from S. D. Ingham, Secretary of Treasury in President Jackson's cabinet.[116] He agreed with the Republicans that slavery was not the natural condition of the working man— black or white. He believed that the repeal of the Missouri Compromise was a conspiracy in which Atchison went to Kansas to organize and left Pierce on the job at Washington. Buchanan now stood on the same platform, and consequently he would support Frémont. This made up nearly all of the important survivors of Jackson's group save Amos Kendall. Not until after the state election, did the Democrats finally get his response in their favor.[117]

The Democrats met the "invasion" as they had planned to do. Though frightened at first, they soon gained the ascendency. They arranged a series of great mass meetings at intervals throughout the state. Of these, one at Philadelphia on September 17, ratification day, was the greatest. They brought talent from all over the United States and arranged an itinerary for each so as to keep every quarter of the state supplied with a continuous list of speakers properly chosen for the section.[118] Pennsylvania was thoroughly stumped and not a stone was left unturned in meeting and combating Republican argument.

The cry of "Union in danger" which had been sounded by Forney at Chambersburg was their heaviest gun. The conservative business interests were appealed to, especially the "cottonocracy" of Philadelphia, which represented many Old Line Whigs families. They were asked to join in saving the Union, especially now that the old issues of bank and tariff were a "theme for the historian.[119] Not only was there response; many of the Old Whigs even became active in the campaign.[120] All Whig precedent from outside the state was used. The public statements of Senators Pearce and Pratt and also Reverdy Johnson of Maryland, of James B. Clay, and Fletcher Webster, of Rufus Choate and others were well circulated. Some of these oracles of whiggery were induced to take the stump.

Robert J. Walker came from his retreat to write a letter on the campaign issues which the committee felt was a performance equal to his Texas letter.[121] This letter, in pamphlet form and in several languages was spread broadcast throughout the country.[122] In logical form he reviewed the Democratic position, and restated the attack on the Republican party as sectional. As for Kansas, the North had an advantage under the Nebraska Bill. Many pro-slavery men in the North were not for carrying the institution there. The North, numerically stronger, could see that the principle was carried out. He believed Kansas would be a free state. As to the Republican purpose which proposed to use a majority at the polls to check slavery, it was "revolutionary and agrarian." "It discards the peaceful arbitrament of the Supreme Court of the United States, the great conservative feature of our institutions; it overthrows the constitution and all its guarantees, and substitutes in their place an elective despotism, by which a majority of the people may abolish, divide, or confiscate, all property at each successive election." Besides this (by way of conclusion and climax) the party endangered the Union. To this point he said:—"I indulge in no menace against the Union. I make no predictions on a subject of so fearful import; but this I can say. The South will not and ought not to submit to degradation. They will not be despoiled by the North of all rights in the common territory; they will not surrender their constitutional guarantees; they love the union of the constitution, the union of equals with equals, and not of sovereign states of the North with the subject states—say rather, conquered provinces of the South. Rather than submit to this, they will adopt the last alternative—*separation.*" In conclusion, he saw slavery gradually melting away, and the Negro disappearing into central America, Mexico, and Africa.

The threat to the Union would reach a larger audience than conservatives and business men, and it was used accordingly. Henry A. Wise organized a convention of the Democratic governors of the slave states to meet at Raleigh, N. C., October 13, the day before the Pennsylvania election. He had circulated calls to the governors about the middle of

September, and had secured a varied response.[123] Whatever this portended it had its influence in Pennsylvania.[124] Only three governors assembled at Raleigh; but the voters of Pennsylvania and of other states who went to the polls on the following day did not know this.

Another feature of the defence of Pennsylvania was a counter-appeal to the workingman. The Republican doctrines and the personality of their candidate when used upon audiences of laboring men by a stump artist like William D. Kelly were a formidable array.[125] First they had to defend Buchanan against the ten cents a day accusation. This they did and gleaned further quotations on the subject from his Independent Treasury speech. Some were as follows:—"That country is most prosperous where labor commands the greatest reward," and "From my soul I respect the laboring man. Labor is the foundation of the wealth of every country, and the free laborers of the North deserve respect for their probity and intelligence. Heaven forbid that I should do them wrong."[126] The Republicans stood for free men—the negro free and in competition with white labor. The Democrats summarized it tersely: "The nigger better than the white laborer."

The party that threatened to break the Union must certainly be a radical party. The Republicans were never less than "abolitionists." Any endorsement by abolition radicals was material; and Fred Douglas's support of Frémont was used as a classic. The public utterances of the Republican leaders were carefully searched for radical and disunion sentiment. Statements like that of Banks on letting "the union slide" were plentiful, and whole columns of quotations were found in the papers. Abolition centers were supposed to furnish the money to "abolitionize" Pennsylvania. It was more than this—it was all of the fanatics combined. Frémont's cabinet was selected for him by the *Pennsylvanian* of July 22.

Cabinet:
Secretary of State—Joshua R. Giddings
Secretary of Treasury—William Lloyd Garrison
Secretary of Interior—David Wilmot
Secretary of Navy—Wendell Phillips
Postmaster General—Senator Hale

Attorney General—Frederick Douglass
Chaplain—Henry Ward Beecher
New members:
    Spoilsman General—O. B. Matteson
    First assistant—N. P. Banks
    Second assistant—Thurlow Weed
    Third assistant—Horace Greeley
Female department:
    Presiding Angel—Abby Folsom
    First assistant—Lucy Stone
    Second assistant—Harriet Stowe
Missionaries
    Africa—Charles Sumner
    Congo Coast—Henry Wilson
    Timbuktoo—Gerrit Smith
    Turkey—President, New York Free Love Society

The influence of the pulpit in politics produced a bitter attack especially upon the Reverend Henry Ward Beecher of "the Church of the Holy Rifles." The "adventurer" candidate, the "wooly horse," was attacked at all points whereat his career and personality were vulnerable. It was enough to tell Pennsylvania that radicalism was abroad in the land.

Another point was to keep as large a gap as possible between the Frémont and Fillmore supporters who were cooperating on the Union State ticket. The Democrats busied themselves proving that the Fillmore electors chosen at the Harrisburg Convention of August 5 had Frémont men among them. Every day brought new evidence in the case. The true friends of Fillmore were to be sold out to abolitionism.[127]

The dual arrangement did result in some awkwardness, and some of the strength of the opposition was lost because of it. Regardless, the Republicans, or more accurately, Unionists, imbued the western and north-western counties with their enthusiasm, and were sure to "cross the Alleghenies" with a majority. It was only a question of the Democrats being able to overcome it in the eastern part. "Here," says Errett, "there was a change in the political atmosphere. There were Frémont men to be found everywhere; but there was no feeling, no enthusiasm for him; and when you came to Philadelphia, there was a chill in the air like that which follows a hail storm."[128]

October 14 brought the result of the canvass. Save in Philadelphia, the day was quiet enough. The Baltimore Americans had arranged to apply their methods in the Quaker city. A boat-load of the "rip raps" landed; but inadvisedly killed an Irishman the day before the election, and were too much in the hands of the law to be effective on eletcion day.[129] The returns showed a close vote, but finally victory for the Democrats. The state offices were carried by a majority of about three thousand. The Congressmen elected were: 14 Democrats, 7 Union, and 4 Republicans (exclusive.) The Legislature held a majority of three on a joint ballot in favor of the Democrats.[130] The "Keystone state of the Federal Arch" had stood.

Indiana was another October state in which the Democrats had a good chance to check the Republican avalanche. The southern sentiment of the population of the lower half of the state and the presence of Know-Nothingism promised success in blocking any kind of a union against the Democracy. January 8, Jackson Day, the Democratic Convention at Indianapolis, adopted orthodox resolutions and nominated Ashbel P. Willard for governor.[131] He was a stump speaker by nature, and well fitted to lead in the type of a contest that soon developed. The "Peoples Convention," after the style of that of 1854, met at Indianapolis, May 1. They heard some enthusiastic Kansas speeches, adopted resolutions for its immediate admission and for no more slave states. To please Know-Nothings, suffrage was to accompany Naturalization, and for liquor law men, they expressed a desire for a constitutional law to check intemperance.[132] Oliver P. Morton was nominated to lead the ticket. He was the strongest possible selection; for he had always been a Democrat, was conservative, and capable as a leader.[133] The opposition, the Peoples Party took care not to be called Republican, and the state ticket represented the various factions that were opposed to the Democrats.

The canvass had all the features of the campaign elsewhere. The Democrats staged a tremendous rally at Tippecanoe battle ground September 3, at which James B. Clay and other noted persons took part. Willard and Morton held a series of debates, and Willard frequently indulged in breaking up a Republican meeting by calling off the Democrats.[134] Colfax and Judge Stuart held a joint debate in the north part of the state, and a wagon load of Republicans while attending one of these near Fort Wayne was set upon by a band of Irishmen and severely beaten.[135] The managers of the Peoples Party refused to accept the services of Julian during the early part of the Campaign, on the ground that he was an abolitionist.[136] They also refused to attempt anti-slavery propaganda in the south part of the state. Late in the canvass Julian entered the southern districts to convince the working people that slavery was at variance with their interests; but he long cherished the theme that "the South" was abandoned to "Fillmorism and Old Linerism."[137] From the standpoint of the true Republican principle, namely: the opposition to slavery, Julian thus summarized the campaign in the Hoosier state:—

> "Know-Nothingism was petted, not because it was with us in principle; but because we were willing to sell our principles for office. Neither the moral or economic bearing of slavery was discussed, while the real issue tendered in the Philadelphia platform, was rarely, if ever, fairly stated from the stump. The general style of our public speaking implied that the admission of Kansas as a free state was the real issue. Border Ruffian outrages and radical disclaimances of "abolitionism" were the regular staple of our orators. What infinite pains were taken to keep the "People's Party" above all taint of suspicion as to the latter abomination! With what emphasis did our leaders asservate that they were not abolitionists, and had no desire to interfere with slavery in the states, or to discuss the relation of master and slave where it existed by law; that our party was exceedingly national, and wonderfully friendly to the union; and at the most we only opposed the *extension* of slavery which the Old Whig and Democratic parties did years ago, whilst we were decidedly opposed to marrying the negro or setting them free among us."[138]

The Republicans failed to "come down to the National Road" with a majority sufficient to overcome that of the Democrats south of it. In fact, the size of the Democratic majority was a surprise to all. Willard was elected by a majority of nearly six thousand.[139] The Democrats carried six

Congressional districts and the Republicans, five. The Democratic majority in the legislature was more than twenty on joint ballot and two senatorships were at their disposal. Indiana was a dark spot on Republican national prospects. No party had yet consented to bear the name, and there were electoral tickets for both Frémont and Fillmore.

The Ohio election came at the same time; but it was generally conceded that the Republicans would carry it. After a lively canvass, the expected came true. The Republicans elected the state officers. The Democrats held eight of the twenty-one Congressional districts which was a great improvement over the 1854 catastrophe. The election in Florida where Know-Nothingism had been strong returned a Democratic governor, and an assurance that she would be of a solid South. An election in Delaware and town elections in Connecticut added to the Democratic triumph.

The drive north which culminated in the October election gave the Democrats practical assurance of success. From now on they fought with a psychological advantage. They claimed the Thirty-fifth Congress, three additional senators from the North, and the presidency. The odds were against the Republicans, and the ardor of their assault was checked.

1. William H. Hull to Howell Cobb, July 14, in *Toombs-Cobb-Slidell Correspondence*, pp. 375-376.
2. George Sanderson to Buchanan, Aug. 12. Buchanan MSS. P.H.S.
3. Malcolm Ives to Buchanan, Sept. 7, A.C.Ramsey to Buchanan, Sept. 27. Buch.MSS. P.H.S.
4. Buchanan to Malcolm Ives, Sept. 10. "My letters from the South are alarming. They are more so, because they contain no bluster; but evince a spirit of cool and calculating determination. It is the madness of folly, the very 'error of the moon' to believe that the Union is not in serious danger."
5. *New York Herald*,Oct.19, "The Presidential Question, Exact Condition of the Fight." Also,H.Wykoff to Buchanan, Oct.21,22, D.Sickles to Buchanan,Oct. 21. Buch.MSS.P.H.S.
6. Bennett to Buchanan, Oct. 22, Wykoff to Buchanan, Oct. 23. Buchanan MSS. P.H.S.
7. *VanBuren's Letter*. An attack in *New York Tribune* (w), July 12, said he had been "badgered" into writing it.
8. "Rynders Address" attacked in *Weekly Tribune*, July 26.
9. *The Albany Atlas and Argos* was the name given the newly combined papers.
10. Fernando Wood to Buchanan,July 28, D.B.Taylor to Buchanan, July 28. Buchanan MSS. P.H.S.
11. Fernando Wood to Buchanan, cited above. Taylor to Buchanan,

cited above. S.A. Bardsley to Buchanan, July 1. Buch. MSS. P.H.S.

12. S.Beardsley to Buchanan, Aug.2. Reports in *New York Tribune* (w), Aug. 2.
13. The nominations in many of the districts showed the old cleavage had left a grave problem there. Ives to Buchanan, cited below.
14. Malcolm Ives to Buchanan, Oct. 11. Buchanan MSS. P.H.S.
15. Geary's Report in *Kas.Hist.Soc.Pub.* vol. IV, p. 523.
16. *Ibid.*, pp. 256-529.
17. Document, *Kan.Hist.Soc.Pub.* vol. IV, p. 530.
18. This band had 1 brass field piece, 7 wagons, 38 U.S.Muskets, 47 Sharps' rifles, 6 military rifles, 2 shot guns, 20 revolving pistols, 14 bowie knives, and miscellaneous arms. Geary's report, p. 537. The Democratic Press made capital out of this equipment.
19. *Kan.Hist.Soc.Pub.*, vol. V, p. 265.
20. Minutes of Geary's administration in *Kan.Hist.Soc.Pub.* vol. IV, p. 719.
21. Convention, Aug. 6, reported in *Springfield Republican*, Aug.7.
22. Ely-Brewster platform, see chapter VII, "The Americans".
23. *Springfield Republican*, May 7. *National Intelligencer*, May 13. *Boston Bee*, May 7.
24. *Boston Bee*, May 26, 31.
25. *Boston Bee*, May 29.
26. *Springfield Republican*, Jan. 30.
27. *Springfield Republican*, July 1. *Boston Bee*, July 2.
28. *Ibid.*, July 1 and 2.
29. *New York Tribune* (w), Aug.2. *Springfield Republican*, July 24 and 26. *Boston Bee*, July 25.
30. *National Intelligencer*, July 31.
31. *Springfield Republican*, Aug. 5 and Aug. 21.
32. *Ibid.* Sept. 3 and *New York Tribune* (w), Sept.6 See also Chapter XI.
33. *National Intelligencer*, Sept. 5.
34. Letters to F.H.Ruggles and S.M.Allen in *N.Y.Tribune* (w), Sept. 27.
35. *N.Y.Tribune* (w), Sept. 27.
36. Pearson,H.G.,*Life of John A. Andrew*, vol. I, p. 66.
37. Quincy,Edmund, *Life of Josiah Quincy*, pp. 511-518.
38. Letter, Aug. 9. See Chapter VII, "Minor Parties."
39. Pamphlet, *Letter of Josiah Quincy, Aug. 30, to Whig Committee of Maine in reply to a letter of J.Z.Goodrich on Choate's Letter.*
40. Pamphlet, *Whig Policy Analyzed and Illustrated by Josiah Quincy*, Oct. 27.
41. Pamphlet, *Joel Parker's Address to Citizens of Cambridge.*
42. Pamphlet, *The Scholar in Politics.*
43. See below, "The October Elections."
44. Speech of James O. Putnam at Rochester, March 3.
45. Defence of President Fillmore by Honorable James Brooks of New York, Cincinnati, May 30.
46. There were two of the Brooks brothers—James and Erastus.

Erastus was national vice-president of the Americans and became their candidate for governor of New York.

47. Pamphlet, *North American Documents: Law's Letter to Gustavus Adolphus Scroggs,* on July 3, 1856.
48. *New York Tribune* (w), July 12.
49. See Chapter X—"The War of Personalities."
50. Pamphlet, *North American Documents. Letters of Law, Marsh, and Schaffer.*
51. *National Intelligencer,* Aug. 3. *New York Tribune* (w), Aug. 30, Sept. 6.
52. Pamphlet written by P. McGill.
53. There was a special animus between Brooks and Greeley. Brooks had engaged in his far-famed controversy with Bishop Hughes while Greeley was a friend of the Bishop.
54. *New York Tribune* (w), Sept. 27.
55. *New York Tribune* (w), Oct. 11.
56. For account, see below.
57. The Democrats had felt the necessity of keeping the Americans in the field in the North, and were working to that end.
58. Pamphlet, *Facts for the People, no. 1. Conspiracy of the Fillmore Leaders to elect Buchanan by inducing honest men to throw away upon Mr. Fillmore votes which would otherwise be cast against slavery extension and for John C. Frémont.*
59. *Proceedings of the Democratic Republican State Convention at Syracuse, New York, July 24.* (Address and Resolutions).
60. *New York Tribune* (w), Sept. 20.
61. Hamilton Fish to James A. Hamilton, Sept. 12. Pamphlet. *New York Tribune,* Sept. 26.
62. *Speech of General Aaron Ward at White Plains,* Sept. 16. Pamphlet.
63. Buchanan's Letter to Tammany Hall, July 2.
64. *Proceedings of the Merchants Great Democratic meeting at the New York Exchange on Thursday, 2d of October, 1856.*
65. Meetings April 11 at Neward, May 25 at Paterson.
66. *New York Tribune,* May 29.
67. Reported in *New York Tribune,* June 6.
68. *Ibid.,* June 12.
69. *Letter of Ephraim Marsh, President of the Philadelphia Convention denouncing Fillmore,* cited above.
70. *New York Tribune* (w), Sept. 27.
71. Davis,W.J., *History of Political Conventions in California,* p. 68.
72. *Democratic State Journal,* April 21. Davis, p. 59.
73. Davis, pp. 59-61.
74. *Democratic State Journal,* Aug. 28. Davis, pp. 65,66.
75. *Democratic State Journal,* Aug. 11 and 28.
76. Davis, p. 74.
77. *Daily Alta California,* Oct. 10,12. The *Alta* was a moving force in the Peoples Party and in securing vindication for the Vigilantes.
78. Davis. pp. 70-73.
79. Fillmore to B.F.Washington, Aug. 30. *Fillmore papers,* vol. II, p. 364.

80. *Democratic State Journal*, July 17.
81. J.A.Stuart to Buchanan, Sept. 13. Buchanan MSS. P.H.S.
82. C.Smith to Buchanan, Sept. 16. Buchanan MSS. P.H.S.
83. Beverly Tucker to Buchanan, Sept. 18. Buchanan MSS. P.H.S.
84. Robert McLean to Buchanan, Oct. 7. Buchanan MSS. P.H.S. McLean along with ex-Governor Thomas were the most active Democrats in Maryland.
85. For account, Schmeckebier, *The Know-Nothing Party in Maryland*, p. 38.
86. Robert McLean to Buchanan, Oct. 13, J.Cadwalader to Buchanan, Oct. 19. Buchanan MSS. P.H.S.
87. C.L.Ward to J.W.Forney, July 23. Buchanan MSS. P.H.S. Ward was national chairman, and Forney state chairman for Pennsylvania.
88. *Pennsylvanian*, July 3.
89. Reported *Pennsylvanian*, Aug. 8.
90. McClure,AK., *Old Time Notes of Pennsylvania*, vol. I, p. 266, gives a good account of Forney's speech and his personal enthusiasm.
91. Bigler to Buchanan, July 15. Buchanan MSS. P.H.S.
92. They bought the *Tiogo Eagle*, C.L.Ward to Buchanan, July 20. Buchanan MSS. P.H.S.
93. Ellis Lewis to Buchanan, Aug. 13. Buchanan MSS. P.H.S.
94. Campbell to Buchanan, Aug. 13. Buchanan MSS. P.H.S.
95. Jones to Buchanan, Sept. 18. Buchanan MSS. P.H.S.
96. Jones to Buchanan, Aug. 16. Buchanan MSS. P.H.S.
97. *National Intelligencer*, March 21.
98. *New York Tribune*, March 27.
99. *Ibid.*, May 14.
100. *Pennsylvanian*, Aug. 7.
101. Wm.M.Chace to Welles, July 17. Welles MSS. L.C.
102. C.A.Dana to Pike, Oct. 5, in *First Blows*, pp. 349-350.
103. *The Evening Bulletin* and *North American*.
104. E.D.Morgan to Welles, July 21. Welles MSS. L.C.
105. Welles to J.T.Heil, Sept. 4. Welles MSS. L.C.
106. Morgan to Welles, Sept. 19. Welles MSS. L.C.
107. C.L.Ward to Buchanan, Sept. 10. Buchanan MSS. P.H.S.
108. Morgan to Welles, Aug. 27. Welles MSS. L.C.
109. E.D.Morgan to Welles, Sept. 11. Welles MSS. L.C.
110. Morgan to Welles, Sept. 19. Welles MSS. L.C.
111. Morgan to Welles, Sept. 30. Welles MSS. L.C.
112. Morgan to Welles, Oct. 8, Chase to Welles, Oct. 11. Welles MSS. L.C.
113. WilliamM.Piatt to Buchanan, June 8, W.H.Hunter to Buchanan, June 9, Thomas I.McCammant to Buchanan,July 19. Buchanan MSS. P.H.S.
114. Pamphlet,*Governor Reeder's Reasons for Voting for Frémont—*
115. Pamphlet, *Infidelity and Abolitionism—An Open Letter to Friends of Religion, Morality, and the American Union.*
116. Pamphlet, *Another Old Line Democrat for Frémont*. Letter to Charles Gibbon, Sept. 22.

117. Letter to *Pennsylvanian*, Oct. 22. *Pennsylvanian*, Oct. 24.
118. Their leading speakers were: Preston from Kentucky; Stewart from Maryland; Floyd from Virginia; Cobb and Johnson of Georgia; Meade of Virginia; A.V.Brown of Tennessee; John VanBuren and Horatio Seymour of New York; Faulkner of Virginia; Levi Woodbury and Toucey of Connecticut; John Appleton of Me.; Thomas C.Fields of New York; I.H.Wright of Mass.;B.F.Hallett, Mass.;Jas.B.Clay,Ky.;J.S.Wells,N.H., Reverdy Johnson,Md.; Rufus Choate,N.H. Home talent: E.B.Schnable, C.R.Buchalew, Richard Broadhead, Wm.Bigler,Josiah Randall.
119. Pamphlet, *Address of the Democratic State Committee to the People of Pa.*
120. Letter of Wm.B.Read, June 30, in *Pennsylvanian*, July 11. Pamphlets: *Speech of Josiah Randall at Chambersburg*, Aug.6 (printed by Dem.State Comm.) *Appeal to Pennsylvania and and the middle states at Somerset, Pa.* Sept.24, *An Appeal for the Union by a Philadelphia Whig.* Seven articles signed "A Whig" in *Philadelphia Evening Journal.*
121. Walker to Buchanan, Oct. 3. Buchanan MSS. P.H.S. The Texas letter referred to was used in the campaign of 1844.
122. Pamphlet, *An Appeal for the Union. Letter of Robt. J. Walker, Sept. 30, written to Dem.Comm. of Pittsburgh.*
123. Wise to Gov.I.W.Lyon of Md. Sept.17, in Wise, *Life of Henry A.Wise,p.* 209. Replies in Wilson, *Rise and Fall*, vol. II, pp. 519-520.
124. *Apropos* this Convention Wise wrote Wilson in 1873 that he feared the security of the Union and wished to be ready to act. He insisted that a like convention would have prevented secession in 1860. Wise, *Life of Henry A. Wise of Virginia*, p. 210.
125. Kelly made numerous speeches and was termed by his opponents "the Prince of Demagogues."
126. This in capitals ran as a column head in the *Daily Pennsylvanian* and was used in pamphlets, circulars, and speeches.
127. Pamphlet, *The Great Fraud by which Pennsylvania is Sought to be abolitionized in October and November—the abolition state ticket and the Abolition Electoral Fillmore Ticket.*
128. Errett in *Western Magazine of History*, vol. X, p. 264.
129. *Pennsylvanian*, Oct. 13. VanDyke to Buchanan, Oct. 13. Buch. MSS. P.H.S.
130. Returns in *Tribune Almanac*, 1857.
131. *National Intelligencer*, Jan. 16.
132. *Ibid.,*May 5.
133. Foulke, *Life of Oliver P. Morton*, vol. I. pp. 48-49.
134. *Ibid.*, vol I, pp. 51-57.
135. *New York Tribune* (w), Oct. 4.
136. Clark, *Life of Julian*, p. 174.
137. Clark, *Life of Julian,pp.* 180-181, quoting *Journal*, Dec. 5., Speech, July 4, 1857, in *Julian's Speeches*, p. 133-134.
138. Speech, July 4, 1857, in *Julian's Speeches*, p. 134.
139. Returns from *Tribune Almanac*, 1857.

CHAPTER XIII

THE VERDICT

The October elections pointed to certain victory for the Democrats. The rejoicing of the victors and the inevitable slump of enthusiasm for the Republican cause raised some questioning as to whether they would continue the fight or not. However, there was still a possibility of Frémont for president. The results in Pennsylvania would have to be reversed and every free state that awaited the November election to register its position, be carried. There was a further incentive in going on record as having fought a good fight.

The Struggle Continued

Although the odds were against them, the Republicans persevered. They claimed that forged naturalization papers had been used to swell the Democratic vote in Philadelphia,[1] and raised the accusation of fraud to offset the reaction to the defeat in the state. They did their best to overcome the effect of Geary's pacification of Kansas, and to make the situation there continue to yield political capital. The report of the Investigation Committee was augmented by a list of further outrages.[2] William Phillips' *Conquest of Kansas* was off the press by the middle of October.[3] Mrs. Robinson, wife of the Topeka Constitution governor was preparing a work on Kansas and the press promised the public something interesting, but the campaign was over before it was finished.[4] Editorials were as sanguinary as ever but there was a strained tone about them. The *Tribune* began a continued story by L. Maria Child, entitled *The Kansas Emigrants*,[5] and a correspondence of ministers in regard to outrages began to appear to fill the waning Kansas column.[6] Letters from the "Prison of the Hundred" took the place of those from "Camp Treason."[7] A national Kansas Committee with headquarters at Chicago[8] did what it could to keep the hue and cry going, but a lull was inevitable.

Public interest was centered in the renewal of the contest in

Pennsylvania, and events there were of national import. The Republican leaders held a conference at Philadelphia and decided to renew their efforts.[9] They attributed their defeat to a number of things:[10] (1) the vote that Fillmore kept from them; (2) charges of Catholicism against Frémont; (3) the German, Welsh, and Quaker voters of Philadelphia had not come out; (4) several counties voted for Buchanan because of the Republican position on the liquor question; (5) in many counties large numbers of voters had remained at home. The total vote was twenty thousand below the regular poll of the state, and that missing vote, a number sufficient to win the election, was claimed for Frémont. With fifty thousand dollars the Republicans believed they could overcome some of the conditions that led to their defeat, and offset the general loss of enthusiasm.

Money came slowly. F. L. Bogue, a New York merchant, was enlisted to secure financial aid.[11] Morgan exerted himself greatly to secure more funds in New York. On October 21 he issued a draft for five thousand dollars and twenty-five thousand, if Frémont were elected.[12] "True men" at Boston were doing the same thing, and Lindley Smith, a merchant of Philadelphia, was doing the same thing there. Chase, Truman Smith, and Cameron went to work in Philadelphia and by October 27 had raised a contingent fund of twenty-five thousand to be paid only in case of Frémont's election, and had twenty-five thousand more, under the same conditions, for use in Philadelphia and other counties.[13] The funds obtained were sufficient to launch a brisk offensive, and the Democrats raised the query: "Could Pennsylvania be bought?"

Votes had been lost to the Republicans because of the position taken by the "south end" of the American allies who had never taken the welfare of the Union party to heart. The *Herald* accused them of misappropriating funds sent from New York,[14] and they were supposed to have sold ten thousand votes of the straight Know-Nothings of Philadelphia to Forney in a "side door transaction."[15] It might never be possible to bring all the Know-Nothings to a position of cooperation, but before this could be put to a test it was necessary to have the Fillmore electoral ticket withdrawn and a union ticket put in its place. On October 7, one week prior to the fateful election, the Frémont state committee had met at Harrisburg and made plans for a union electoral ticket.[16] They arranged for a mass convention at the same city on October 15, the day after election. Here they would select delegates for another convention at Harrisburg on October 21. This convention was to agree upon a union ticket, and a plan of union was tendered. Separate tickets were to be printed on which twenty-six names would be the same. One electoral vote was to be sacrificed by placing the name of Frémont at the head of one ticket and Fillmore at the other. The vote of the state was to be cast for both candidates in proportion as the popular vote stood. In event the entire vote would elect either candidate, it was agreed to cast it in his favor.

The plan for union did not work smoothly. The Americans turned down this and several other propositions.[17] John P. Sanderson, Know-Nothing chairman, refused to take action, and was later accused of suppressing the call for the mass convention. Finally a committee from the "North American" supporters of Fillmore broke the ice by a direct approach to the Sanderson committee.[18] Sanderson responded by sending a committee to the Republicans. His committee came back with a report on the call for the convention October 21, and the proposed plan of union. This brought the issue to a crisis. A majority of the Sanderson committee voted their approval of the ticket already in the field, and the *American Organ* printed their ticket with great unction.[19] Several of the Sanderson committee withdrew to cooperate with the "North Americans" and Republicans in their Union convention. The die had been cast; union could not be complete.

There was no longer any occasion to treat with Sanderson, and on October 20, the day before the Union Convention, Gibbon published his appeal to the Republicans.[20] This gave rise to the complete airing of the transaction over the ten thousand Philadelphia votes. Sanderson had at first taken the initiative in inviting a conference to form the union electoral ticket; but had gone to Washington and thereafter had refused to sanction a conference. Finally he asked Gibbon, the Republican chairman, to come to his office, since he had Forney's answer, and to enter at the side door. Gibbon, who was a Quaker, hesitated to enter offices by the side door, and was informed that he need not come.[21] The convention denounced the action of Sanderson and read a list of condemnatory resolutions from local councils. They adopted the plan for the ticket as already outlined by the Republicans.

The Democrats immediately countered the new offensive. They worked to keep the ultra Fillmore men who refused union steady in their position and to draw as many of them as they could to Buchanan. As a camouflage, they accused the faction that refused to enter the union of doing so in order to keep the South from abandoning Fillmore.[22] It was necessary to retain the effect of Wise's Governors' Convention. Radical statements of Southern leaders were used to prove that the South would surely destroy the Union, if Frémont succeeded.[23] The value of the Union was figured out in dollars and cents and presented to the Philadelphia merchants.[24] The only antidote was southern evidence to the contrary, and October 25 Kenneth Raynor attempted to save the day by writing a letter declaring that the South was only making a bluff to prevent concentration on Frémont in the North.[25] On November 1 he carried the doctrine to Philadelphia.[26] Raynor's efforts were not effective, and the Democrats made the most of their advantage. They made *A Final Appeal to Pennsylvania* in which they reviewed the entire situation, and pointed out how an honest Pennsylvanian had brought peace to Kansas, which operation was but the fore-runner of the making of a new free state.[27]

Arrangements similar to the one in Pennsylvania were attempted in other states. In Indiana, though there was little hope of regaining the state, some politicians thought a union on an electoral ticket feasible. It was attempted, a call for a joint convention appeared, and efforts made to make the movement live.[28] Little ever came of the movement. Attempts to combine were made in states that had not had October election to show conclusively the necessity of alliance in order to defeat the Democracy. An arrangement was tried in New Jersey similar to that in Pennsylvania[29] but with little success. A call was circulated in Illinois,[30] but apparently without response. The Fillmore ticket in most of the states was there for the purpose of remaining distinct and drawing off votes, and a union with it was impossible.

In several of the northern states there were occurrences that had a bearing on the outcome of the election. In California where both Frémont and Fillmore had been paraded as Pacific Railroad men, the Democrats made it a local issue; but had kept silent about their candidate. A while before election a letter from Buchanan was printed which was everything the most ardent Californian could desire.[31] This appearance was long enough before election day to give the letter time for a thorough circulation, and still not sufficient time for it to reach the Lower South. In Michigan the Democrats threatened to defeat Howard for Congress, which would be serious since he had been chairman of the Kansas Investigation Committee. Seward was sent to aid in the canvass for Howard.[32] In Massachusetts Burlingame's return to Congress was in doubt. He was threatened by a combination possible only in the complex politics that accompanied the last struggles of the Know-Nothings, and there was considerable interest as to the return of the man who had accepted "Bully" Brooks' challenge. Sumner's return to the Senate was likewise a point of interest in Bay State politics. Enthusiasm was to be the big factor in assuring it. On election day the martyr made a triumphal entry into Boston and the *Pilot*, though a supporter of Buchanan, pronounced it the greatest demonstration since the coming of Kossuth.[33]

The Results

The eventful day of the general election came at last, and Buchanan was made president of the United States.[34] New England went solidly for Frémont. There was still the bar-sinister of Americanism in Massachusetts, Connecticut, and Rhode Island; but its fate was sealed. The principle of opposition to slavery had triumphed. Massachusetts would return Sumner to the Senate and it was not far in the future that Banks would take the control of the state away from Gardner. There would be no more attempts of Americanism to dominate as an anti-slavery party.

The Atlantic seaboard states added but one to the Frémont column. New York went for him by an ample plurality over Buchanan, his closest competitor. The Republicans swept the state offices and controlled the legislature. Twelve seats in Congress went to the Democrats who were united with the Fillmorites in the election of four of them. The result in New

York had an important place in the future of the politics of the country. A Republican victory in the Empire State gave her prestige in party conclaves. The thorough defeat of Fillmore indicated that Americanism that sought to dominate the country by offering a compromise on the slavery controversy could never again have "a bulwark in the North." In Pennsylvania the returns showed that Buchanan had carried the state, not by a plurality, but by a majority of over a thousand votes. This was all that the Democrats could wish; but they were doomed to disappointment. Much animus had been generated by the campaign and the assembling of the legislature showed that the Democrats had a precarious majority of two or three. Attempts to reward Forney for his work by giving him a senatorship failed. Simon Cameron secured the three Democratic votes necessary to elect a Republican, and went to Washington as the first contribution of Pennsylvania to the party. Buchanan either would not or could not give Forney a place that he would accept. In this the man who had "slipped in at the side door" to save Pennsylvania, saw the hand of the South controlling the president he had done so much to elect and keeping him from a well-merited reward.[35] New Jersey went for Buchanan by an ample plurality. Two "fusion" candidates were elected to Congress and three Democrats. The "fusion" candidate for governor was elected. The elections in both Pennsylvania and New Jersey left the Republicans in an unsatisfactory position. The basis of the formidable attack they had made on the Democrats was still that of cooperation with other parties on the principle of opposing slavery. There must be further assimilation.

In the northwest, Ohio followed the course marked out by the October returns, although Frémont won by only a plurality. Likewise, Indiana had undergone no change of heart, and "Buch and Breck" carried the Hoosier state. Buchanan also carried Illinois by a plurality. Bissell, the Republican candidate for governor, won over Richardson. The Democrats took five of the nine seats in Congress, and had good majorities in the legislature. They had the lion's share in the state but Richardson, Douglas' *alter ego*, who was to be given the governorship to recompence the loss of the speakership was defeated by nearly five thousand votes. The election was not a final verdict on the control of the state, and in only two years Douglas' term in the Senate expired. Michigan gave Frémont a large majority, Bingham was re-elected governor, and Howard, the only candidate for Congress whose seat was considered in danger, was returned. The victory was complete. The next year Cass' seat in the Senate would be vacant and Zachariah Chandler was his logical successor. Going from Cass to Chandler marked the passing from one political era to another. Wisconsin also gave the Republicans a thorough victory. In Iowa where the Fillmore ticket had strength enough to cause the Republicans a great deal of anxiety, Frémont won by a plurality. Except for Illinois and Indiana where a large part of the population was of southern origin, the Republicans held the Northwest. The political empire of Douglas had been reduced to two states and even there his political supremacy was challenged.

California and the border states with but one exception went to Buchanan. Republican strength in California awaited the time that Broderick would be killed and the slavery issue alienate the two wings of the Democracy of the state. The border state elections indicated how far the Republicans might penetrate into slave territory. In the Wheeling district of Virginia Frémont polled two hundred and ninety-one votes. In Kentucky, he received 314; in Delaware, 308; and in Maryland, 281. The reward for a continued effort to make a showing in the slave states had been less than twelve hundred votes, and showed that the idea that the poor white of the South would support an attack on the South, was visionary. Maryland alone went for Fillmore. It was the only slave state the Americans had been able to save from their "sectional" antagonist, and they had not carried even one of the free states.

The South was a unit for Buchanan. In some states Fillmore was given a heavy vote, and his total in all the slave states was 479,465 as compared with 609,587 for Buchanan. The electoral vote stood: Buchanan, 173; Frémont, 114; and Fillmore, 8. The Democrats had the control of the nation for another four years, but they had also the problem of harmonizing North and South on the program they had pledged for Kansas.

The Aftermath

Although the Democrats triumphed, the new party on slavery made substantial gains. The Americans had been defeated in their last strongholds in the North, and would not seriously interfere again. That opposition to slavery was to be the great issue in the North had been demonstrated, and with it the future of the Republican party was practically assured. The next Congress would be Democratic, but the opposition would be more homogeneous and more clearly Republican. Every free state had an organization. The national machinery had been completed and used once. All these were very definite accomplishments.

It was also possible to profit by the lessons taught in the campaign. The Democratic party had swept the South and at the same time carried a considerable part of the North. So long as it held Pennsylvania in its grip and Douglas was master of two of the states of the Northwest, there was no hope for Republican success. Still the future did not seem dark. If squatter sovereignty meant one thing in the North and another thing in the South, the possibility of Republican victory lay in the breaking of the Democracy along this line of cleavage. Greeley had nailed its dual promise on slavery in the very last breath of the campaign.[36] In the short session of the Thirty-Fourth Congress the Republicans argued that Buchanan was sustained in the North on a promise of freedom to Kansas.[37] Aid was to come from the camp of the enemy. The work of Stephen A. Douglas during the Buchanan administration was necessary to the first Republican victory.

A great many things might be done to give the party unity and vitality. The discordant elements could be adjusted with time. After the first struggle as a party, the old free-soil elements that had pioneered were sufficiently submerged to make it possible to get closer to Whig doctrine. The next platform might include planks not found in the Buffalo Platform of 1848. Pennsylvania was yet to be won and a tariff plank would be possible in 1860. There was also much to be done to make the finances of a campaign easier. Getting money spontaneously from the people had not been successful enough to yield the best results, and Greeley admitted that where they had one dollar for Pennsylvania and New York

the"Fillmoreans and Buchaniers had ten."[38] The addition of a
tariff plank to their platform might put them in position to
secure a stronger financial backing. Still, the Republicans
would continue to experience difficulty in raising funds. The
greatest sources of financial aid could not be tapped by a
party whose triumph threatened to lead to civil war.

One of the first requisites of future success was to keep the
discouragement of defeat from demoralizing so loosely knit
an organization. The *National Era* printed numerous statements from the Republican press to prove that they were not
disheartened. Its own reaction was that fraud and tempor-
izing with Know-Nothingism had lost them the vital northern
states. Another time both these could be met and for the
present the party accepted the verdict without a thought of
applying the Democratic precept of destroying the union because they had failed.[39] Greeley, the oracle of the new political
faith, summed up their adjustment to the inevitable.[40] They
were not discouraged and were confident of a future. Their
showing had been good for a party that was less than six
months old in five of the free states.[41] Much of their voting
strength had come from the Americans, and better results
could be expected when this party had had a longer time to
adjust itself to the new conditions. The struggle to make
Kansas free must also be continued. They were also to use
their strength to reform the ballot box and prevent the recurrence of frauds like those in October that had beaten them
out of the victory. Facing the future, they were to forget the
past: "Republicans, the past is past, and its duties, well or il
discharged are no more; and each day has its own responsi
bilities, and wise are they who have the sagacity to discove
and the virtue promptly and faithfully to discharge them."

The Republicans acted on the promise that better thing
lay in the future, and continued to shape ends towards tha
objective. The chairman of the national committee issued
call for a conference on the welfare of the party.[42] The Re
publican Association of Washington issued an address to th
Republicans of the United States which summed up what the
had done and what they intended to do.[43] Clephane collecte
and published the most valuable documents of the campaign.
The same year that the document collection was printed Hel

er's *Impending Crisis* was given to the country with the aid and endorsement of the Republicans. There was no intention of giving up the struggle in Kansas. Greeley alone had fifteen thousand dollars in his *Tribune's* Kansas fund. The radical abolitionists were not willing to accept the adjustment to the situation made by the Republicans. They called a convention at Worcester, Massachusetts, with the purpose of seceding from the Union, and they reviewed the work of the Republicans in the campaign, and pronounced their method a failure.[45] This further purging of radicalism, aided the new party in keeping everything in readiness to continue the struggle to drive the Democracy out of the North.

The Republicans, in truth, never quitted the field, and they had as an added incentive the welfare of an organized party. The new party had already become a vested interest of a political future of the men who had broken their old alliances. If it died, their career might die with it, and in a new alignment, other leaders be at the van. The fact is, that without this first attempt, the Republican party as it came to American history, must have been different. Their great and all-important issue was non-extention of slavery. It became obvious before the Buchanan administration was half gone that Douglas' "Popular Sovereignty" applied as the northern end of the Democracy had promised to apply it, would accomplish the end the Republicans sought. The same time also witnessed the "Little Giant" in insurrection and read out of the administration party because, he insisted on the unimpaired working of his measure as he interpreted it. Here was the Democracy of the Northwest, an old and established party, standing for a principle that assured freedom to the territories. With their *raison d'etre* absorbed by the older party, the logical sequence was that the Republicans should come flocking to Douglas and his supporters. But they did not come. A new party with leaders and following had already been created. Though they sought the same end, as Douglas, they would seek it in terms a little more radical, would tread ground a little more dangerous—a performance they had already trained themselves to do—and thereby continue to live.

The Republican leaders, though not new to politics, made a new school. The coming of new schools has always been given due notice in our history. Among them, the Republican leaders in their first national contest stand second to none in significance. The position they took in the face of the almost certain dissolution of the union in event of their success marked a new departure. It ran counter to the councils of the school of Clay and Webster who in all their wranglings, turned always to domestic tranquillity as the paramount issue. Here was a group that would accept the logic of a "higher law."

In connecting a constituency with this well-defined leadership, it must be remembered that the creative campaign of 1856 was staged as a young man's movement. "Young America" had had its place in politics for some time, and the radical nature of the new party made fitting application of it. The leader chosen was a young man, an adventurer from the farthest west, and the war crys were new and revolutionary. Men voting for the first time cast their ballot for Frémont. With a large part of the voting population of the North accepting their position in face of the threat of disunion, schooling themselves to act regardless of consequences, sweeping towards unity, on a tidal wave of enthusiasm, and keen for victory, a new force was born in the Free States in 1856.

It was a new force indeed. Its leaders must live by, or die with the infant party, and to live meant to crowd nearer and nearer the verge of the crisis that the prosecution of their principles ever threatened to bring. Young and enthusiastic men were found and oriented in a new atmosphere that disregarded consequences. In fact, a new psychology was taught and a new political genus known as "stiff-backed Republican" appeared. He would vote for the prescription of slavery extension, and would fight if certain contingencies arose. With a South already a unit on the slavery question, this newcomer sought to destroy the Democracy in the North and by the numerical preponderance of the Free States, control the country on a counter-sectional issue. This was portentious of great events.

1. McClure in *Old Time Notes*, vol.I, p. 258, says that nearly a score of men were later convicted on the charge of fraud at the ballot box at this election.
2. Pamphlet, *An Authentic Account of Outrages in Kansas since the Appointment of the Kansas Investigation Committee and not*

included in *Their Report to the House of Representatives . . . By an Officer of the Commission.*

3. First notice in *New York Tribune,* Oct. 11.
4. Robinson, Sara T.L., *Kansas, Its Interior and Exterior Life.* The first notice of the book in the *New York Tribune* was Nov. 7.
5. *New York Tribune,* Oct. 23.
6. *Ibid.,* Oct. 29.
7. *National Era,* Nov. 6.This referred to the men Geary had captured and held for trial.
8. Account of organization in Chicago *Daily Democratic Press,* July 25.
9. Morgan to Welles, Oct. 15. Welles MSS. L.C. *Pennsylvanian,* Oct. 20. McClure says that Henry Wilson was the hopeful man of the group that met at Philadelphia, that Cameron, Weed, and Blair decided to fight but were not sanguine. *Recollections of Fifty Years,* p. 45.
10. Chace to Welles, Oct. 21. Welles MSS. L.C.
11. Morgan to Welles, Oct. 25. Welles MSS. L.C.
12. Morgan to Welles (private), Oct. 22. Welles MSS. L.C.
13. Morgan to Welles (private), Oct. 27. Welles MSS. L.C.
14. *New York Herald,* Oct. 17, clipped in *Pennsylvanian,* Oct. 20.
15. Gibbon—Sanderson Correspondence, *National Era,* Oct. 20. For account, see below.
16. William S. Garvin to Buchanan, Oct. 10. Buch.MSS. P.H.S. *New York Tribune* (w), Oct. 18.
17. Morgan to Welles, Oct. 18. Welles MSS. L.C.
18. *Pennsylvanian,* Oct. 18.
19. *Daily American Organ,* Oct. 21.
20. Gibbon-Sanderson correspondence cited above.
21. Holliday says that Henry Wilson and Truman Smith had been watching Gibbon; for they feared his Quaker conscience, and when he lost the vote, Wilson reprimanded him. Holliday's Address, *Kan.Hist.Soc.Pub.*,vol.V, p. 54.
22. *Pennsylvanian,* Oct. 22.
23. For a list of threats, see Wilson, *Rise and Fall,* vol. II, p. 519.
24. Mueller,H.R., *Whig Party in Pennsylvania* p. 231.
25. Raynor's Letter Oct. 25. *New York Tribune,* Oct. 31.
26. Speech of Kenneth Raynor at Philadelphia, Nov. 1, in Cluskey, W.M., *Political Encyclopedia,* pp. 481-485.
27. Pamphlet, *The Last Appeal to Pennsylvania.*
28. Reported in Indianapolis, *State Sentinel,* Oct. 22,24.
29. Morgan to Welles, Oct. 27. Cited above.
30. Copy in Trumbull MSS. L.C.
31. *Sacramento State Journal,* Oct. 18. *Daily Alta California,* Oct. 22.
32. Pamphlet, *The Slaveholding Class Dominant in the Republic,* Speech of Seward at Detroit, Oct. 2.
33. *Boston Pilot,* Nov. 15.
34. Statements in regard to the returns are based on reports in *Tribune Almanac* of 1857; table in Cluskey's *Political Encyclopedia,* p. 244, and various newspapers.
35. It became the burden of Forney's contention that not only did Buchanan's subserviency to the South prevent his appointment,

but it also resulted in his refusal to carry out "Justice to Kansas," the point on which alone Pennsylvania was carried. Forney attributed the enmity of the South to the fairness of his work in presiding during the speakership election.

36. The *New York Tribune,*Nov. 4, clipped an article from the *Richmond Whig* attacking the *Lancastrian* for maintaining that the election of Buchanan meant non-extension.
37. Cluskey, *Political Encyclopedia,* pp. 441-447. This was considered important enough to be given a place among political documents.
38. Greeley to Pike, Aug. 6, *First Blows,* pp. 346-347.
39. *National Era,* Nov. 13.
40. *New York Tribune,* Nov. 6.
41. Connecticut, Rhode Island, New Hampshire, Pennsylvania, New Jersey.
42. Morgan to Welles, Nov. 6. Welles MSS. L.C.
43. Address dated Nov. 27, Cluskey's *Political Encyclopedia,* pp. 486-488.
44. Clephane, Lewis, *Republican Campaign Documents,* 1857.
45. Pamphlet, *The Kansas Struggle,* 1857.

BIBLIOGRAPHY

I. *MANUSCRIPT COLLECTIONS*

Buchanan, James	Pennsylvania Historical Society
Burke, Edmund	Library of Congress
Chase, Salmon P.	Library of Congress and Pennsylvania Historical Society
Clayton, John M.	Library of Congress
Coryell, Lewis S.	Pennsylvania Historical Society
Corcoran, W. W.	Library of Congress
Crittenden, John J.	Library of Congress
Donelson, A. J.	Library of Congress
Everett, Edward	Massachusetts Historical Society
Fessenden, William Pitt	Library of Congress
Giddings, Joshua R.	Library of Congress
Higginson, Thomas W.	Harvard Library
Julian, George W.	Library of Congress
Mann, Horace	Massachusetts Historical Society
Marcy, William L.	Library of Congress
McLean, John	Library of Congress
Pierce, Franklin	Library of Congress
Seymour, Horatio	New York Educational Bldg. Albany
Sherman, John	Library of Congress
Sumner, Charles	Harvard Library
Trumbull, Lyman	Library of Congress
Van Buren, Martin	Library of Congress
Washburne, E. B.	Library of Congress
Washburn, Israel	Library of Congress
Welles, Gideon	Library of Congress
Winthrop, Robert C.	Massachusetts Historical Society
Gundlach Collection	Missouri Historical Society of St. Louis
Treat Collection	Missouri Historical Society of St. Louis

II. *PUBLISHED PERSONALIA*

Ambler, Charles H., Correspondence of R. M. T. Hunter, Annual report. of American Historical Association, 1916, vol.II.

Baker, G. E., Works of William H. Seward, Boston, 1884.

Works of Charles Sumner, Lee and Shepard, Boston, 1883.

Moore, John Bassett, Works of James Buchanan, Philadelphia, 1908.

Nicolay and Hay, Complete Works of Abraham Lincoln, Gettysburg Edition.

Pierce, Edward L., Memoirs and Letters of Charles Sumner, 1878—1894.

Phillips, U. B., Correspondence of Robert Toombs, Alexander H. Stephens, and Howell Cobb. Annual Report of the American Historical Association, 1911 vol II.

Severance, Frank H., Fillmore Papers, vols. V and VI., Publications, Buffalo Historical Society.

Tyler, Lyon G., Letters and Times of the Tylers, Richmond, 1885.

III. *THE PRESS*
Washington, D. C.

National Era, Free Soil, Library of Congress

Daily Union, administration organ, Pennsylvania Historical Society

Daily Sentinel (clipped) Buchanan paper
National Intelligencer, Whig neutral. Pennsylvania Historical Society
American Organ, official American organ. Library of Congress

Pennsylvania

Pennsylvanian, Philadelphia, Buchanan official organ. Pennsylvania
          Historical Society
North American, Philadelphia, American-Republican. Pennsylvania His-
          torical Society
The Lancastrian, Lancaster, Buchanan's official paper (clipped)
The Gazette, Pittsburg, Republican (clipped)

New York

Evening Post, Free-Soil Democrat-Republican   (clipped)
Courier and Enquirer, Whig-Republican (clipped)
Times, Henry J. Raymond, Whig-Republican   (clipped)
Herald, Hard Democrat supported Republicans. Library of Congress
Tribune, Whig-Republican.   Pennsylvania Historical Society
Express, American Fillmore organ   (clipped)
Albany Evening Journal, Whig-Republican.   New York Historical So-
          ciety

New England

Springfield Republican, Whig-Republican. American Antiquarian So-
          ciety
Boston Bee, American, Governor Gardner's official paper. Boston Public
          Library
Boston Pilot, Irish-Democratic.   Boston Public Library

The North West

Enquirer, Cincinnati, Democratic. Library of Congress
Ohio Statesman, Democratic. Library of Congress
State Sentinel, Indianapolis, Democratic. Indiana Historical Society
Democrat, Chicago, Republican   (clipped)
Argus and Democrat, Madison, Democratic.   Wisconsin Historical So-
          ciety
Wisconsin State Journal, American-Republican.   Wisconsin   Historical
          Society
Milwaukee Free Democrat, Abolitionist-Republican (clipped)

Border States and South

Missouri Democrat, St. Louis, Blair-Benton organ. St. Louis Public
          Library
The Republican, St. Louis, Whig pro-slavery. Missouri Historical So-
          ciety, St. Louis
The Herald of Freedom, Lawrence, Free State (clipped)
The Richmond Enquirer (clipped)
Alta California, San Francisco, Vigilance Committee—Republican. Li-
          brary of Congress
Democratic State Journal, Sacramento, Democratic. Library of Congress

Radical Press

The Liberator, Boston. Pennsylvania Historical Society

Anti-Slavery Standard, New York. Pennsylvania Historical Society
The Independent, New York, (clipped)

IV. *PAMPHLETS*

(The following is not an exhaustive list.)

A. Compilations

Facts for the people—A general Selection of Documents for Republicans.
Reminiscences of Past and Present Times.
Republican Campaign Edition for the Million—Republican Platform.
     lives of Frémont and Dayton, etc.
The Republican Pocket Pistol—a collection of facts for Freemen.
The Republican Scrap Book.
Fillmore and Donelson Songs.
Campaign Song Book. Frémont Songs for the People.
Prize Republican Songster. Songs from all over the Union, competing
     for prizes offered by the Philadelphia Republican Club.
Republican Campaign Songster.
The Freemans Glee Book.
Frémont Songs. 12 selections.

B. Speeches, Sermons, and Addresses

Allison, John of Pa, The Republican Party—its Necessity and its
     Mission, in House of Representative, Aug. 6.
Armstrong, Rev. G. D. Politics and the Pulpit.
Benjamin, Judah P. of Louisiana on the Kansas Question, delivered in
     the Senate, May 2, 1856.
Billinghurst, Charles of Wis., A Review of the President's Message in
     House of Representatives, Aug. 9, 1856.
Bliss, Philoman of Ohio, Complaints of the Extensionists, their Falsity,
     in the House of Representatives.
Brenton, S. of Indiana, on Kansas contested election, in the House,
     Mar. 20, 1856.
Brooks, James, Defense of Mr. Fillmore, before a meeting of the
     American Party held at Cincinnati, Friday evening, May 30.
Brooks, Preston L., Disunion Document. speech at Columbia, S. C.,
Broom, Jacob of Pa., Defense of Americanism in House of Represent-
     atives, Aug. 4, 1856.
Brown, Aaron V., An Address on the Parties and Issues of the Presiden-
     tial Election before the Keystone Club of Philadelphia.
     Aug. 15.
——————————, Address Before the Democratic Association of
     Nashville, June 24.
Buffington, James of Mass., Position of Mass. on the Slavery Question,
     in House, Apr. 30.
Burlingame, Anson of Mass., Defense of Mass., in House of Represent-
     June 21.
Burnett, Henry of New York, on Admission of Kansas and the political
     effects of Slavery, House, June 30, 1856.
Cadwalader, John of Pennsylvania, on the subject of Slavery in the
     Territories, House of Representatives. Mar. 5, 1856.
Carey, Henry C., Address to voters of Burlington County upon the im-
     portance of the approaching presidential election.

292   *The Early History of the Republican Party*

Clay, Clement C. Jr. of Ala., on the Contest in Kansas and the plan
    and purpose of Black Republicanism. Senate, Apr. 21.
Clay, Cassius M. of Ky., Speech before the Young Men's Republican
    Union of New York (*Tribune*, Oct. 24).
Cochrane, John, Speech delivered before the young mens Democratic
    union club, Apr. 9.
Colfax, Scuyler of Indiana, the "Laws" of Kansas, House of Repre-
    sentatives, June 21st.
Cragin, A. H. of N. H., Jefferson against Douglas, in House, Aug. 4th.
Curtis, G. W. The Duty of the American Scholar to the Politics of
    the Times. Aug. 5 before Literary Society of Wesleyan U.,
    Middletown, Conn.
Delavan, Edward C. a speech at a meeting of the Friends of Fillmore
    at Ballston, Aug. 9.
Door, James A. of New York Bar, Address, Justice to the South, Oct. 8.
Dougherty, Daniel, Oration delivered before the democracy of the city
    and county of Philadelphia in Independence Square, July 4.
Darnell, W. S. of Mass. The Kansas Contested Election, in House.
    Mar. 18.
Day, Timothy C., of Ohio. The Democratic Party as it was and as it
    is, in the House, Apr. 23, 1856.
————————————, The Humbug and the Reality, an address to
    his constituents.
Douglas, Stephen, A. Speech on Kansas territorial affairs, Senate, Mar. 20.
————————————, Reply to Senator Collomer on Kansas ter-
    ritorial affairs in Senate, Apr. 4.
Elder, Dr. William, of Philadelphia, Emancipation. Its Conditions and
    Policy. At Tremont Temple, Boston.
Field, David Dudley, Reasons why naturalized citizens should vote for
    Frémont. Delivered at Troy, N. Y.
Fillmore, Millard, Three Speeches at Albany, Newburg, and Rochester.
Foster, Eden B., A North Side View of Slavery, a Sermon on Crime
    against Freedom in Kansas and Washington, Aug. 31st.
Foster, Frederick, Great Speech of Hon. Frederick Foster.
Frothingham, O. B., The Last Signs. A sermon.
Giddings, Joshua R., Privileges of the Representatives. Privileges of
    the People. Speech at the trial of Preston Brooks.
    July 11.
Grow, Galusha A. of Pa., Affairs in Kansas, a speech in the House,
    Mar. 5th.
Hall, Nathaniel, The Lord Reigneth. Sermon preached at the First
    Church, Dorchester, Mass., June 1st.
Hall, Robert B., of Mass., Speech on the assault of Sumner in the
    House, July 12th.
Harlan, James of Ia., Admission of Kansas, speech in Senate, Mar. 27.
Hickman, John, of Pa., Kansas Contested Election, speech in the
    House, Mar. 19.
Hale, John P. of N. H., The Wrongs of Kansas. Speech in the
    Senate, Feb.
Henry, C. S., Plain Reasons for the Great Republican Movement, etc.
    Remarks made at a public meeting in Geneva, N. Y.,
    July 19.

Holbrook, John C., Our Country's Crisis, a discourse delivered at
    Dubuque, Ia., July 6.
Jay, John Esq., America Free or America Slave—an address on the
    state of the country at Westchester County, New York.
    Oct. 8.
Johnson, Andrew, Speech on the political issues of the day, delivered
    before the citizens at Nashville, July 15th.
Kelley, William D., Address at West Philadelphia Hall, Sept. 4th
——————————————, Address at Spring Garden Hall, Sept. 9th.
——————————————, Address at Spring Garden Hall, Sept. 16th.
Marshall, S., of Illinois, the Insanity of the Times, and the Present
    Condition of Political Parties, in the House, Aug. 6th.
Mulfor, Isaac S., An address on the Relation of the General Govern-
    ment to Slavery, at Camden, N. J.
Morgan, E. B. Fillmore's Political History and Position, in House of
    Representatives, Aug. 4th.
Morrill, Justin S. of Vt. Admission of Kansas. House of Represent-
    atives, June 26th.
Parker, Joel, Non Extension of Slavery and Constitutional Responsi-
    bility. Address before the citizens of Cambridge, Oct. 4th.
Parker, Theodore, A New Lesson for the Day.
Perkins, G. W. Facts and Duties of the Times, a Sermon delivered
    before the First Congregational Church of Chicago.
Perry, John J. of Maine, Freedom national—Slavery sectional—speech
    in the House May 1st.
Porter, Noah, Civil Liberty. A sermon at Framington, Conn. July 13th.
Postes, George Thatcher, Fellowship with Slavery. A sermon in First
    Cong. Church. Meriden, Conn., June 29th.
Pugh, George E. of Ohio on the condition of affairs in Kansas Terri-
    tory, in Senate, May 26th.
Putnam, James O., American Principles. Speech delivered at a Fillmore
    and Donaldson Ratification meeting in Rochester.
    Mar. 3, 1856.
Randall, Josiah, of Philadelphia. Speech at Chambersburg, Aug. 6th.
Reed, William B., Address on Leaving the Whig and Joining the
    Democratic Party.
——————————, Appeal to Pennsylvania. Speech delivered at a meet-
    ing of the friends of Buchanan and Breckenridge at
    Somerset, Penn., Sept. 24th.
Roy, J. E., Kansas—Her struggle and Her Defense. Discourse preached
    in Plymouth Cong. Ch., Chicago, June 1st.
Sammons, Address delivered at the opening of the American State
    Council at Syracuse, Aug. 26th.
Sears, Edward H., Revolution or Reform. A discourse occasioned by
    the present crisis. Preached at Wayland, Mass.
    June 15th.
Seward, William. H., Plymouth oration. Dec. 21, 1855.
——————————, Immediate Admission of Kansas into the Union, in
    Senate, Apr. 9.
——————————, Speech against Douglas Second Enabling Bill, in Sen-
——————————, ate, July 2.

—————————, Concerning Kansas and the Constitutional Freedom
—————————, of Debate, June 16.
—————————, Speech on the Army Bill in the extraordinary session
of the Senate.
—————————, Immigrant White Labor or imported Black African
Slave Labor. Speech at Oswego, N. Y. Nov. 3.
—————————, The slaveholding Class Dominant in the Republic.
At Detroit, Oct. 2.
Seymour, Horatio, Speech at Springfield, Mass. July 4.
Sherman, John W., of Ohio. Speech in reply to Mr. Stephens of Ga.
and Review of Oliver's Minority Report, House.
July 30th.
Stephens, Alexander H. of Ga. Speech on the Bill to Admit Kansas as
a state under the Topeka Constitution, House,
June 28th.
Stewart, James A. of Md. Powers of the Government of the U.S.
Federal, State and Territorial. House, July 23.
Sumner, Charles, Faneuil Hall Speech, Nov. 2, 1855.
—————————, Crime Against Kansas, in Senate, May 19—20.
Tappan, M. W. of N. H. Modern Democracy the ally of Slavery
House of Rep. July 29.
Toombs, Robert, Lecture delivered in Tremont Temple, Boston, June 24
Trumbull, Lyman, Illinois, Affairs in Kansas Territory. Speech in Sen-
ate, Mar. 14.
Trofton, Mark of Mass., Kansas Contested Election. In House, Mar. 12
Tyson, J. R. of Pa. Speech on Sumner Assault. House, July 12.
Ullman, Daniel, The Course of Empire. An oration before the order
of United Americans.
Wade, Edward, of Ohio. The Slavery Question. Speech in House.Aug. 2
Wall, James W., Speech on accepting the nomination for Congress
Burlington, N. J.
Ward, Aaron V., Speech at the great Democratic mass meeting at
White Plains, New York, Sept. 16.
Washburn, I. Jr. of Maine, The Contested Election. Speech in the
House, Mar. 14.
Waldron, Henry of Michigan, Kansas Affairs. Speech in the House
Apr. 8.
Wilson, Henry, of Mass., Personalities and Aggressions of Mr. Butler
In Senate, June 13.
—————————, Speech in Senate, Feb. 18.
Zollicoffer, Felix K., of Tennessee. State of Political Parties. In House

C. Political Letters and Addresses

Allen, Thomas G., Letter to Col. Thomas B. Florence Representativ
in 34th Congress from 1st district of Pa. Aug. 1
Bernard, David D., Letter from, on Political Conditions of the Country
Blair, Frances P., Letter to the Republican Association of Washington
D. C. Dec. 1, 1855
—————————, A Voice from the Grave of Jackson. Letter to
public meeting in New York held Apr. 29.
—————————, General Jackson and James Buchanan. Letter from

F. P. Blair to the public. Aug. 15.

———————, Letters to his neighbors. Silver Spring. Sept. 17.

———————, Facts for the People. Another letter from Francis P. Blair.

Caruthers, Samuel, Letters to his constituents.

Chote, Rufus, on the Presidential Question, in Boston Courier, Aug. 14.

Chambers, John. Letters to Hon. Harlan Ingram, R. G. Wright, Gen. George W. Bowman, and Democratic members of the legislature.

Clay, James B. A letter from. July 14 in Terre Haute Journal.

———————, Letter to James Buchanan.

Colwell, Stephen. The South: a letter from a friend in the North with specific reference to the effects of disunion upon slavery.

Freedley, Edwin T. The Issue and its Consequences.

Ingham, S. D. Another Old Line Democrat for Fremont—Letter of former Secty. of Treas. under Jackson, Trenton, Sept. 2.

Magruder, J. B. Presidential Contest of 1856 in Three Letters.

Marshall, S. S. The Real Issue. Union or Disunion. Letter on the Parties and Politics of the day, to the Freemen of the 9th Congressional district of Ill.

Law, George—Letters from George Law, Ephraim Marsh, and Chauncey Schaffer.

Marsh, Ephraim—Reasons for supporting Col. John C. Frémont.

Pearce, James A. and Pratt, Thomas G.—Old Line Whigs for Buchanan and Breckenridge. Letters to the Whigs of Md.

Quincy, Josiah. Remarks on the Letter of the Hon. Rufus Chote to the "Whig State Committee of Maine written in answer to a letter of the Hon. John Z. Goodrich.

Ramsen to Rynders. Slavery or Freedom—A strange matter. Several letters.

Reeder, A. H., Reasons for Voting for Frémont.

Scott, Henry D. Letters to his constituents of Indiana.

VanBuren, Martin. Letter of ex-Pres. VanBuren, June 28.

Walker, Robert J. An Appeal for the Union. Letter to the Democratic Committee of Pittsburgh. Sept. 30.

Watkins, A. G., Letters on the Presidential Question.

Address of the Democratic State Central Committee to the People of Pa.

An Appeal for the Union by a Philadelphia Whig.

An Appeal to the Conservative Masses—North and South—to end agitation forever against slavery by decided action now.

Democratic Stampede in Michigan. Patriotic appeal.

The Last Appeal to Pennsylvania.

D. Controversial—Slavery, Economics, Politics

Bailey, Dr. G., Facts for the People, published monthly, Washington, D. C.

Baker, Henry, M. D. Two Chapters from Oligarchy and Hierarchy.

DeBows Review—The Relative Political Status of the North and South.

Evening Post—Letters addressed to the Friends of Freedom and the

Union by Hampden

For Free Democrats.

Foot, Samuel, late Judge of Supreme Court of New York—Reasons for Joining the Republican Party.

Green, Samuel B. A pamphlet on equal rights and privileges to the people. Nov. 1, 1856.

Ganse, H. D. Bible Slaveholding Not Sinful—a reply to "Slaveholding Not Sinful" by Samuel B. Howe. D.D.

Infidelity and Abolitionism—an open letter to the Friends of Religion, Morality, and the American Union.

Ingersoll, C. J. African Slavery in America.

Jagger, William—Information acquired from the best authorities with respect to the institution of slavery.

Morris, Charles—The Olive Branch or the Evil and the Remedy.

Nott, Samuel—Slavery and the Remedy or Principles and Suggestions for a Remedial Code.

Quincey, Josiah--Whig Policy Analyzed and Illustrated.

Randolph, Samuel—A plea for the Gospel Scheme for the Abolition of Slavery.

Reply to Dr. Dewey's Address delivered at the Elm Tree, Sheffield, Mass. with extracts from the same.

Stringfellow, Thornton, Scriptural and Statistical Views in favor of Slavery.

Life of John Thompson, a Fugitive Slave.

The Fearful Issue to be Decided in November next etc.

The Five Predatory Tribes; or the Bolters Factions Analized.

The Great Fraud by which Pa. is sought to be Abolitionized in Oct. and Nov. The Abolition State Ticket and the Abolition Electoral Fillmore ticket.

The Hireling and the Slave, Poems with a political aspect.

The Record of George William Gordon. The Slave Trade at Rio de Janerio.

The Responsibility of the North in Relation to Slavery.

Weston, George M. The poor Whites of the South.

——————— Will the South Dissolve the Union?

——————— The Federal Union it must be preserved.

——————— Who are Sectional?

——————— Who are and who may be slaves in the United States?

——————— Southern Slavery Reduces Northern Wages.

Words of Council to men of business by a man of business.

E. Nativism

Brownlow, W. G. Americanism contrasted with Foreign Romanism and Bogus Democracy, etc. Nashville. 1856.

Bachellor, E. G. "Footprints of Sam."

History of the Rise, Progress, and Downfall of Know-Nothingism in Lancaster County by two expelled members.

Beesley, Samuel C. Immigration, its Evils and Consequences.

Know-Nothing Platform Containing an account of the Roman Catholic Hierarchy.

Report of the Majority Committee on Secret Societies made to the

House of Delegates of Maryland, Mar. 3, 1856.
Secret Circular of Know-Nothings of Philadelphia.
Senator Brooks and † John, Archbishop of New York (controversy). Mar. 6, 1855.
The Catholic Question in Politics comprising a series of letters addressed to George D. Prentiss Esq. of the Louisville Journal by a Ky. Catholic.
The Sons of Liberty, 1776 and 1856.
Twelve Letters under the signature of Madison on the American Question by a distinguished Virginian.

F. Personalities—Buchanan, Fillmore, and Fremont

Facts for the People, no. 1.—Mr. Buchanan's Low Wage doctrine.
Independent Treasury Speech of Buchanan.
James Buchanan—His Doctrines and Policy as exhibited by Himself and Friends.
Justice to "Buch." Papers containing several reasons why Jas. Buchanan should receive the distinguished consideration of the people.
Life of Honorable James Buchanan as written by Himself and set to music by an old democrat, to the tune of "Poor old horse, Let him die." Price, half a Jimmy. Lancaster, near Wheatland.
Memoirs of James Buchanan of Pa. by Democratic State Central Com.
Plain Facts in Favor of Jas. Buchanan for President.
Short Answers to Reckless Fabrications Against the Democratic Candidate for President—James Buchanan.
The Agitation of Slavery—Who commenced it and who can end it! Buchanan and Fillmore compared.
Which—Fillmore or Buchanan, by Anna Ella Carroll of Md.
A Review of Pierce's Administration showing its only popular measures to have originated with the Execeture of Millard Fillmore, by Anna Ella Carroll.
Is Millard Fillmore an Abolitionist?
Union Safe. The contest between Fillmore and Buchanan. Frémont crushed by Lewis C. Levin. To Americans of Pennsylvania.
The Executive Acts of Ex-President Fillmore with Reasons for his Election.
The Siamese Presidents—an invocation to their High Priest Gas. Translated from the original Choctaw and Hebrew by Nemo.
The Life and Administration of President Fillmore. Reasons for his election to the presidency.
John C. Frémont. Is he honest, is he capable.
Facts and Figures for Frémont and Freedom. Is he honest, is he capable? Read and judge.
Colonel Frémont's private and public character vindicated by James Buchanan.
Colonel Frémont's Religion—The Calumnies against him exposed by indisputable proof.
Colonel Frémont Not a Roman Catholic.
Frémont's Romanism Established. Acknowledgement by Archbishop Hughes. How Frémont's Nomination was brought about. Hughes, Seward, Frémont, and the Foreigners.

Frémont—only seventeen working days in the United States Senate—
    His whole civil life.
Frémont the conservative candidate. Correspondence between Hon.
    Hamilton Fish, the United States Senator of New York and
    Hon. Jas. A. Hamilton, son of Alexander Hamilton.
Das Leben—Colonel John C. Frémont.
Life, Explorations, and Public Services of John C. Frémont. Author-
    ized campaign edition.
Life of Frémont—only unofficial edition.
Life of John C. Frémont: Refuting the charge of Romanism, etc.
Life of Colonel Frémont: by Greeley and McElrath.
Charles E. Prichett, John C. Frémont, his character, achievements, and
    qualifications for the presidency and other matters concerned
    therewith.
The Election and the Candidate. Gov. Reeder in Favor of Frémont.
    Reasons for electing Frémont.
Senate Executive Document No. 63, 34th Congress, 1st Session.
Who is Frémont by one who has long known him socially, financially,
    and politically.

G. Kansas

The Kansas Struggle of 1856, in Congress and in the presidential cam-
    paign, with suggestion for the future.   1857
Defense of Kansas, by Henry Ward Beecher.
Majority Report of the Senate Committee on Territories, March 12,
    1856, by Judge Douglas.
Minority Report of the Senate Committee on Territories, March 12,
    1856, by Judge Collamer of Vt.
Conspiracy Discolsed. Kansas affairs. Read! Read! Read!
House of Reps. Report no. 200. (Report of Select Committee.)
Dunn's Bill. Hypocracy of Black Republicanism in Congress as estab-
    lished by the official journal of the House of Reps.
Kansas in 1856. An authentic account of the outrages in Kansas since
    the appointment of the Kansas investigation committee, and
    not included in their report to the House. By an officer of the
    Committee.
Kansas and the Constitution by "Cecil."
The Kansas Territorial Act. S.356.
Organization of the State Government in Kansas and the Inaugural
    Address of Gov. Robinson.
The Border Ruffin Code in Kansas. Toomb's Kansas Bill, dissected.
The Crime of Kansas. Let the South Respond. Approved and signed
    by D. R. Atchison and others.
The Issue Fairly Presented.—The Senate Bill for the admission of
    Kansas as a state—Democracy, Law, order, and the will of the
    majority of the whole people of the territory against Black
    Republicanism, usurpation, revolution, anarchy, and the will
    of the meagre minority.
To the People of the United States by the executive committee of the
    New England Emigrant aid society. (A response to Douglas'
    Report of Mar. 12.)

H. Special Issues: Foreign vote, Fugitive Slave Law, Sumner Assault

Letter of Dauiel O'Connell on American Slavery and letter of Salmon P. Chase in reply to Daniel O'Connell.

The Popes Bull and the Word of Daniel O'Connell.

The Murder of Keating by Herbert. To the Voters and Working Men of the First Congressional District. (Pa).

The Killing of Thomas Keating. An address from Irishmen of Washington City to the citizens of the United States.

The American Papers.

Warrende Stimme eines alten Pennsylvani Deutschen Bauren aus Beiten der Revolutschen und Washington.

Case of Passmore Williamson.

Fugitive Slave Law, from New York Independent. Oct. 31.

The Fugitive Slave Law—unconstitutionality of the Fugitive Slave Act. Decision of the Supreme Court of Wisconsin in the case of Booth vs. Ryecroft.

Case of the Hon. Charles Sumner by M. S. Perry M. D.

Slavery and its Tendencies—Letter from Jas. Watson Webb to the *New York Inquirer,* May 24.

Massachusetts Resolution on the Sumner Assault, the Slavery Issue. Speeches of Senators Butler, Evans, and Hunter.

The Sumner Outrage—a full report of the meeting of citizens in Cambridge, June 2.

I. Broadsides and Caricatures

Circular for Labor vote.

Facts for the People no. 1. The Conspiracy of the Fillmore Leaders to elect Buchanan.

Republican Bulletins by Frémont and Dayton, 10th Ward Club of Philadelphia.

No. 1 Who is John C. Frémont.
No. 2 Issues with Slavery
No. 3 Tyranny of the Slave Power
No. 4 Twenty Reasons for Leaving the Democratic Party
No. 5 Henry Clay on Republican Principles

The New Democratic Doctrine. Slavery not to be confined to the Negro Race but to be made the universal condition of the laboring class of society. Young Men's Frémont and Dayton Central Union of New York.

J. Proceedings of Conventions and Rallys

Celebration of the 4th of July by the Jackson Democratic Association of Washington.

Official Proceedings of the National Democratic Convention held in Cincinnati, June 2-6.

Official Proceedings reported by the *Express.*

Official Proceedings of the Republican Convention in the city of Pittsburgh, Pa., on Feb. 22, 1856.

Proceedings of the Convention of Radical Political Abolitionist held at Syracuse, N. Y. June 26, 27, 28, 1855.

Free Soil, Free Speech, and Free Men. Proceedings of the Dem. Rep. State Convention at Syracuse, July 24, 1856.
Proceedings of the Merchants Great Democratic Meeting at the New York Exchange on Thursday, Oct. 20, 1856.
Proceedings of the State Convention of the Nat. Democracy of the State of New York, held at Syracuse, Aug. 23, 1855.
Declaration of the Republican Association of Baltimore.

General Sources:

Committee Reports. First and Second Sessions, 34th Congress.
Congressional Globe. First and Second Sessions, 34th Congress.
Journals of the Senate and of the House. First and Second Sessions, 34th Congress.
Messages and Papers of the Presidents by J. D. Richardson.
Political Text Book or Encyclopedia (1857) by M. W. Clusky.
Republican Campaign Documents (1857) by Louis Clephane.
Republican Party Conventions. 1856—64. Minneapolis. 1893.
Republican Party Convention. 1856—1892. by H. H. Smith, Washington 1896.

Frémont Material:

Benton, Thomas Hart, Thirty Years View. New York. 1854—56.
Bigelow, John, Memoirs of the Life and Public Services of John Charles Frémont. New York. 1856 (Campaign Biography)
Cleland, Robert G., History of California—The American Period, New York, 1922.
Frémont, John C., Memoirs of My Life, etc. Chicago and New York. 1887.
Frémont, John C., Letters to Editors of National Intelligencer . . . . . June 13, 1854. Senate Mis. Doc. 67. 33d Cong. 1st session.
Frémont, John C., Geog. Memoir of Upper Cal. in Illustration of his map of Oregon and Cal. 1848. Senate Mis. Doc. 1848. 30th Congress. 1st session.
Frémont, John C., Report of Exploring Expedition to Rocky Mountains in the year 1842 and to Oregon and North California in the years 1843—4. Senate Ex. Doc. 174, 28th Congress, 2d session.
Frémont, John C., Message from the President communicating the proceedings of the court-martial in the trial of Lieut. Col. Fremont, with his defense and speeches and documents on the California claims. 1846—7. Washington, 1848.
Frémont, John C., California Guide Book. New York. 1849.
Frémont, Mrs. Jessie Benton, Souvenirs of My Time. Boston. 1882.
Meigs, W. M., Life of Thomas Hart Benton. Philadelphia. 1904.
Nevins, Allen, John C. Frémont the West's Greatest Adventurer. New York. 1928.
Nicollet, I. N., Report on Upper Mississippi. House doc. 52 in vol.II, 28th Congress, 2d Session.
Proceedings of a National Railroad Convention held at Philadelphia, 1850.
Quaife, M. M., Jas. K. Polk, Diary during Presidency, 1845—9. Chicago. 1910.
Rogers, J. M., Thomas Hart Benton. Philadelphia. 1905.
Smucker, Samuel V. N., Life of Col. John C. Frémont and his narration

of explorations and adventurers in Kansas, Nebraska, Oregon, and California. New York and Auburn. 1856.

Schafer, Joseph, History of the Pacific North West. New York. 1905.

Smith, Justin H., The War with Mexico. 2 vols. New York, 1919.

Upham, C. W., Life, Explorations, and Public Services of John Charles Frémont. Boston. 1856 (Campaign Biography)

Monographs:

Alexander, DeAlva S., Political History of State of New York. New York, 3 vols. 1906.

Boucher, Chauncy S., In Re That Aggressive Slavocracy. Miss. Valley Historical Review. vol 8. pp. 13—79.

Brand, Carl F., History of the Know-Nothing Party in Indiana. Ind. Mag. Hist. June 1922.

Catterall, Mrs. H. C. T., Antecedents of Dred Scott. Am. Hist. Rev. vol. 26.

Church, C. A., History of the Republican Party in Illinois 1854—1912. Rockford, 1912.

Cole, Arthur C., Centennial History of Illinois.Springfield.3vols.1919.

Commons, John R., Horace Greeley and the Working Class Origin of the Republican Party. Pol. Sci. Qr. 24, No. 3. 1908.

Cross, Ira, The Origin Principles and History of the American Party in Iowa. Journal of History and Politics. vol. 4, pp. 526—599.

Curtis, Francis, Republican Party in the U. S., New York, 2 vols., 1904.

Davis, Winifield J., History of Political Conventions in California, 1849—92. Publications Cal. State Lib., no. 1, Sacramento, 1893.

Davis, Elmer, History of the New York Times. Times print, 1921.

Desmond, H. J., Native Americanism. American Catholic Quarterly Review, vol. 27, pp. 747—60.

Errett, Russell, Formation of Republican Party in 1856, in Magazine of Western History vol. 7.

    ”   ”   Republican Nominating Conventions, 1856—60, in Magazine of Western History, vol. 10

Flower, Frank M., History of the Republican Party embracing etc . . . . Springfield, Ill., 1884.

Giddings, Joshua R., History of the Rebellion, Its Authors and Its Causes. New York, 1864.

Gilman, A. F., The Origin of the Republican Party. Pamphlet.

Hall, B. F., The Republican Party and its Presidential Candidates 1856. (Campaign Document)

Hayes, George M., A Know-Nothing Legislature. Am. Hist. Asso. Report, 1896

    ”   ”   The Causes of Know-Nothing Success, Am. Hist. Rev., vol. 3, p. 67.

Holliday, Col. Cyrus K., The Presidential Campaign of 1856. Kas. Hist. Soc. Pub. vol. 5, pp. 48—60.

Howe, Daniel Wait, The Genesis of the Republican Party. 1908. (pamphlet)

Julian, George W., The First Republican Convention, Am. Hist. Rev., vol. 4,

Kleeberg,G. S. P., The Formation of the Republican Party as a National Political Organization. New York. 1911. Columbia University Study.

Long, John Davis, The Republican Party: its History, Principles, and Problems. New York. 1888

Mueller, Henry R., History of the Whig Party in Pennsylvania. New York. Columbia University Study. 1922.

Nevins, Allan, The Evening Post—A Century of Journalism. New York. 1922.

Nichols, Roy F., The Democratic Machine, 1850—1854. New York 1923. Columbia University Study.

"   "   Some Problems of the First Republican Presidential Campaign. Am. Hist. Rev., vol. 28,

Pelzer, Louis, Origin and Organization of the Republican Party in Iowa. Iowa Journal of History and Politics, vol. 4,

Schmeckebier, Lawrence F., The Know-Nothing Party in Maryland, 1899. Johns Hopkins Study.

Scisco, Louis D., Political Nativism in New York, New York, 1901. Columbia University Study.

Scroggs, William O., Filibusters and Financeers. The Story of Wm. Walker and His Associates, New York. 1916

Sioussat, St. George L. Tennessee and National Political Parties 1850—60, Am. Hist. Assn. Report Oct. 1, 1914.

Smith, Theodore Clark, The Liberty and Free Soil parties in the North West, (Harvard Historical Studies. vol. 6, 1897)

Stanwood, Edward, A History of the Presidency. Boston, 1898.

Streeter, Floyd B., Political Parties in Michigan, 1837—1860. Lansing, 1918.

Turner, A. J., Genesis of the Republican Party.

Wilson, Henry, Rise and Fall of the Slave Power, 3 vols. Boston, 1874.

Biography, Autobiography, and Reminiscense:

Abbott, Lyman, Henry Ward Beecher. Boston, 1903.

Abbott, Lyman, Reminiscences. New York, 1915.

Allen, Alex., G. V., Life and Letters of Phillips Brooks. New York. 3 vols. 1901.

Bancroft Frederick, Life of William H. Seward. New York, 2 vols. 1900.

Barnes, Thurlow W., Memoir of Thurlow Weed. Boston, 1884.

Barre, W. L., The Life and Public Services of Millard Fillmore. Buffalo. 1856. (Campaign Biography)

Bayard, Samuel J., A Sketch of the Life of Com. Robert F. Stockton with an appendix, etc. . . .New York, 1856. (Campaign Biography)

Bigelow, John, Retrospections of a Busy Life. New York, 1909.

Binney, Charles C., Life of Horace Binney with Selections from His Letters. Philadelphia. 1903.

Birney, William, James G. Birney and His Times. New York. 1890.

Boutwell, George S., The Lawyer and the Statesman and the Soldier. New York, 1887.

Boutwell, George S., Reminiscence of Sixty Years in Public Office. 2 vols. New York. 1902.

Brigham, Johnson, Life of James Harlan, in Iowa Biographical Series,

1913.

Butler, William Allen, A Retrospect of Forty Years 1825—1865. New York, 1911.

Chamberlain, Ivory, Biography of Millard Fillmore. Buffalo, 1856. (Campaign Biography)

Conway, Moncure Daniel, Autobiography Memories and Experiences of, in 2 vols. Boston, 1905.

Crane, William C., Life and Select Literary Reminscences of Sam Houston of Texas. 2 vols., 1884.

Curtis, George Ticknor, Life of James Buchanan, 2 vols., New York, 1883.

Dearborn, J. W., Sketch of Life and Character of Hon. Amos Tuck. Pamphlet, 1888.

Detroit Post and Tribune, Life of Zach. Chandler. Detroit, 1880.

Dickinson, J. R., Speeches and Correspondence of Daniel S. Dickinson. New York, 1867.

Dix, Morgan, Memoirs of John A. Dix. 2 vols. New York, 1883.

DuBois, Jas. T. and Mathews, Gertrude S., Galusha A. Grow—Father of the Homestead Law. Boston, 1917.

DuBose, John W., Life and Times of William L. Yancey. Birmingham, 1892.

Fessenden, Frances, Life and Public Services of William Pitt Fessenden, 2 vols. Boston, 1907.

Field, H. M., The Life of David Dudley Field. New York, 1898.

Foote, Henry S., Casket of Reminiscences. Washington, 1874.

Forney, John W., Anecdotes of Public Men. New York, 1873.

Foulke, William Dudley, Life of Oliver P. Morton Including His Important Speeches. Indianapolis, 1899.

Fuess, Claude M., The Life of Caleb Cushing. New York, 1923.

Garrison, William Lloyd, William Lloyd Garrison, 1805—1879. Story of His Life Told by His Children, 4 vols. Boston, 1894.

Going, Charles Buxton, David Wilmot—Free-Soiler. New York, 1924.

Greeley, Horace, Recollections of a Busy Life etc., New York, 1868.

Gresham, McA., Life of Walter Quenton Gresham, 1832—95, 2 vols., Chicago. 1919.

Grinnell, Josiah, B., Men and Events of Forty Years. Boston, 1892.

Hamlin, Charles E., Life and Times of Hannibal Hamlin. Cambridge, 1899.

Higginson, Mary Thatcher, Thomas Wentworth Higginson—The Story of His Life. New York, 1914.

Hoar, George F., Autobiography of Seventy Years, 2 vols., 1903.

Hollister, O. J., Life of Schuyler Colfax. New York, 1886.

Horton, R. G., Life and Public Service of James Buchanan Esq. New York. 1856. (Campaign biography)

Houston, Sam., Life of Sam Houston, political biography. New York, 1854.

Hunter, Martha T., Robert M. T. Hunter. Washington, 1903.

Johnson, Allen, Stephen A. Douglas. New York, 1908.

Jones, Charles Henry, Life and Public Services of J. Glancy Jones, 2 vols. Philadelphia, 1910.

Julian, George W., Political Recollections, 1846—1872. Chicago, 1884.
  „   „   Life of G. W. Julian by G. Clark Julian, Ind. Hist.

Collection. vol. II.
„   „   Speeches on Political Questions by Geo. W. Julian
with an introduction by Maria Child. New York,
1872.
„   „   Life of Joshua R. Giddings.
Kerr, Winfield Scott, John Sherman, His Life and Public Services, 2
vols., Boston, 1908.
Koerner, Gustav, Memoirs, 1809—1896. 2 vols., Cedar Rapids, 1909.
Konkle, Burton Alva, The Life and Speeches of Thomas Williams,
1806—1872. Philadelphia, 1905.
Linn, William A., Horace Greeley. New York, 1903.
Merriam, George S., The Life and Times of Samuel Bowles, 2 vols.,
New York, 1885.
McClure, Alexander K., Old Time Notes in Pennsylvania, 2 vols.,
Philadelphia, 1905.
McClure, Alexander K., Recollections of Half a Century. Salem, Mass.,
1902.
Parker, William B., Life and Public Services of Justin Smith Morrill.
Boston, 1924.
Pearson, Henry Greenleaf, The Life of John A. Andrew, 2 vols., Boston,
1904.
Pelzer, Louis, Augustus Cascan Dodge in Iowa Biographical Series, 1908.
Pike, James S., First Blows of the Civil War. New York, 1879.
Poore, Ben Perley, Perley's Reminiscences, 2 vols., Philadelphia, 1886.
Quincey, Edmund, Life of Josiah Quincey. Boston, 1867.
Remelin Carl Gustav., Life of Charles Remelin from 1814—1892
written by himself in Cincinnati between 1890—1892. Cincin-
nati, 1892.
Schuckers, J. W., Life and Public Services of Salmon Portland Chase.
New York, 1874.
Seward, Fredrick W., Reminiscences of a War-Time Statesman and
Diplomat, 1830—1915. New York, 1916.
Sherman, John, Recollections of 40 years in House, Senate and Cabinet,
2 vols., Chicago and New York, 1895.
Slater, William, Life of James W. Grimes, Gov. of Iowa 1854—58 and
Senator of U. S. 1859—1869. New York, 1874.
Stanton, Henry B., Random Recollections. New York, 1886.
Turpie, David, Sketches of My Own Times, Indianapolis, 1903.
Villard, Henry, Memoirs of Henry Villard—Journalist and Financier,
1835—1900, 2 vols., 1904.
Warden, Robert B., An Account of the Private Life and Public Services
of Salmon P. Chase. Cincinnati, 1874.
Weed, H. A., Autobiography of Thurlow Weed, 2 vols., Boston, 1884.
Weiss, John, Life and Correspondence of Theodore Parker, 2 vols.,
New York, 1864.
White, Andrew D., Autobiography of Andrew D. White, 2 vols., New
York, 1905.
Winthrop, Robert C. Jr., A Memoir of Robert C., 2 vol., Boston, 1897.
Wise, Henry A., Recollections of Thirteen Presidents. New York, 1906.
Wise, Burton Hoxall, Life of Henry A. Wise of Virginia, 1806—1876.
New York, 1899.

Woodburn, James Albert, Life of Thaddeus Stevens. Indianapolis, 1913.

Kansas Material:

Brown, G. W., False Claims Truthfully Corrected. Rockford, 1902.
Connelley, Wm. E., Kansas Historical Society Publications. This series of publications contains practically every important document on the early history of Kansas.
"   An Appeal to the Record, Topeka, 1903.
"   James Henry Lane, The Grim Chieftain of Kansas. Topeka, 1899.
"   Life of John Brown, The Last of the Puritans. Topeka, 1900.
Fleming, W. L. The Buford Expedition to Kansas. Ala. Hist. Soc. Reports, No. 7.
Gihon, John H., Geary's Administration in Kansas. Philadelphia, 1866.
Malin, J. C., The Pro-Slavery Background of the Kansas Struggle. Miss. Valley Hist. Rev., vol. 10.
Phillips, William, Conquest of Kansas by Missouri and Her Allies. 1856.
Robinson, Charles, The Kansas Conflict. New York, 1892.
Robinson, Sara T. L. Kansas, Its Interior and Exterior Life. 1856.
Thayer, Eli, The Kansas Crusade. New York, 1889.
Villard, Oswald Garrison, John Brown: A Biography Fifty Years After. Boston, 1910.
Wilson, Hill P., John Brown Soldier of Fortune. Boston, 1918.

INDEX

Republican Party, ground broken for in Appeal to Independent Democrats, 20; position on slavery, 20; origin of, 20-21; extent in 1854, 25; victory in Vermont in 1855, 32; extent in Northwest in 1855 34; important victory in Ohio in 1855, 35-37; organization of national machine, 48-51; call for organization convention at Pittsburgh, 52; elects Banks Speaker of 34th Congress, 58-59; holds first convention at Pittsburgh, 59-61; develops publicity machinery, 67-68; attitude towards foreign affairs, 98; organized in Connecticut and Rhode Island, 127-128; call for first nominating convention, 177-178; convention at Philadelphia, 179-185; platform of, 195-198; makes appeal for Irish and German vote, 217-218; opens campaign, 232-233; takes the offensive in the North, 250-260; attempts to reverse Pennsylvania election, 277-278; influence of election on morale, 283-285.

Rhode Island, election of 1854, 21; election of 1855, 32; election of 1856, 127

Richardson, William A., Democratic candidate for speaker of 34th Congress, 54; 57, 281

Rives, W. C., 151

Roberts, Lieutenant Governor, 224, 263

Robinson, Charles, 111, 124, 164, 193, 206

Robinson, Sara T. L., 276

Rowe, John, 262

Ruggles, Frances H., 186, 187

Russell, Colonel, 213

"Sack of Lawrence," 101, 103, 227

Sanderson, George, 246

Sanderson, John P., 278, 279

Schaffer, Chauncey, 180, 186, 214, 255

Schurz, Carl, 218

Scott, Henry D., 55

Scott, General Winfield, 12, 151

Seibles, I. I., 144

Schenck, Robert C., 172

Seward, William H., leads "Wooly Heads" in New York, 23; re-election to U. S. Senate, 32; joins Republicans, 33; opposes formation of Republication machine, 48; moves for admission of Kansas as a free state, 119; 155, 157, 158, 159; defeated for Republican nomination, 159-160; 166, 167, 172, 177, 182, 183, 204, 212, 224, 256

Seymour, Horatio, 231, 232, 234, 247, 248, 257

Shannon, Wilson, governor of Kansas Territory, 110-11, 228, 229

Sherman, John, on Kansas Investigating Committee, 118

Sickles, Daniel E., 144

"Slave Power," 76-78, 81, 85

Slidell, John, 222

Smith, General Persifer, 228, 229

Smith, Gerrit, 60, 149, 268

Smith, G. W., 124

Softs, 12, 146-147, 247, 248, 250

Soulé, Pierre, 98, 99

Spaulding, Judge, 157, 173

Spooner, Thomas, 39, 155, 156

"Squatter sovereignty," 114, 196, 249

St. Louis Democrat, source of propaganda on Kansas, 108

Stanton, H. B., 263

States rights, in Garner Case, 89-90, in Wisconsin politics, 90

Stevens, J. L., 234

Stevens, Thaddeus, 93, 183

Stockton, Commodore, 136, 168, 171, 172, 180, 181, 190, 191, 258

Stone, A. P., 48-52, 158, 177, 178

Stowe, Mrs. Harriet Beecher, 75, 268

Stringfellow, Thornton B., 75

Sumner, Charles, 78; assault on, 126, 221-223; 155, 160, 161, 167, 184, 256, 258, 268, 280

Sumner, Colonel, 123, 228

Tammany, 257

Tappan, Lewis, 149

Tennessee, election of 1856, 237-238